ICONS OF STYLE

Ariana Grande

Published in 2025 by Welbeck
An Imprint of HEADLINE PUBLISHING GROUP LIMITED

1

Cataloguing in Publication Data is available from the British Library

ISBN 9781035425143

Printed and bound in China

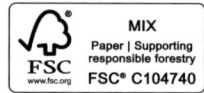

HEADLINE PUBLISHING GROUP LIMITED
An Hachette UK Company, Carmelite House
50 Victoria Embankmen, London EC4Y 0DZ

The authorised representative in the EEA is Hachette Ireland,
8 Castlecourt Centre, Dublin 15, D15 XTP3, Ireland (email: info@hbgi.ie)

www.headline.co.uk
www.hachette.co.uk

ICONS OF STYLE

Ariana Grande

The story of a fashion legend

Caroline Young

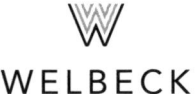

WELBECK

Introduction **8**

CHAPTER 1

Style Trajectory
16

CHAPTER 2

The Signature Style
112

Index **220**
Credits **224**

CHAPTER 3

Key Pieces
150

CHAPTER 4

Impact
210

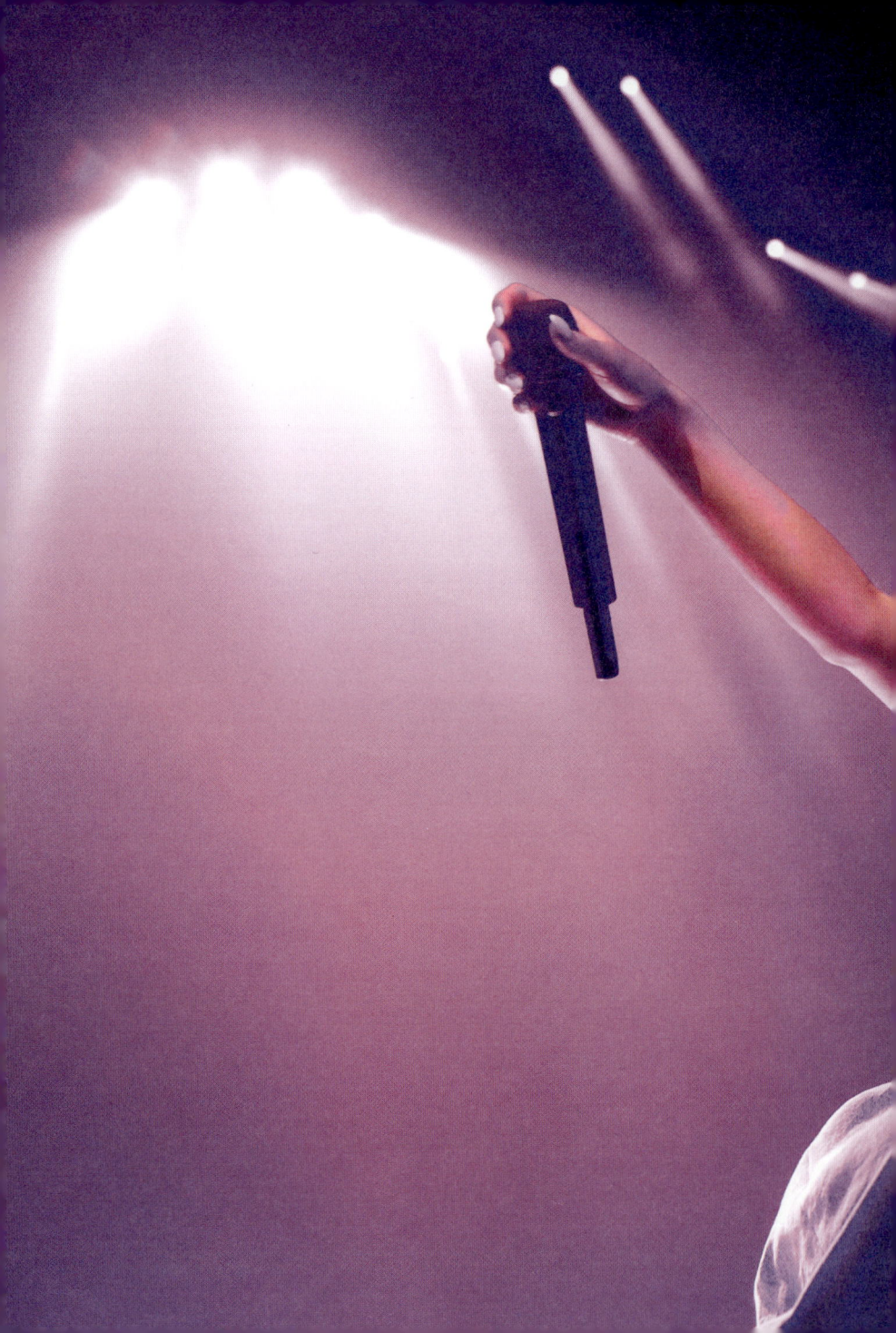

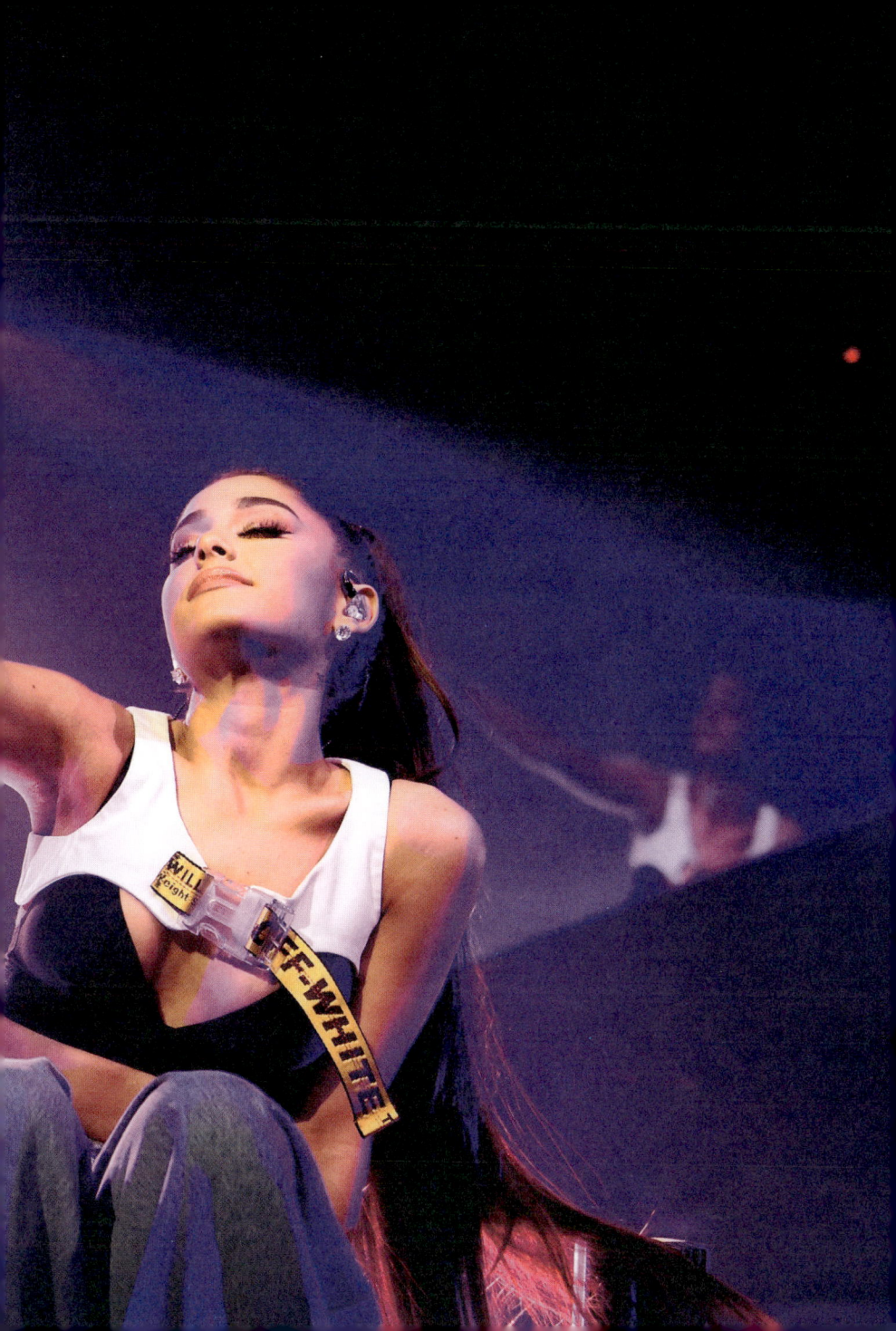

Introduction

The oversized sweater. The thigh-high boots. The ponytail. Ariana Grande is one of the few stars whose image is instantly recognizable through her signature elements. She perfected the sexy street style aesthetic, matured to haute couture and vintage elegance in recent years, but always with the ultimate touch – the waist-length ponytail, worn high or low, or half-up, depending on the mood.

Emerging as a child star with a loyal following among tween audiences for her roles in Nickelodeon's sitcoms *Victorious* (2010–13) and *Sam & Cat* (2013–14), she was able to transition from cherry-red hair and cute prom dresses to an edgier style as she achieved stratospheric success. She was the pop icon with the soaring four-octave vocal range, and with every new album, she became sleeker and more sophisticated, tweaking her image to suit her growth.

For 2013's debut studio album, *Yours Truly*, she chose 50s A-lines, waved hair and nude heels to give her slight 5ft frame some height. With the 2014 follow-up, *My Everything*, she introduced the ponytail and the cat ears, and threw on slouchy sweatshirts and thigh-high boots in an ode to Nancy Sinatra and the Swinging Sixties. *Dangerous Woman* (2016) was a raunchier change of direction, and the album cover's *Playboy* bunny ears and bustier a clear indication of intent.

PREVIOUS On stage in Phoenix, Arizona for the Dangerous Woman tour in February 2017.

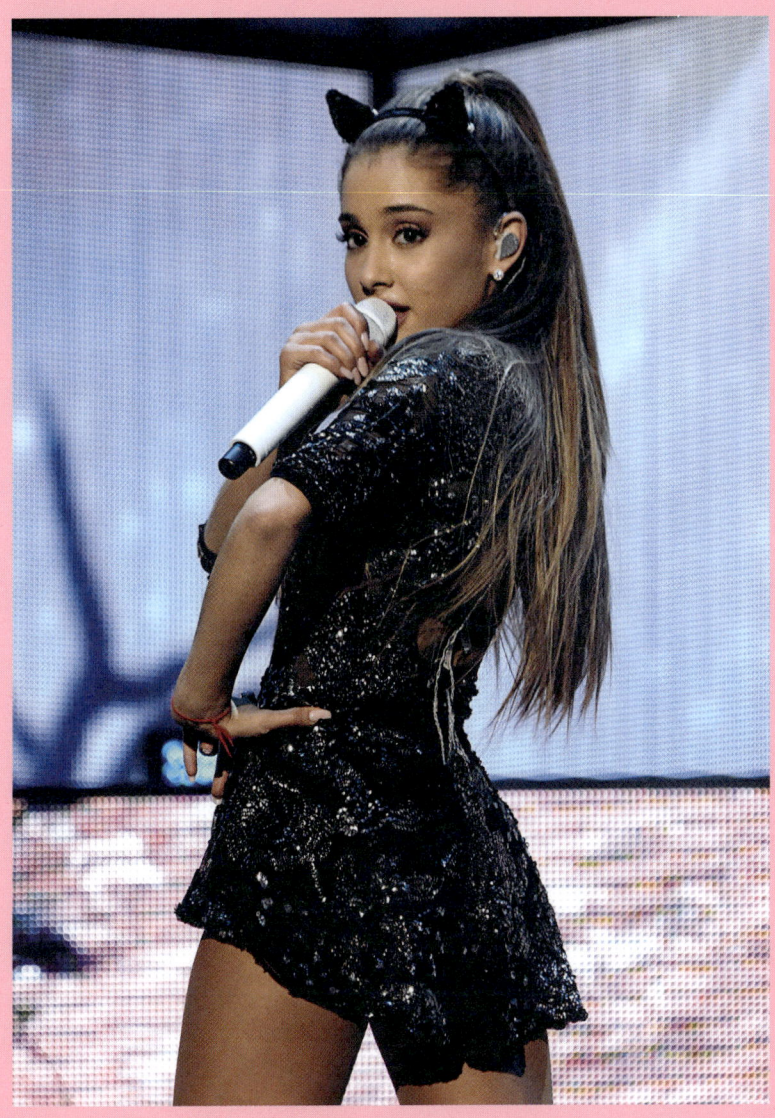

ABOVE At the iHeartRadio Music Festival, September 2014, at the MGM Grand, Las Vegas. Ariana's high ponytail and cat ears were her signature look for the *My Everything* era.

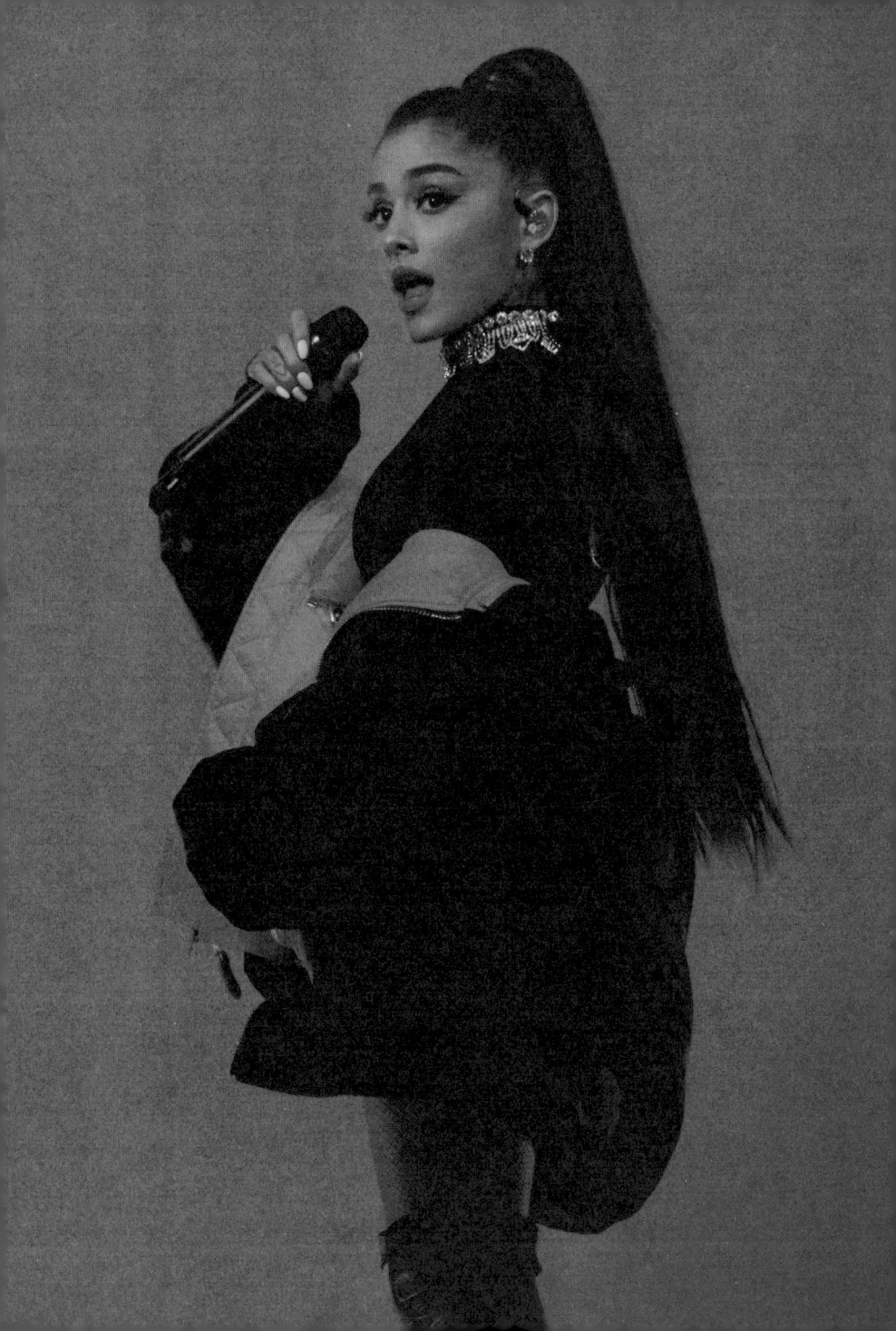

After the devastation of an terrorist attack that targeted her Manchester concert on 22 May 2017, Ariana came back with a message of recovery and love. She organized a "One Love" concert in the city with some of the biggest names in music including Coldplay, Liam Gallagher, Miley Cyrus and Justin Bieber, and, dressed in jeans, a sweatshirt and heels, she was now the great unifier whose soaring vocals brought people together. *Sweetener* in 2018 was a response to the trauma of the terrorist attack, and as part of her recovery, she bleached her hair, chose sweet lampshade tunics, over-the-knee boots and oversized sweaters for her public appearances with fiancé Pete Davidson.

The following year, *thank u, next* (2019), with its trap sounds and theme of loving yourself, was the most personal of her career and placed her at the very top of her industry. She reinvented herself again in 2020, when her cat eye make-up, backcombed hair and 60s styling of *Positions* was a celebration of love, romance and healing.

Ariana retreated from her music to return to her theatrical roots and play the good witch Glinda Upland in the *Wicked* films. When she released 'Yes, And?' in January 2024 as her first single after a three-year hiatus, it was a clapback to all the scrutiny that had been directed at her: that she was too thin, she applied too much fake tan, her ponytail was tired and her love life too complicated.

Streetwear and over-the-knee boots for the Dangerous Woman tour, February 2017.

"Ariana Grande is absolutely iconic. The ponytail is iconic. ... She owns that space... she owns the ponytail. If you put that silhouette behind a screen and backlit it, everyone in the world would see that and say,

'That's Ariana Grande.' And that's powerful!"

LAW ROACH

Over the years there have been the critics who have objected to the contrast of her sweet lampshade dresses and overtly sexy thigh-high boots, particularly because she looked so young for her age despite being 20 when she released her debut album. Ariana has always been a mix of contradictions. She can be both lollipop sweet, with the dimple and angelic voice, and the epitome of super polished, feminine glamour; she can be accessible in her high-street choices and cat's ears, and a couture sophisticate in Versace and Vera Wang. At times she makes up for her diminutive stature with volume – the gowns with layers of tulle, the stage costumes with big shoulders and platform boots, and the soaring vocals that reach each note with a light touch.

As approachable, sweet and friendly as she is in interviews, she's also a fierce campaigner against casual misogyny, the double standards where she's labelled a diva and the hypercritical voices on social media who attack women's appearances. She's a powerful defender of LGBTQ+ rights and this is expressed through her stage performances that invite her audience to enter a rainbow world of positivity, and her promotion of genderless dressing.

Stylist Law Roach elevated Ariana's red carpet and off-duty appearances by introducing her to haute couture and the latest streetwear labels. He helped her hone a style that was unique and completely true to her, while always with that swing of the ponytail. As Roach once said: "Ariana Grande is absolutely iconic. The ponytail is iconic. The A-line skirts are iconic. The over-the-knee boots are iconic... the lampshade look is authentic to her, she owns that space... she owns the ponytail. If you put that silhouette behind a screen and backlit it, everyone in the world would see that and say, 'That's Ariana Grande.' And that's powerful!"

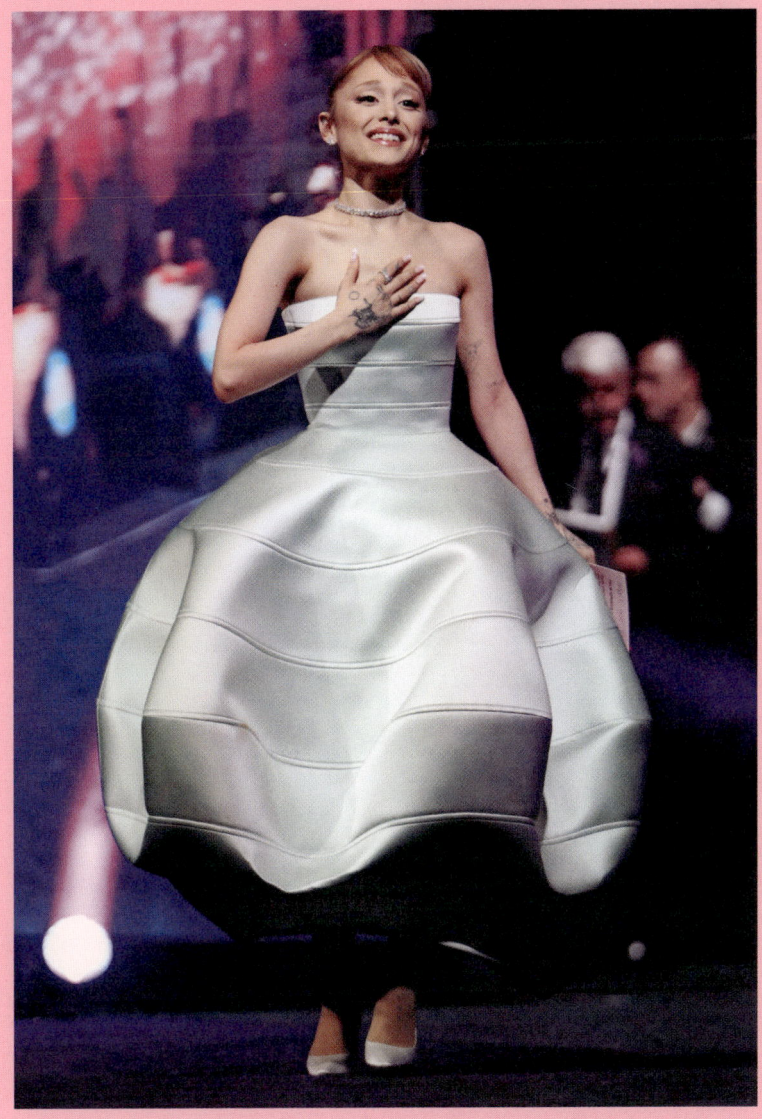

Walking onstage to collect her Rising Star award at the 36th Annual Palm Springs International Film Awards in January 2025, in a custom-made metallic "bubble" dress by Louis Vuitton.

Style

CHAPTER 1

Trajectory

The early years

Even though her childhood was spent in the breezy Florida sunshine, Ariana Grande-Butera, born on 26 June 1993, was much more drawn to colder weather. "I'm like, please bring me the cold and the clammy and the clouds," she once joked. She preferred rehearsing on local theatre stages and mimicking the legendary Judy Garland in front of the TV to hanging at the beach and was fascinated by the dark and macabre, "like a mini-Helena Bonham Carter".

She and her older brother Frankie were raised in a gated community of Mediterranean-style homes in Boca Raton, a city by Palm Beach, and with her mom, Joan, the owner of her own communications equipment business, she was surrounded by strong women role models. Joan moved with Ariana's father – Edward Butera, a graphic designer – from Brooklyn to Florida just before Ariana was born. The two would divorce when Ariana was eight. She described Joan as not "really the housewife type" and a "badass, independent woman" rather than the "cookies-in-the-oven type". Joan favoured the goth look, one Ariana would describe as "modelled after [fictional character] Cersei Lannister's." She said, "We've always had a very weird, like, Addams Family sense of humour. My mom's fabulous, but I've never seen her in anything but black."

Performing in the Broadway show *13*, in October 2008.

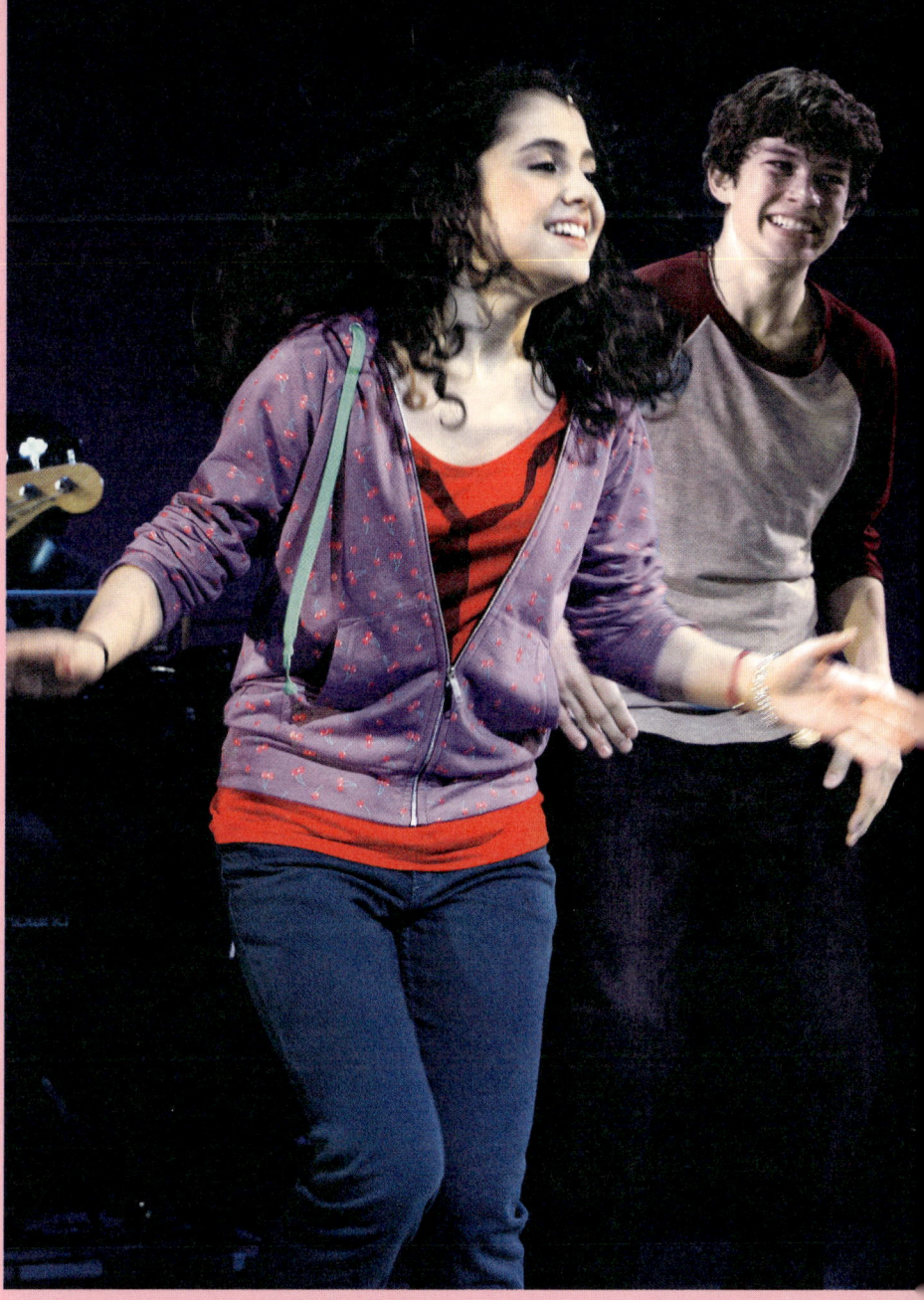

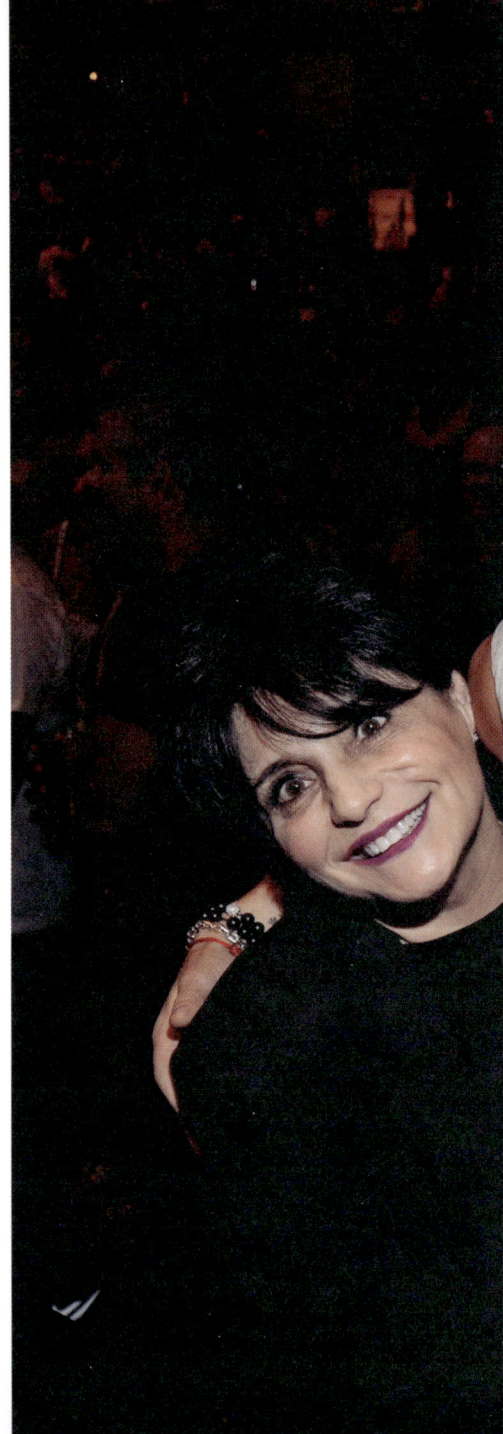

With mom Joan and brother
Frankie, watching Madonna
perform at Madison Square
Garden in September 2015.

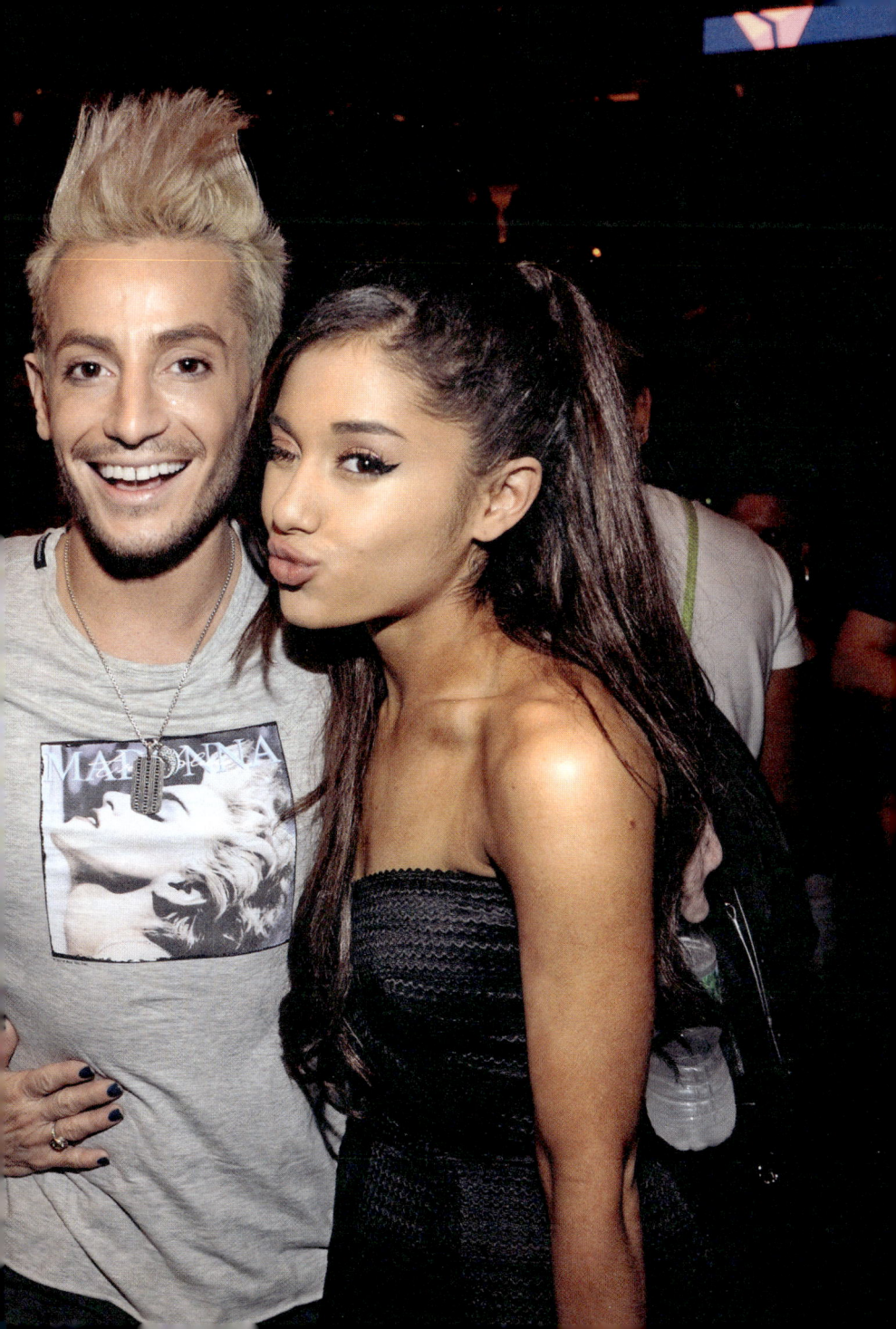

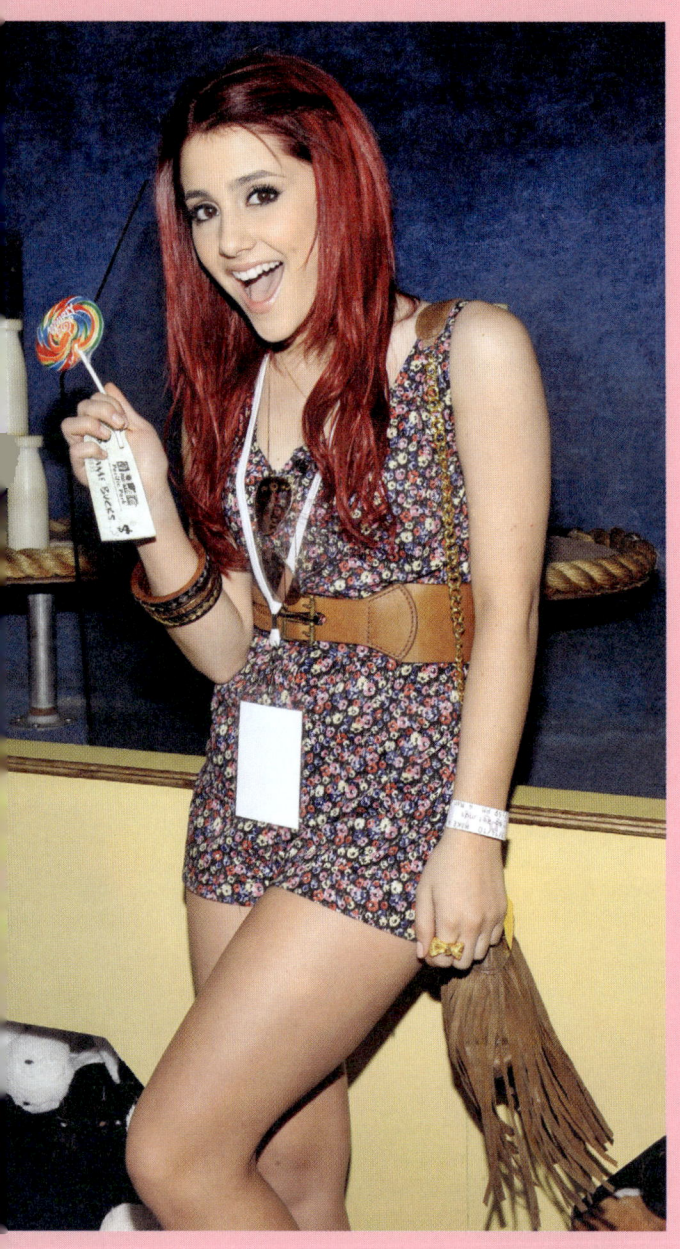

She painted a picture of herself as a strange child drawn to horror, who had a *Jaws*-themed birthday party at the age of two, and who would "run around my house in a *Scream* mask with a hockey stick – it's how I expressed myself." She was fascinated by the dark macabre of Tim Burton, of twisted horrors like *The Ring* and *Paranormal Activity* and the magical fantasies *The Lord of the Rings* and *Harry Potter*. Yet at the same time she was also drawn to vintage femininity. She adored the Parisian elegance of Audrey Hepburn and Coco Chanel, which would be reflected in later fashion and make-up choices, the doe-like Hepburn eyes with heavy lashes and eyeliner flicks, and the simple femininity of a strapless dress.

Her family would gather on the sofa to watch old Hollywood musicals together or go to the theatre to see *Jersey Boys* over and over again, and by the age of the three she was already belting out songs on the home karaoke machine. From a young age Ariana worshipped the divas and gay icons – Madonna, Whitney, Mariah, Celine – who were strong and fierce, yet so precise, and she mimicked them as she perfected her own vocals. It was soon apparent that she had been gifted with a beautiful voice, and to feed her desire to perform, she joined a local theatre group, where she was cast as the lead in *Annie* at the age of eight. She was also given the chance to perform the national anthem at local ice hockey games and was singing karaoke on a cruise ship vacation with her family when eight-time GRAMMY winner Gloria Estefan happened to be in the audience and praised her talents, and encouraged her to keep going.

In a floral playsuit at a Make-A-Wish Foundation event, Santa Monica, March 2010.

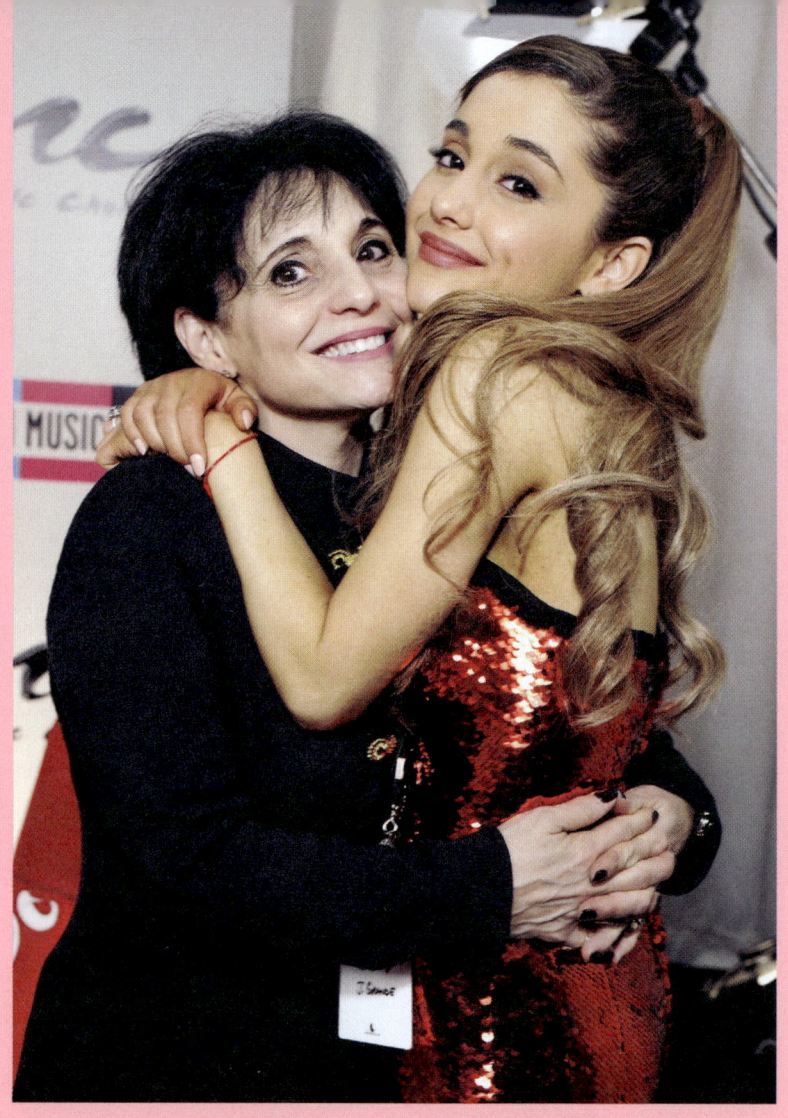

ABOVE With mom Joan at the 2013 American
Music Awards in Los Angeles.

OPPOSITE With her nonna, Marjorie Grande, at the
American Music Awards in November 2016.

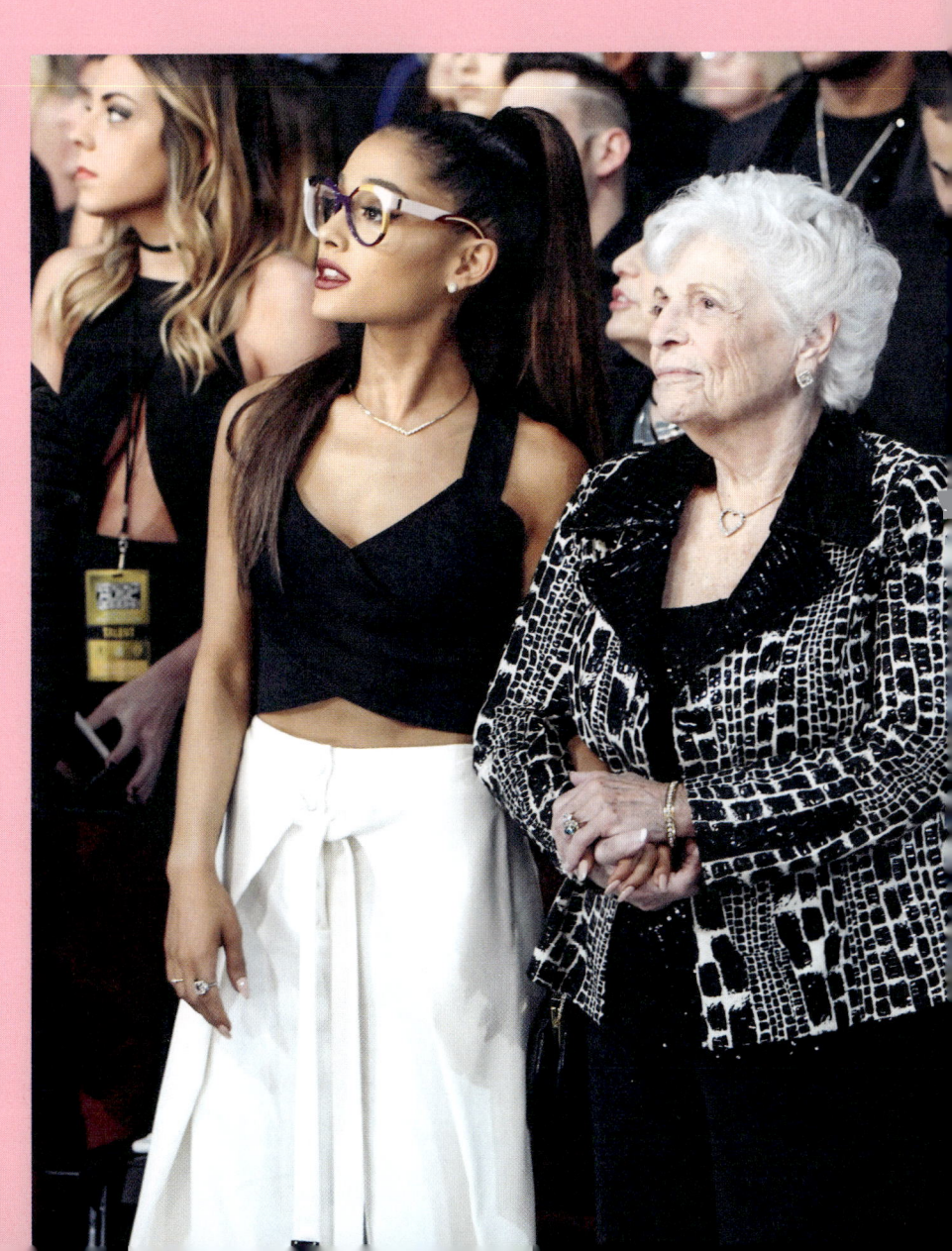

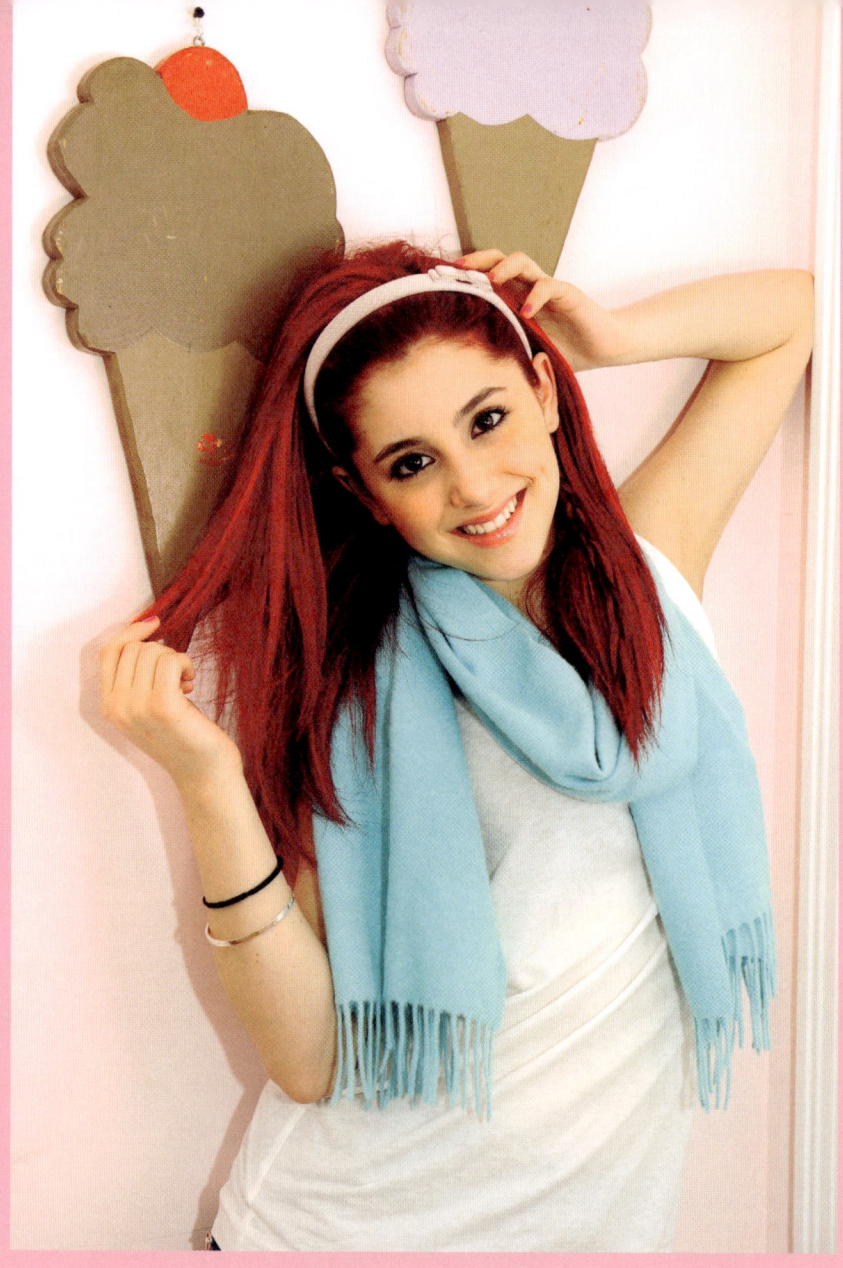

As Cat Valentine in publicity photos
for *Victorious,* in 2010.

Ariana secured an agent while in freshman year in high school and in 2008 she won the role of Charlotte on the Broadway musical 13. With her dark curly hair, dimples and high-energy, she caught the eye of television execs and after being flown to LA for a screen test for Nickelodeon, the 15-year-old was cast as Cat Valentine in a new show, *Victorious*, set in a performing arts school, which first aired in 2010. Cat was happy, bubbly, a little dim-witted and at times tempestuous, and Ariana dyed her hair the colour of red velvet cupcakes to immerse herself in the role.

Given the success of *Victorious*, and Ariana's popularity as a tween icon who arrived at the Nickelodeon Kid's Choice Awards in cute strapless prom dresses and shopped for her own affordable brands online, she was then cast in a spin-off show, *Sam & Cat*. But she was much more interested in following a music career: "I started in musicals because I wanted to sing. I never liked acting. I auditioned for TV to get a platform to get a record deal and then I fell in love with acting because it was fun," she later reflected.

During the period she was transitioning from Broadway to television, she had begun experimenting with writing her own songs, making use of a Boss RC-50 Loop Station, as inspired by another idol, singer-songwriter Imogen Heap. She dreamt of doing music full-time, but whenever she insisted to her agent and manager that her sound was R&B, they dismissed these thoughts. Instead, she took advantage of her huge popularity in launching her own YouTube channel in January 2007, where she uploaded videos of herself singing covers of Adele, Whitney Houston and Mariah Carey.

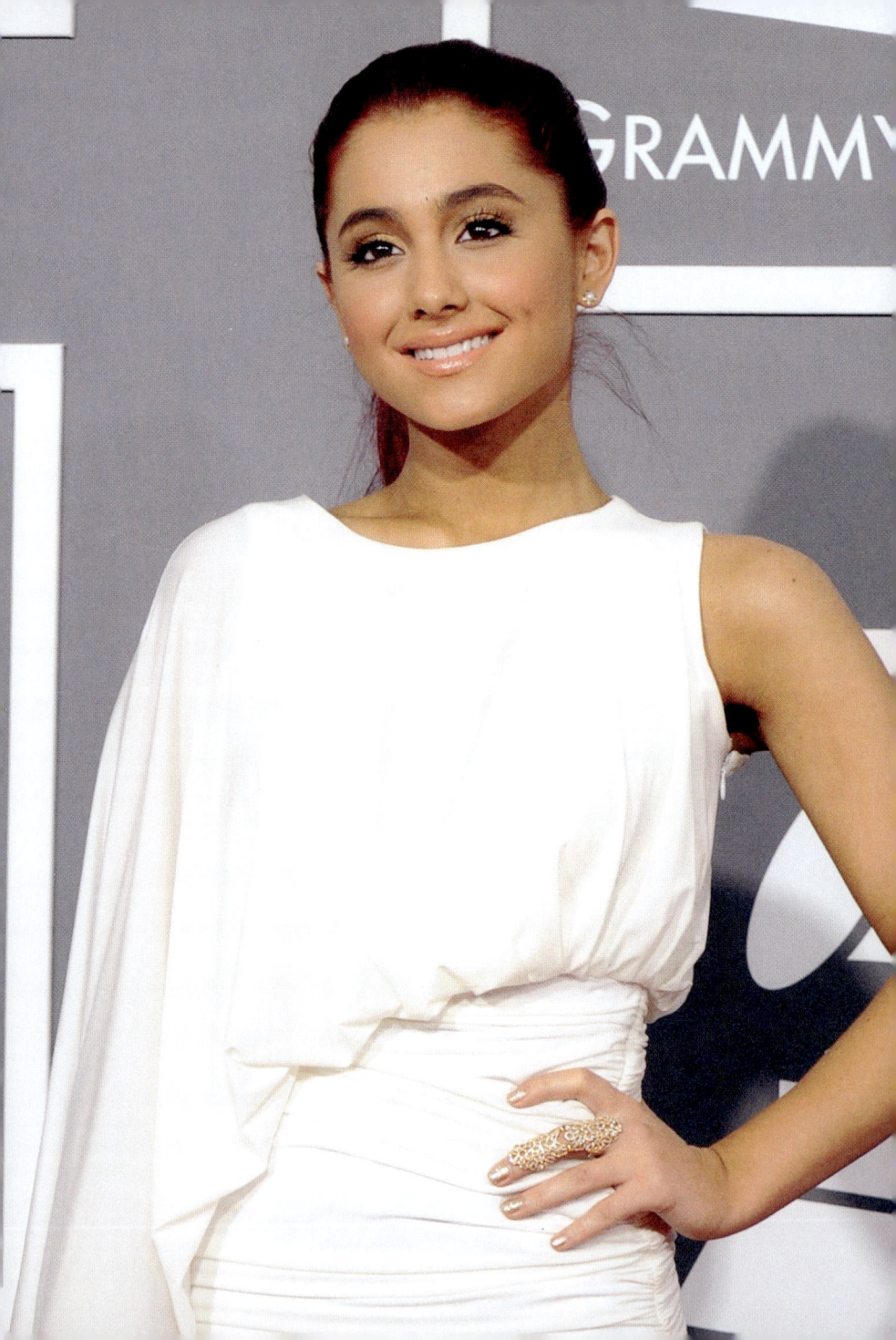

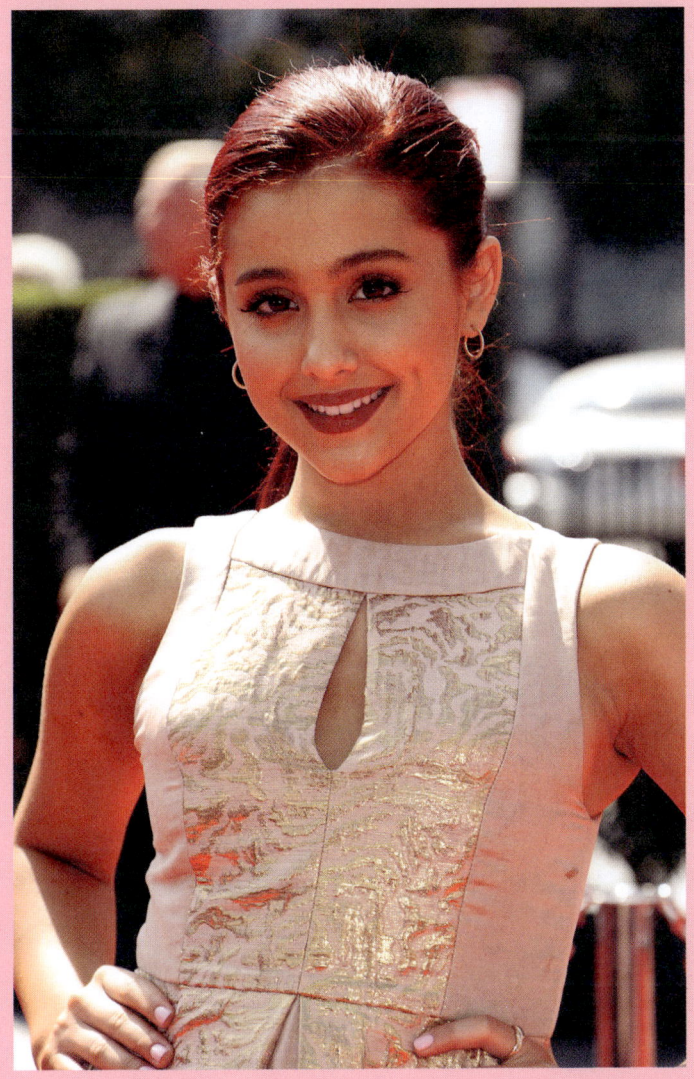

ABOVE Arriving at the 2011 Creative Arts Emmy Awards at Nokia Theatre, Los Angeles, wearing a gold dress she bought online.

OPPOSITE In a BCBG asymmetrical dress at the Grammy Awards in February 2011.

Monte Lipman, the founder and chief executive of Republic Records, spotted the recordings on YouTube and signed her up when she was 17. Rather than R&B, her label pushed her toward bubblegum pop and a sweet, girlish style to appeal to those who knew her as Cat Valentine.

In December 2011 she released a first single, 'Put Your Hearts Up', accompanied by a music video where she performed with CGI butterflies as if on the set of a 50s musical, but she later told *Rolling Stone* in 2014 that it "was geared toward kids and felt so inauthentic and fake... For the video, they gave me a bad spray tan and put me in a princess dress and had me frolic around the street. The whole thing was straight out of hell." She felt trapped in a confused world where she was half playing her television persona and half trying to be herself. She insisted it was all wrong for her,and the saccharine pop was scrapped in favour of a new sound. "One minute I was Cat Valentine," she recalls, "and the next I was singing R&B and making out with [Pittsburgh rapper] Mac Miller." When *Sam & Cat* was cancelled after one season of the show in 2014, she was now able to shake off the tween idol status and reinvent her style.

Ariana's off-duty style for an interview with SiriusXM in July 2011 in New York City.

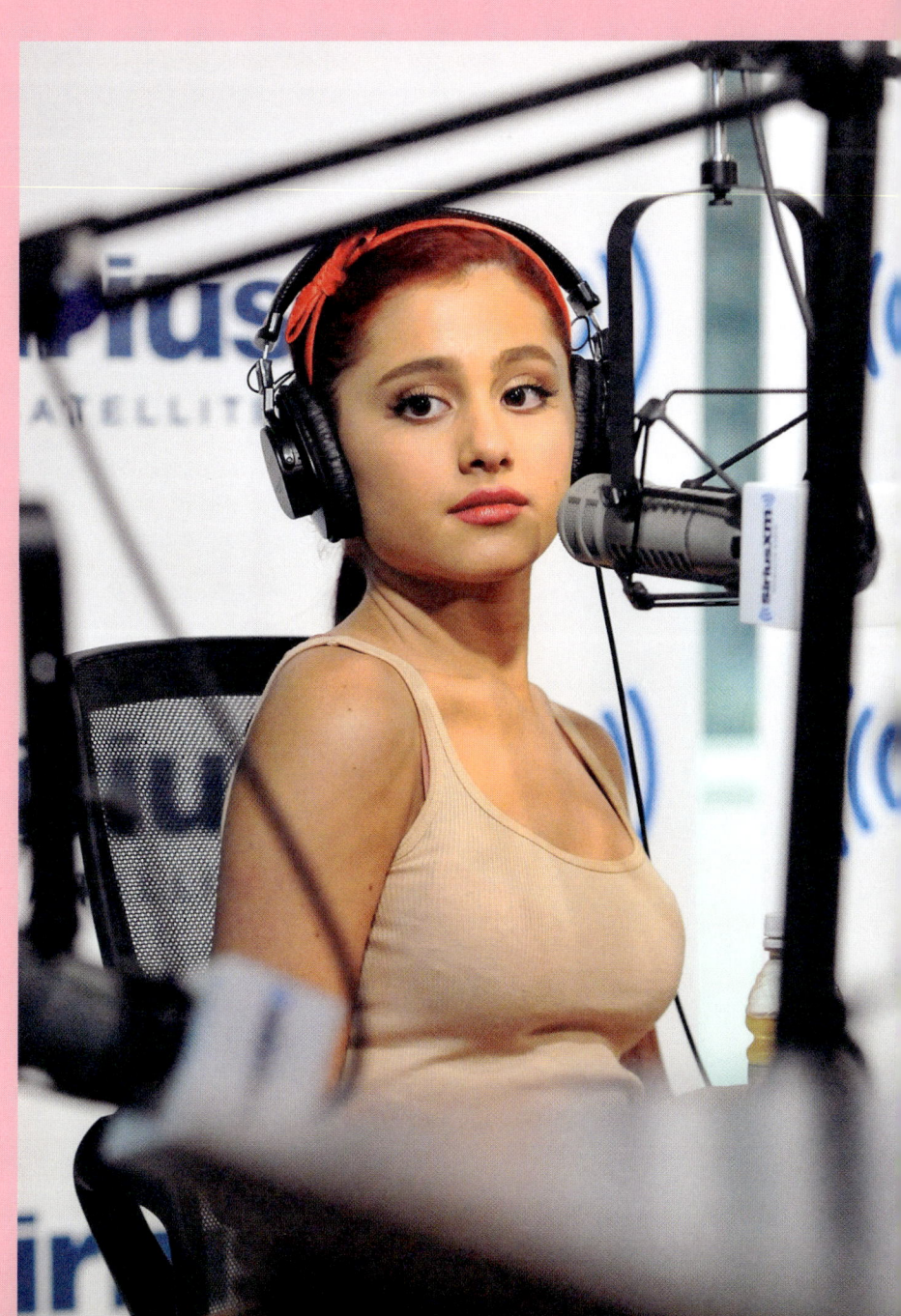

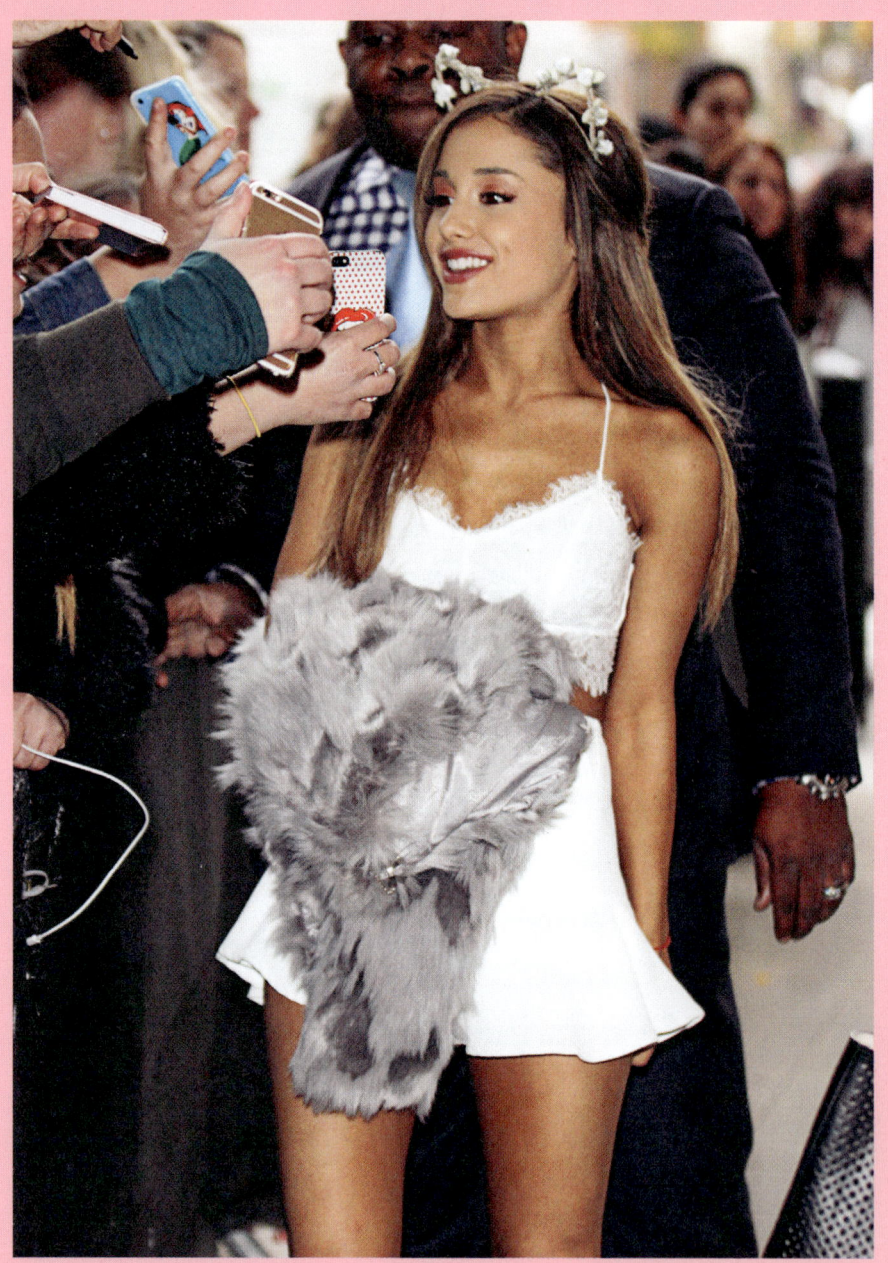

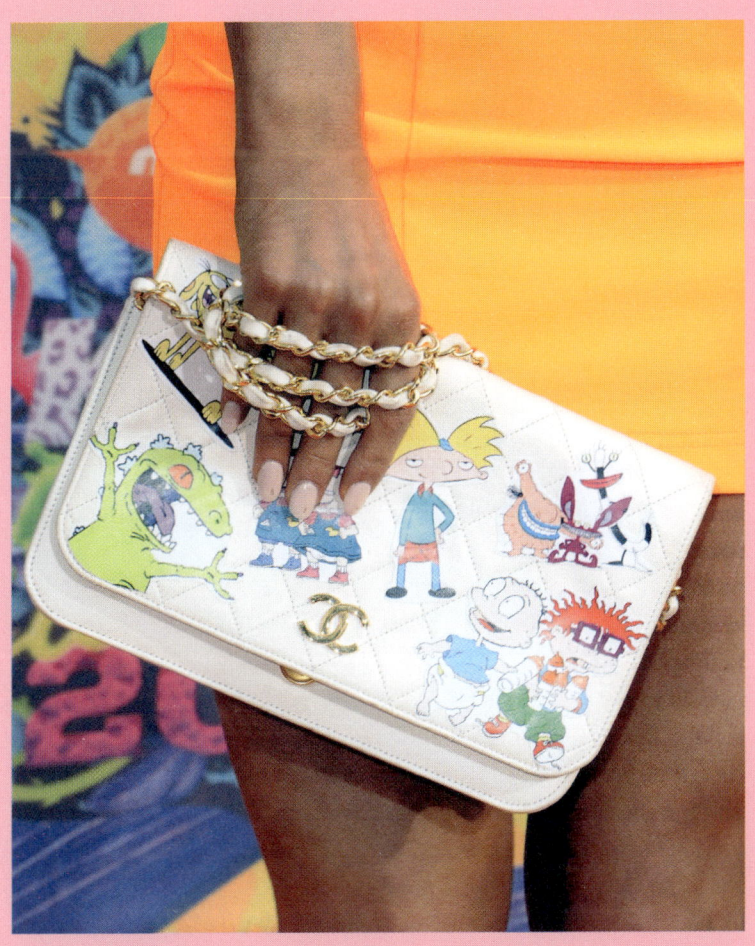

ABOVE Keeping her Nickelodeon origins close to her, with
a custom-decorated Chanel clutch at the Nickelodeon
Kid's Choice Awards in Los Angeles, March 2014.

OPPOSITE Arriving at the BBC Radio 1 studios
in London, in December 2014.

OVERLEAF Strapless prom dresses, heels and Audrey Hepburn
– Ariana in her closet at home in Los Angeles, getting ready for
the Nickelodeon Kids' Choice Awards in March 2012.

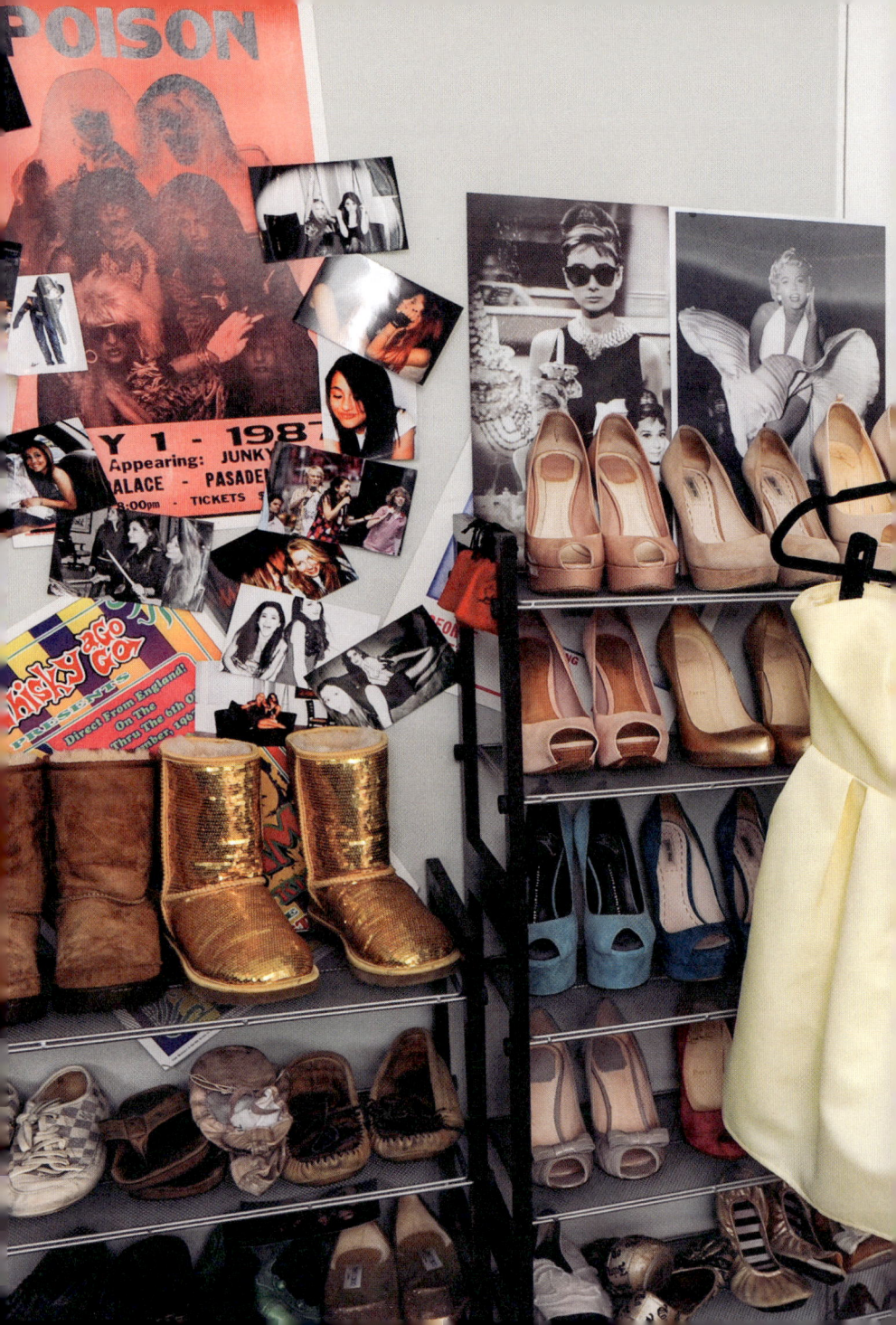

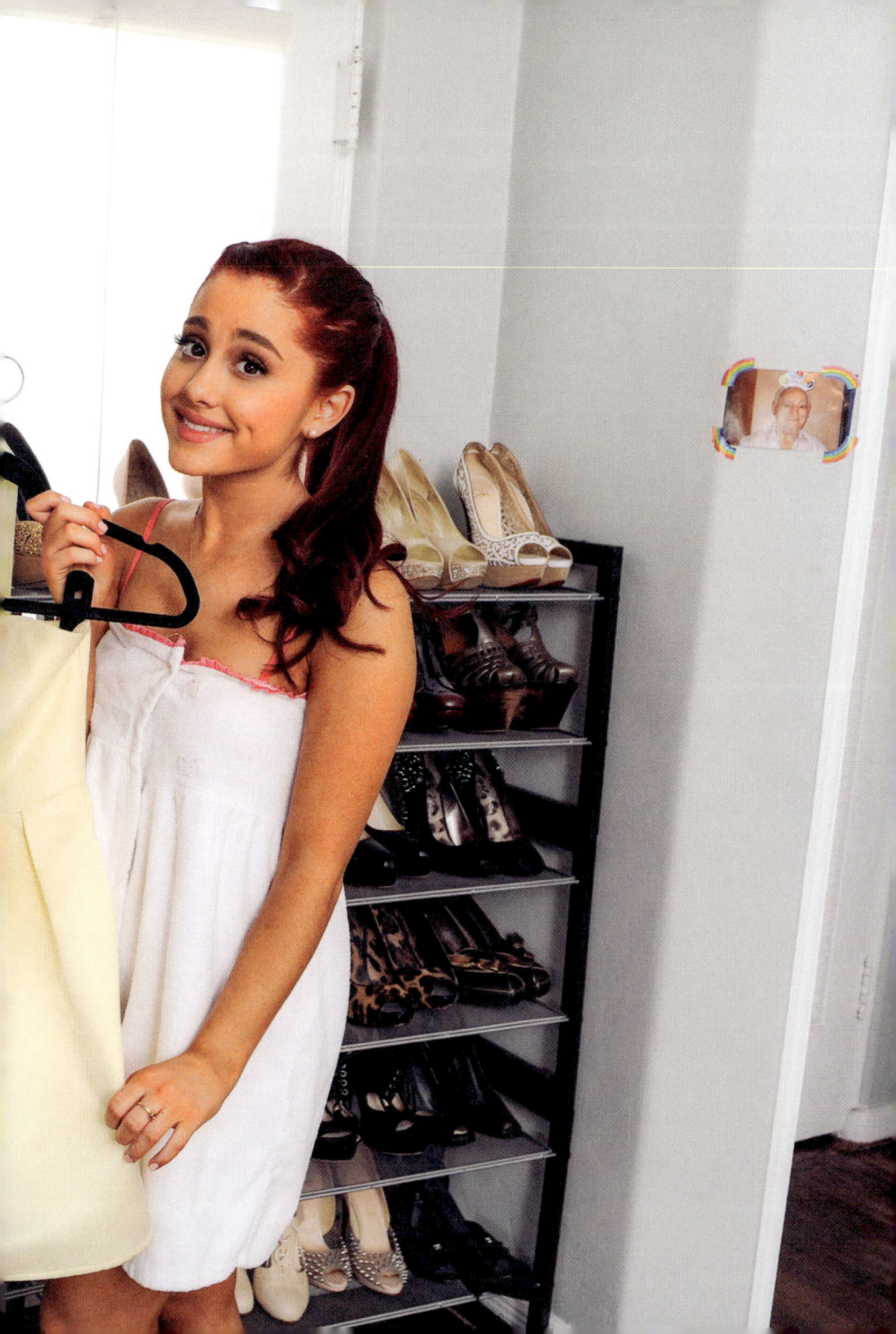

"One minute I was Cat Valentine,

*and the next
I was
singing
R&B"*

ARIANA GRANDE

Yours truly

Ariana's debut album, *Yours Truly*, released at the end of August 2013, entered at No. 1 on the US *Billboard* 200 chart. It was a tribute to the romantic, soulful vibe of her favourite era, the 60s, and girl groups like the Chiffons and the Shangri-Las, who were the soundtrack to her grandparents' lives. If 'Put Your Hearts Up' was candy floss for the Nickelodeon generation, then Ariana proved that she had the vocal talents to move beyond her television origins and 'The Way', her 2013 duet with Mac Miller, helped shift her further from Cat Valentine.

Initial teaser publicity shots for the album pictured Ariana kneeling on a bed of roses, wearing a white basque and stockings, but the reaction against this overtly sexual image was so strong that she scrapped it in favour of a moody, contemplative black and white image. She might have been 20 years old on the album's release, but her fans still thought of her as the teenage girl of Nickelodeon.

She insisted that she wasn't comfortable flaunting her body; rather she wanted the focus to be on the music and her impressive vocals: "I don't want people to talk about my choices or how little I'm wearing. I just want the conversation to be about the music and what I'm creating. I don't see myself as sexy and I'm not comfortable being sexy and dressing sexy. I don't see myself ever becoming a sex symbol."

Performing 'Break Free' at the iHeartRadio Music Festival in September 2014.

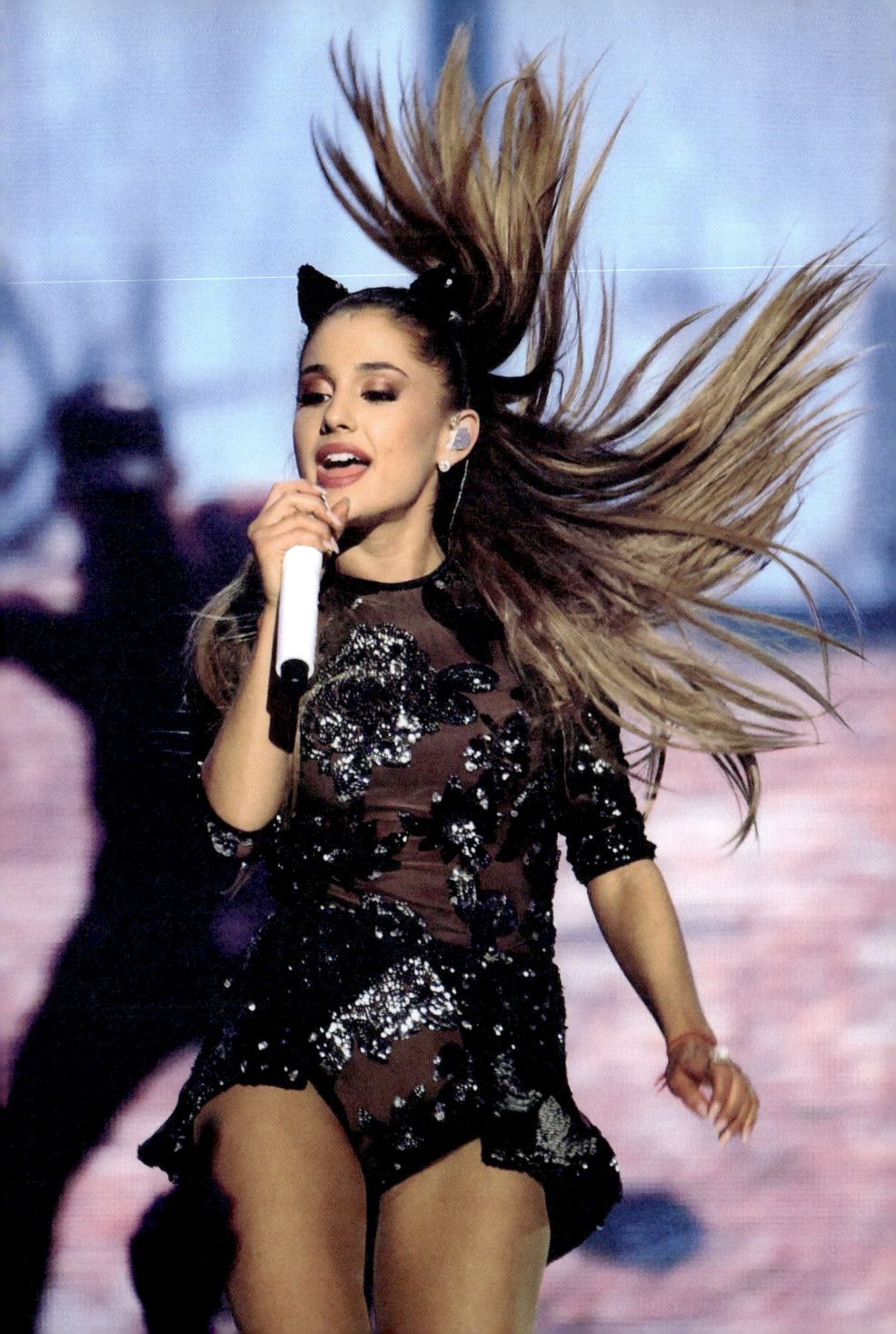

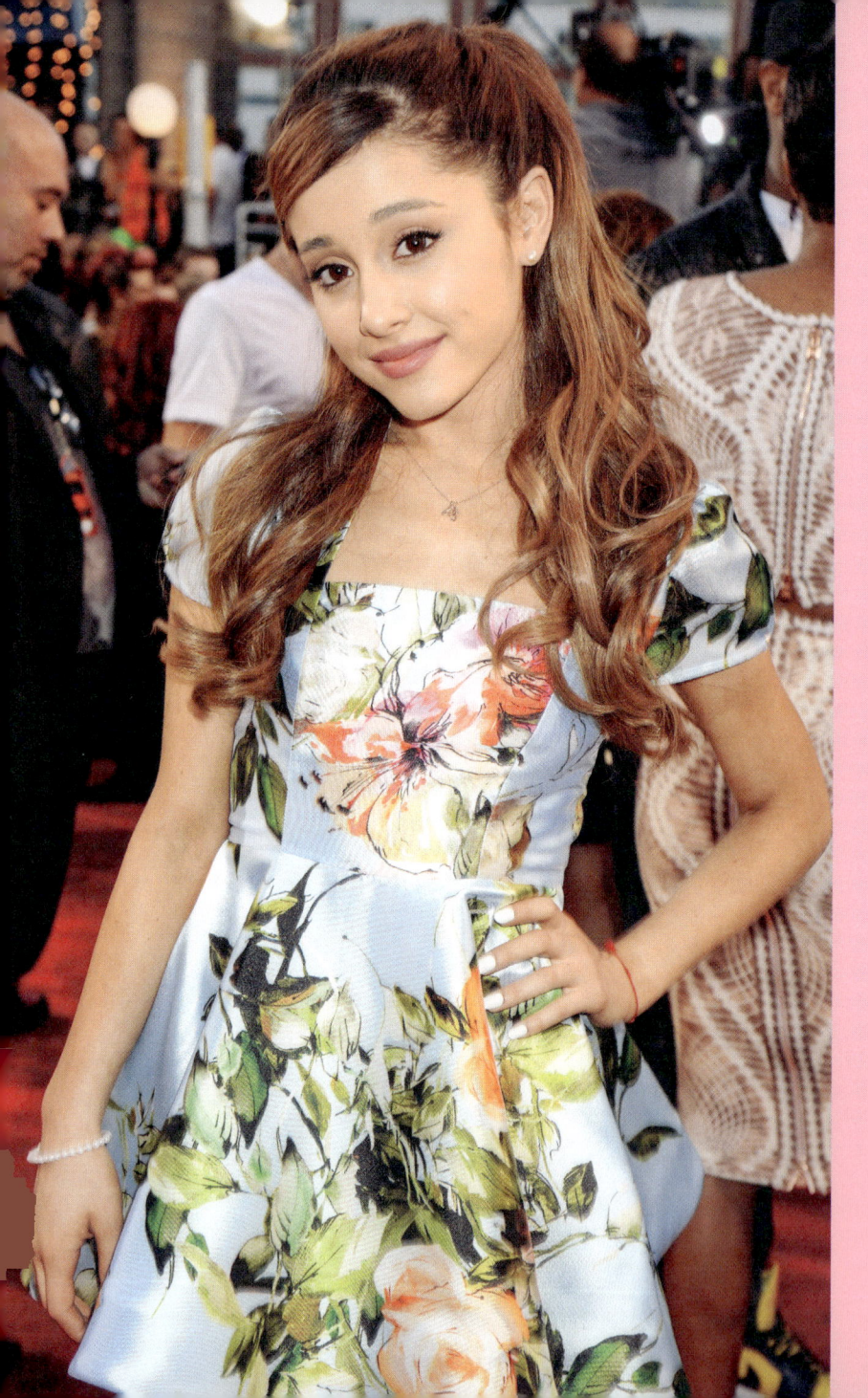

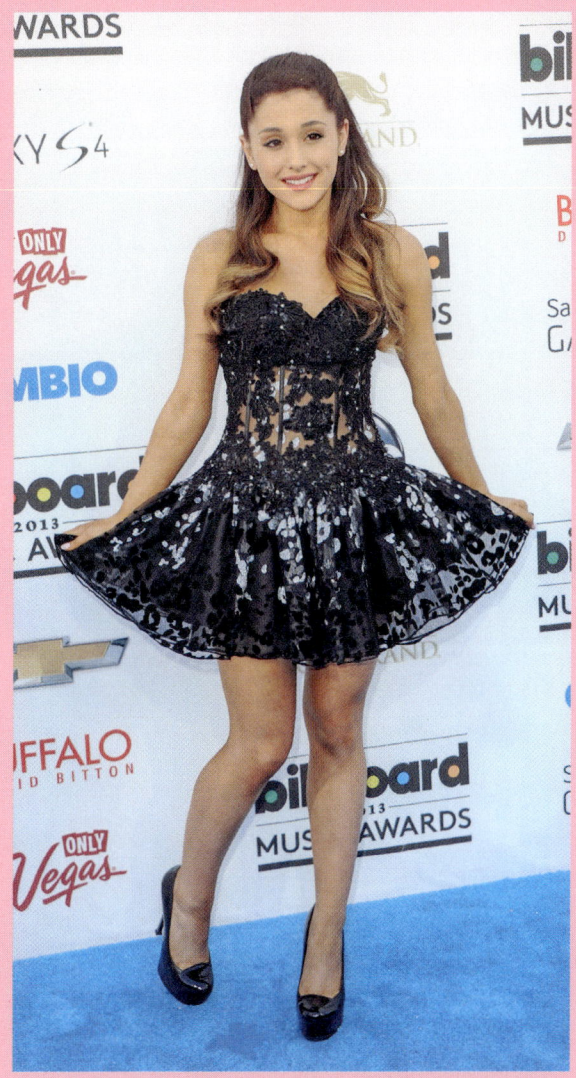

ABOVE Ariana arriving at the 2013 Billboard Music Awards at MGM Grand Hotel & Casino, Las Vegas in a sequined Jovani minidress.

OPPOSITE At the 2013 MTV Video Music Awards, wearing a floral minidress by *Project Runway* designer Kenley Collins.

She spoke out about how she wanted to challenge the hypersexuality of female pop stars, at a time when Miley Cyrus had provoked a backlash for her flip from Disney teen to twerking at the MTV VMAs.

Rather than swing naked on a wrecking ball, Ariana chose to follow a more demure aesthetic with a wardrobe of strapless minidresses, which she herself often bought online. "I wanted to be a little 50s pinup girl," she told the *New York Times*. "A good girl, Goody Two-Shoes, Audrey Hepburn, classic, safe, feminine, soft, girlie."

As a guest on the chat show *Jimmy Kimmel Live!* in October 2013, she wore a sparkling skater dress with five-inch heels to perform two tracks from the album, 'Right There' and 'My Way'. This was now becoming the classic Ariana style, "very girly, retro inspired, feminine floral things. I'm not very edgy. Although that's kind of detrimental because it's in." When asked by fans in an interview in *Glamour* magazine if she was born wearing a strapless dress and five-inch heels, she laughed and said, "I guess I decided probably about a year and a half ago. I think I got most comfortable in my style quite recently. I was never comfortable because I was always trying to wear what was trendy, but it never felt right on my body or in my skin. It felt wrong. I was finally like, hey, fashion and style can be just about self-expression, about what makes you feel stylish."

She named her favourite shoe designer as Saint Laurent, and while she found dancing in high heels tough, she had learnt how to get used to it: "My feet hurt really badly at the end of the shows, but it's fun. While it's happening it's fun. I feel tall."

"*I was always trying to wear what was* **trendy**, *but [...] fashion and style can be just about self-expression, about what makes you* **feel stylish**."

ARIANA GRANDE

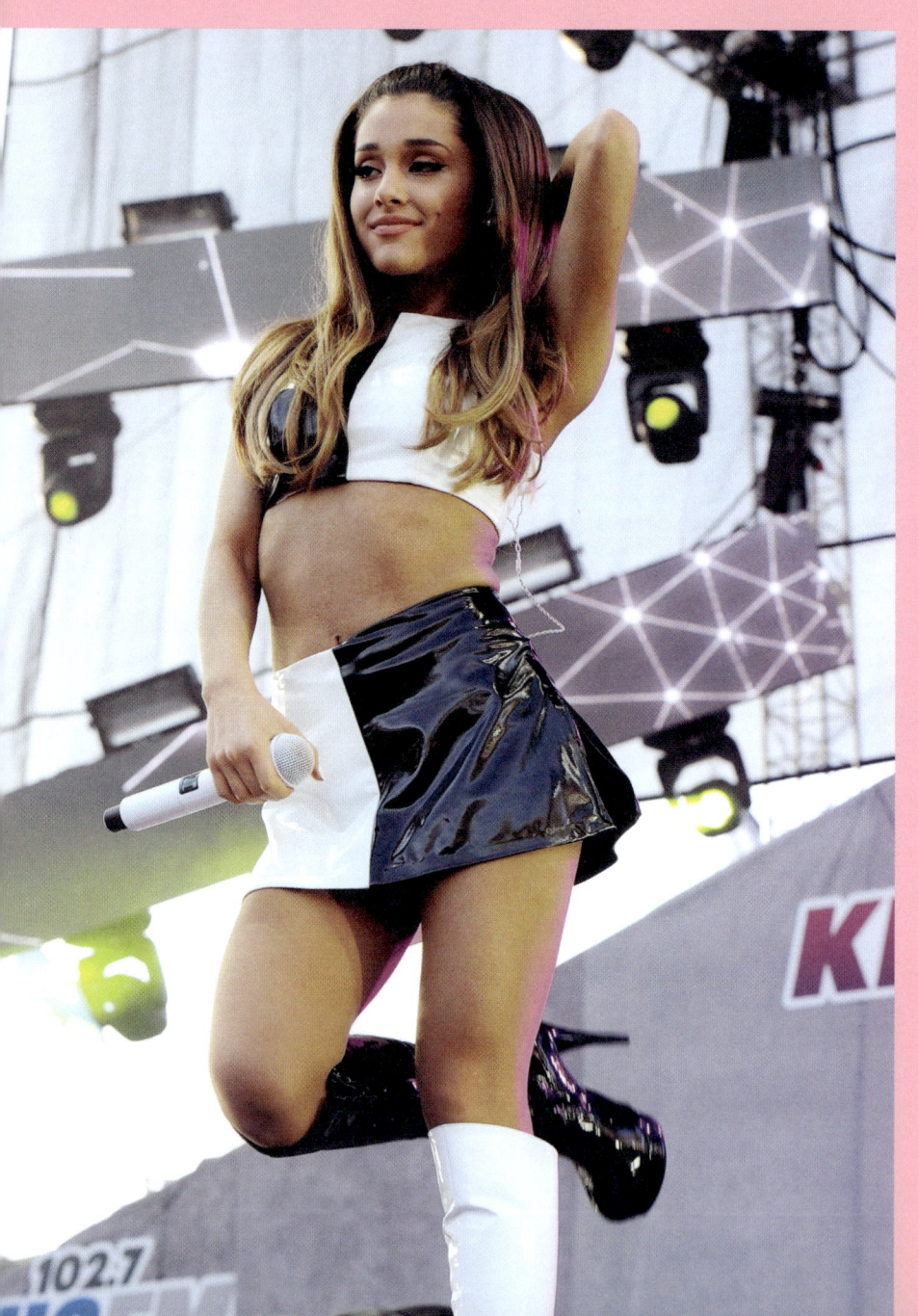

My everything

When Ariana arrived at the White House in April 2014 to perform at the annual Easter Egg Roll, she unveiled a new Nancy Sinatra-esque look. The oversized purple sweater worn as a dress, the white platform boots and the backcombed hair all hinted at a shift in style for her upcoming single 'Problem' with the Australian rapper and songwriter Iggy Azalea.

She now described her influences as "a lot of those older artists from the fifties and sixties. I'm super influenced by that, especially Ann-Margret, Nancy Sinatra and Marilyn Monroe. When I was younger, I used to dress like Audrey Hepburn all the time, but that got a little boring." Ariana had been teasing a Mod look on Instagram in anticipation of new music and the cover artwork for 'Problem' featured the singer reclining in a black bodice and white thigh-high boots, while in promotional performances she chose large sunglasses, black and white minidresses and go-go boots, as if stepping into a 60s Pop Art dream.

OPPOSITE Showcasing a new 1960s Mod aesthetic at 102.7 KIIS FM's Wango Tango in May 2014, Los Angeles.

OVERLEAF Performing 'Problem' with Iggy Azalea at the 2014 Billboard Music Awards.

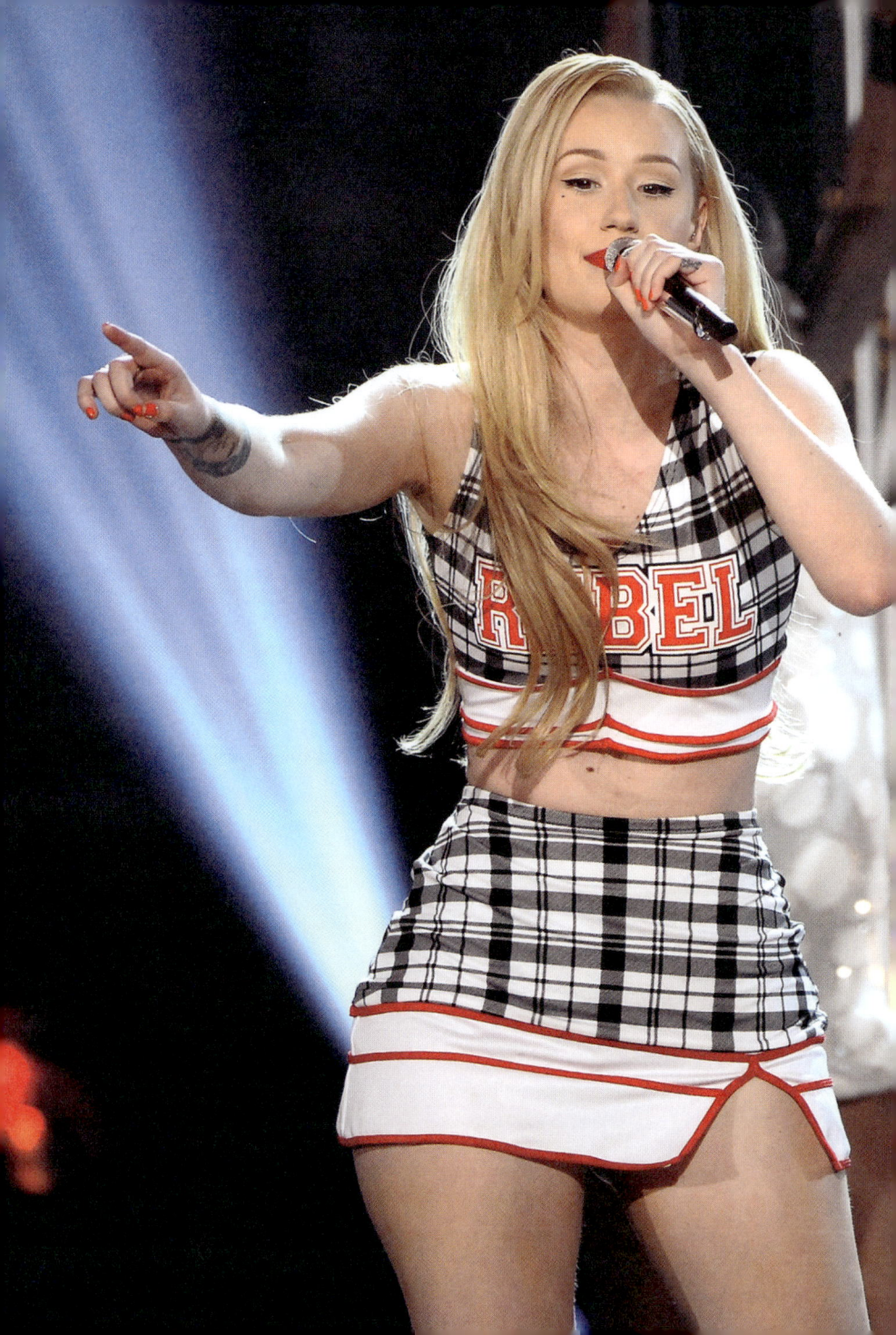

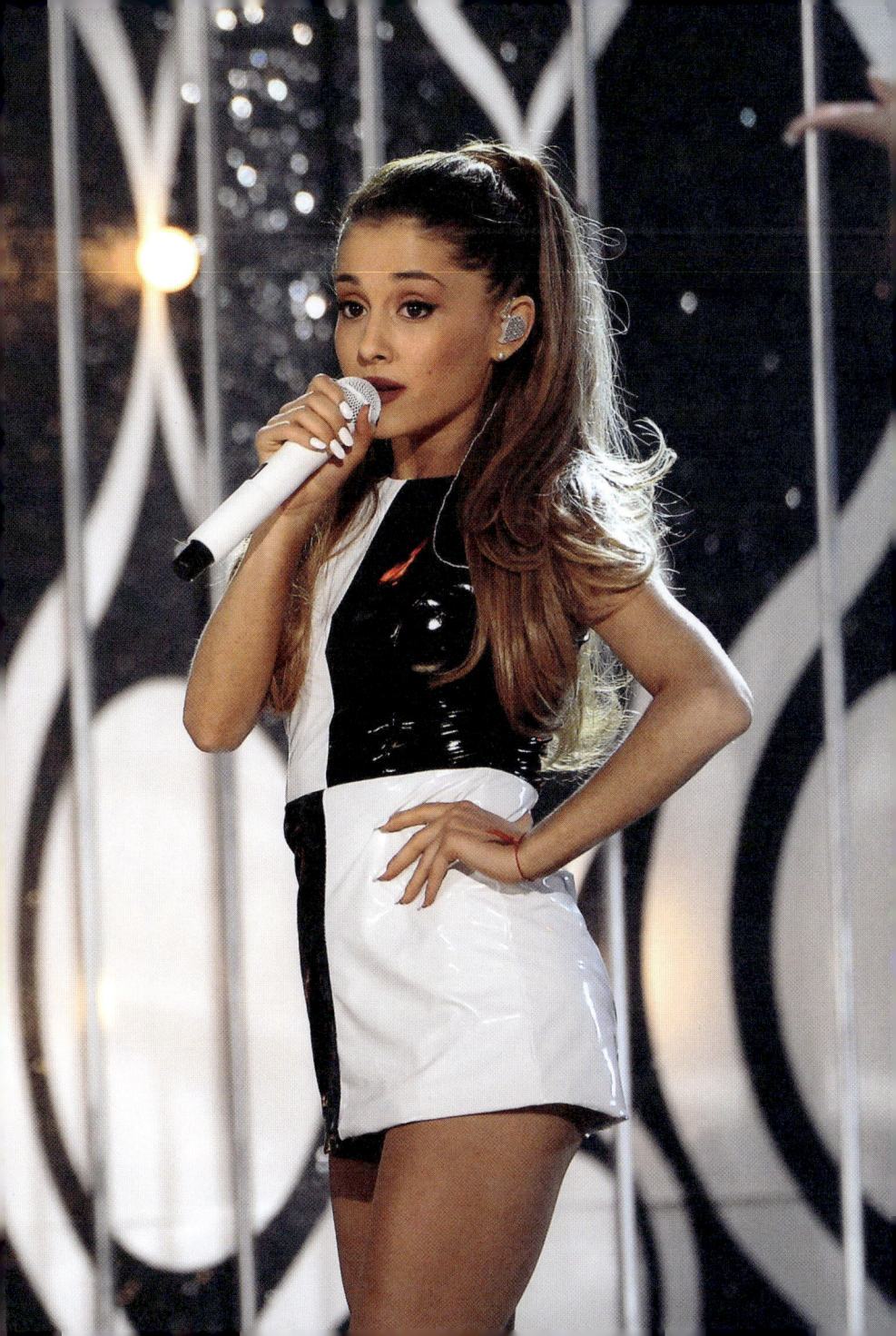

Her second album, *My Everything*, was a chance to evolve her sound and to push the boundaries of her image, which had so far been cautiously managed. Kneeling on a stool in white heels and a black top and shorts, and with her hair pulled into a half-ponytail, it was much more kittenish and coquettish.

Ariana's stage outfits were also becoming more playful, this time adding cat ears to her ponytailed hair and teaming sky-high heels with bodysuits. But there were some factions who warned her about being too grown-up, particularly given that the teen sitcom *Sam & Cat* was still airing, with the final episode shown in July 2014. After watching her perform 'Problem' at the Radio Disney Music Awards, the *Miami Herald* in May 2014 pleaded with her not to go "all Miley on us" as she "eschewed her usual sweet-and-sensible-girl outfit for a black leather bodice and practically painted-on leggings" and paired it with white boots and Mickey Mouse ears.

The album dropped on 25 August 2014 and went straight to the top of the *Billboard* 200. More adult in content, it incorporated pop and EDM alongside the 90s R&B showcasing her light yet powerful vocals. The track lists were a roll call of cool collaborators – The Weeknd, A$AP Ferg, Big Sean and Childish Gambino.

At the iHeartRadio Music Awards in May 2014 in Los Angeles.

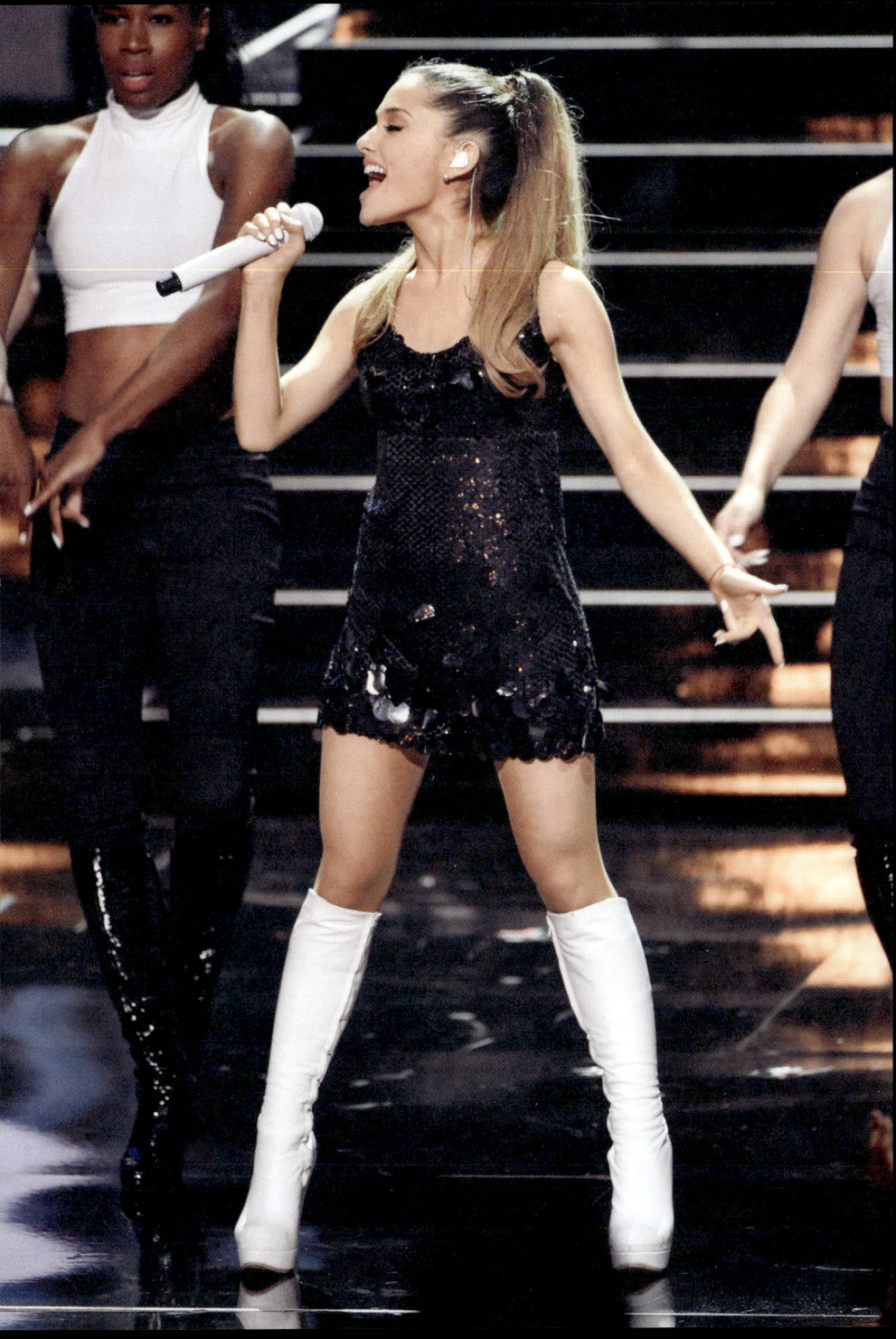

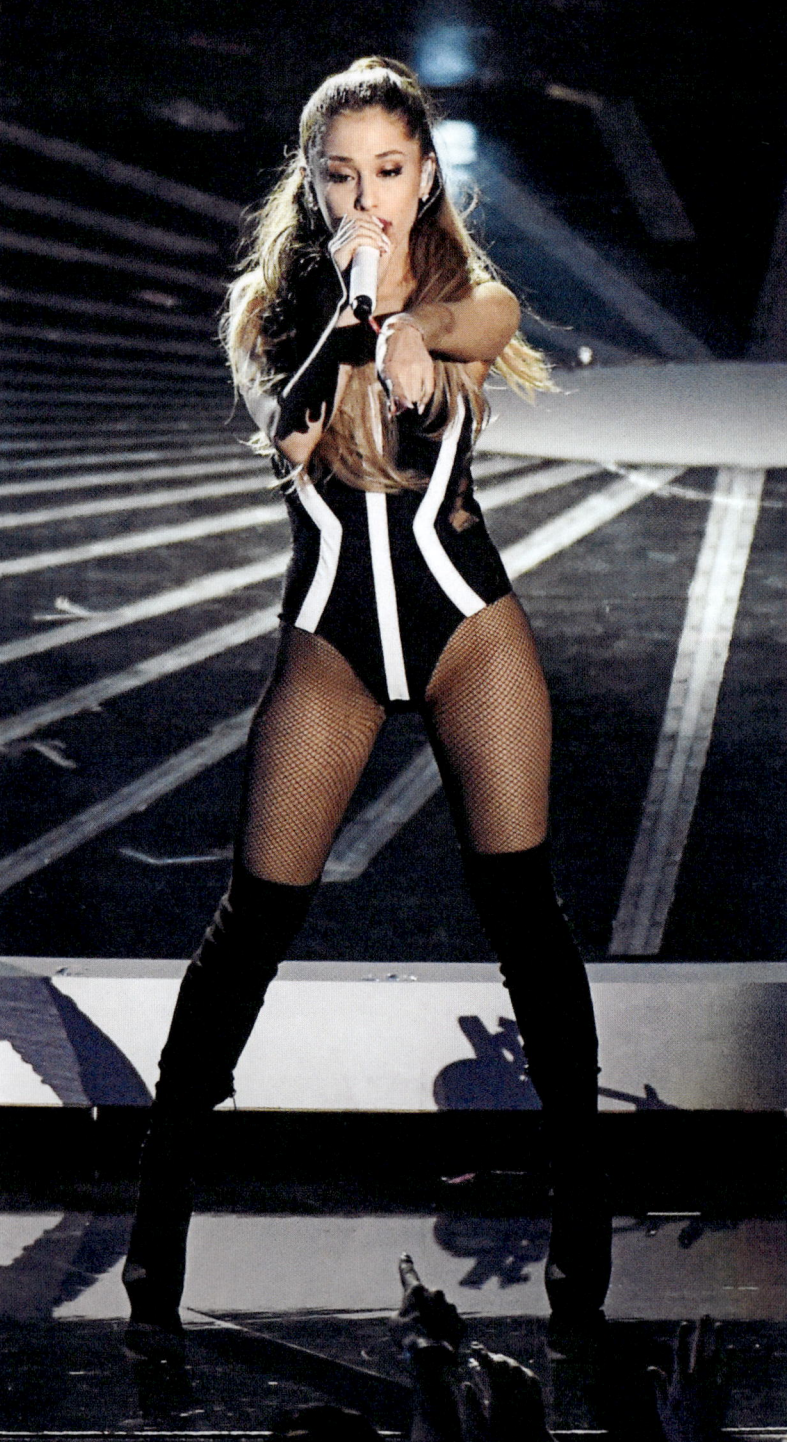

She was aware of the need to grow musically and stylistically, yet she was continually mistaken for being younger. Iggy Azalea had thought she was still a child when she initially turned down the offer of doing a collaboration on *Yours Truly* before their smash success with 'Problem'.

In the 60s sci-fi inspired music video for the second single, 'Break Free' – a collaboration with producer Zedd – Ariana played a *Barbarella*-style sex kitten dancing with CGI aliens in platform go-go boots, bodysuits and Paco Rabanne style metal bra and skirt. For the boisterous 'Bang Bang', with Jessie J and Nicki Minaj, she was the coquettish Ariana from the album cover as she knelt on her bed in high white heels and a white two-piece outfit.

With its melancholic, soaring lyrics over the EDM backing track, 'One Last Time', released in February 2015, was accompanied by an apocalyptic hand-held camera music video and this time Ariana was in off-duty sportswear.

'Love Me Harder', a duet with The Weeknd, was the raunchiest song of her career so far and with its suggestive lyrics, it was, as the *Los Angeles Times* described in August 2014, a "darker (and more fully realized) R&B jam than anyone probably expected from a 21-year-old singer once known for her endless supply of pastel princess dresses". It had been a surprising collaboration between the two, given her origins as a child star, but further signalled the way she was mapping out her new persona.

Ariana performing 'Bang Bang' at the 2014
MTV Video Music Awards.

"I don't know why people are so shocked by me," she said in an interview with *Time* in August 2014. "I guess it's because of the character I played so long [in *Victorious* and *Sam & Cat*] being such a Goody Two-Shoes. But I also think that people have a misrepresentation of me as a person because I'm friendly and I like to meet people and I like to talk to people and make people laugh. Sometimes people can confuse my niceness for weakness in a way – or ditziness or stupidity."

Ariana was unafraid to stand up for herself or to rail against the social media commentators who trolled women's bodies. She was particularly affected by comments after she and Nicki Minaj performed together at the NBA's All-Star Game in February 2015. She tweeted: "stop trying to make people feel badly about their bodies. it's okay to be different ... to be curvy or to be thin. when did it become socially acceptable to comment on what you think is 'wrong' with other people's bodies?"

She proved that her strength lay in her vocals when she was the music guest on *Saturday Night Live* in September 2014, singing a pared-back acoustic version of 'Break Free' sitting on top of a piano and with the cat's ears, ponytail and 60s heavy-lashed eyes, before breaking out into the EDM accompaniment.

In floral Dolce & Gabbana at the 2014 Grammy Awards.

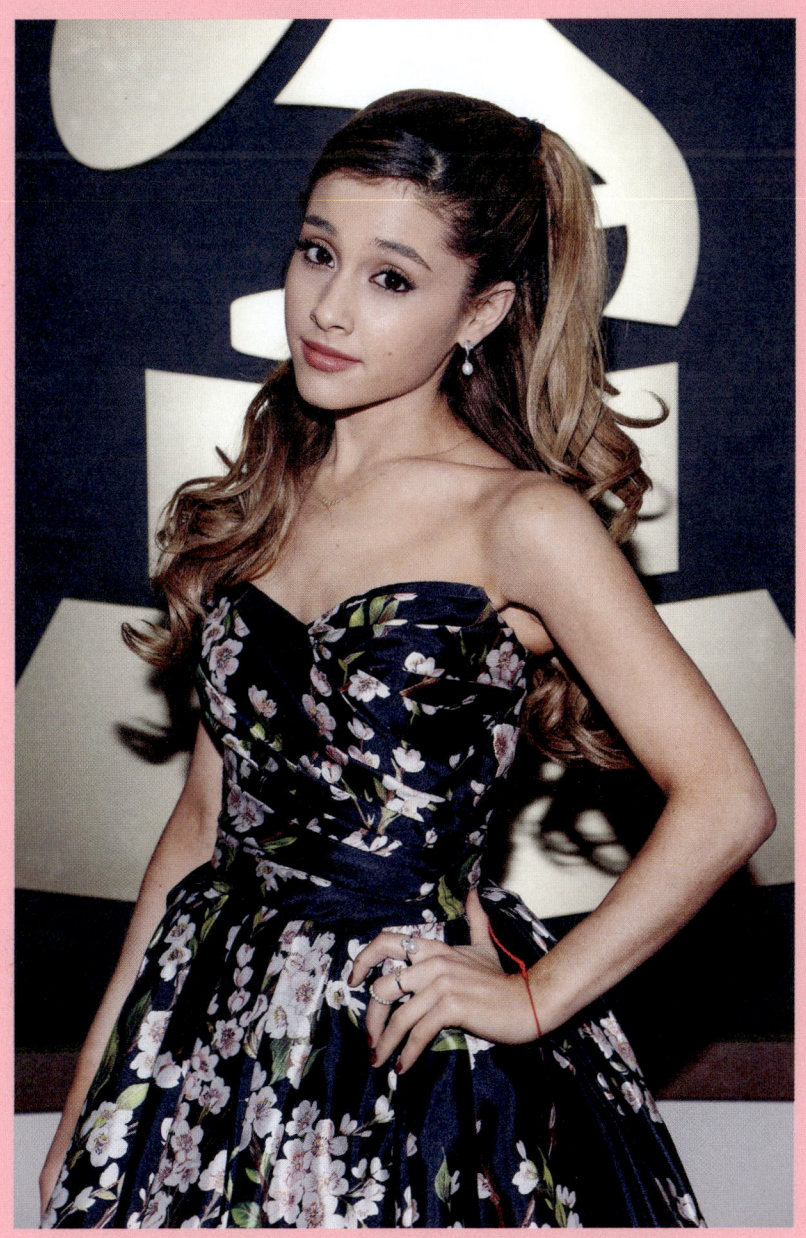

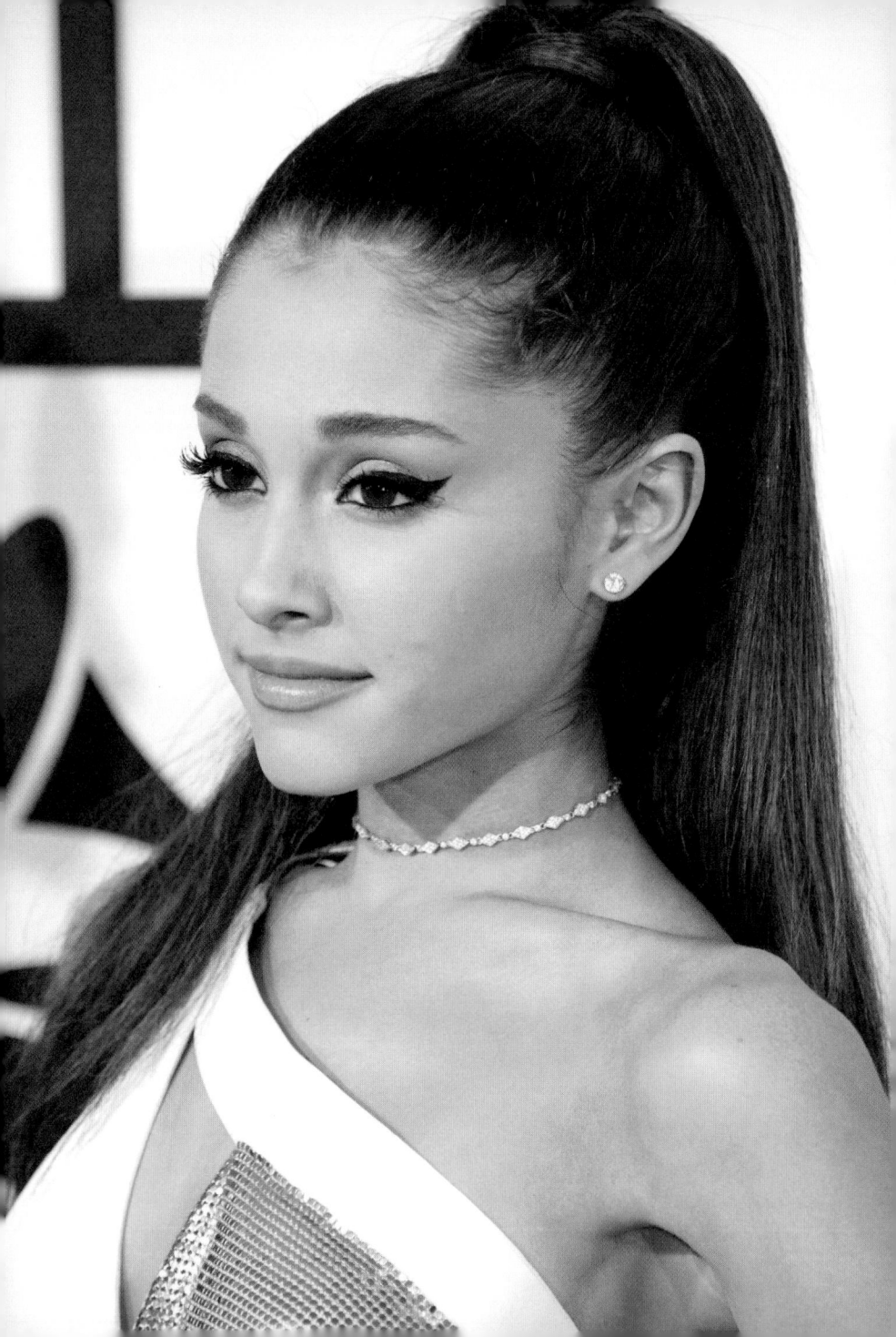

The cute cat ears were now a big part of Ariana's performer style and a teenage Etsy maker, Nhan-nhi "Lillian" Nguyen, from Hawaii, revealed to the press that the singer had ordered a white pair and a purple pair of her kitty-ear headbands to be delivered to her Beverly Hills home and had then worn them on stage. But it wasn't all cat ears and bodysuits, as she still enjoyed the Audrey Hepburn-style dresses, such as the floral strapless Dolce & Gabbana silk gown that she wore to the Grammy Awards in January 2014. In her downtime, she was now teaming her signature ponytail with over-the-knee boots and an oversized sweatshirt or jacket, such as her late grandfather's, to honour him after he passed away at the age of 90 in July 2014.

My Everything was nominated for Best Pop Vocal Album at the 57th Grammy Awards in 2015 and Ariana arrived on the red carpet chicer than ever in a white and silver chain metal Versace from the Spring 2014 ready-to-wear collection. "I look back at the things I wore yesterday and cringe!" she told *Cosmopolitan* in 2014. "I'm not used to the whole red carpet thing yet, but I'll get there... I'll get used to it."

She had been upset by some of the online comments about her floral Dolce & Gabbana at 2014's Grammys and now, when she took to the stage to perform 'Just a Little Bit of Your Heart' in deep purple satin Versace, it was the launch of a visually and musically mature Ariana.

A white and silver chain metal Versace dress and a high ponytail at the 2015 Grammy Awards signalled a move towards haute couture.

Dangerous woman

Ariana's third album had been provisionally titled *Moonlight*, but when she settled on *Dangerous Woman*, it represented a rawer lyrical maturity that really allowed her vocals to take centre stage. Produced by Swedish pop magician Max Martin, it crossed from 50s retro to dance, hip-hop, trap and the sensual electro of 'Into You'. There were also a range of collaborators, including Nicki Minaj on 'Side to Side', Lil Wayne on 'Let Me Love You', Macy Gray on 'Leave Me Lonely' and Future on 'Everyday'.

As the new album's title communicated a message of intent, she revealed that the inspiration had come from the 1975 novel *Woman at Point Zero* by Egyptian author and activist Nawal El Saadawi, who writes, "They said, 'You are a savage and dangerous woman.' I am speaking the truth. And the truth is savage and dangerous."

The 2015 single 'Focus' had originally been planned as the lead single, but it was dropped in favour of the lyrically suggestive title track 'Dangerous Woman', and when released in March 2016, it went straight to the top of the charts in the United Kingdom, and debuted at No. 2 on the *Billboard 200*. Ariana had brought on board self-described "image architect" Law Roach to guide her into a sophisticated, sensual era for her red-carpet looks, her personal wardrobe and her music videos.

An empowering woman. Ariana in a Bryan Hearns leather skirt and Calvin Klein bra for the Dangerous Woman tour, in Phoenix, Arizona on 3 February 2017.

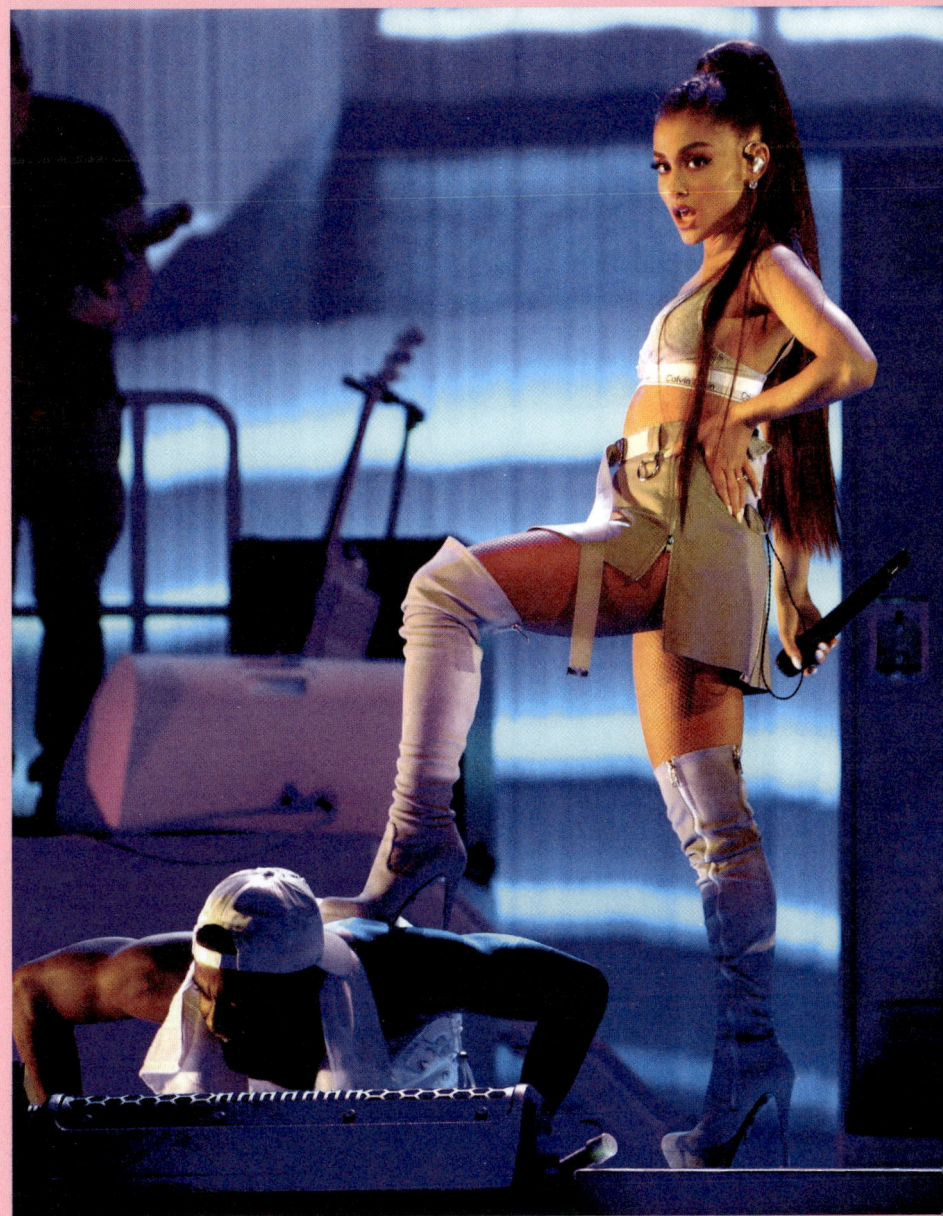

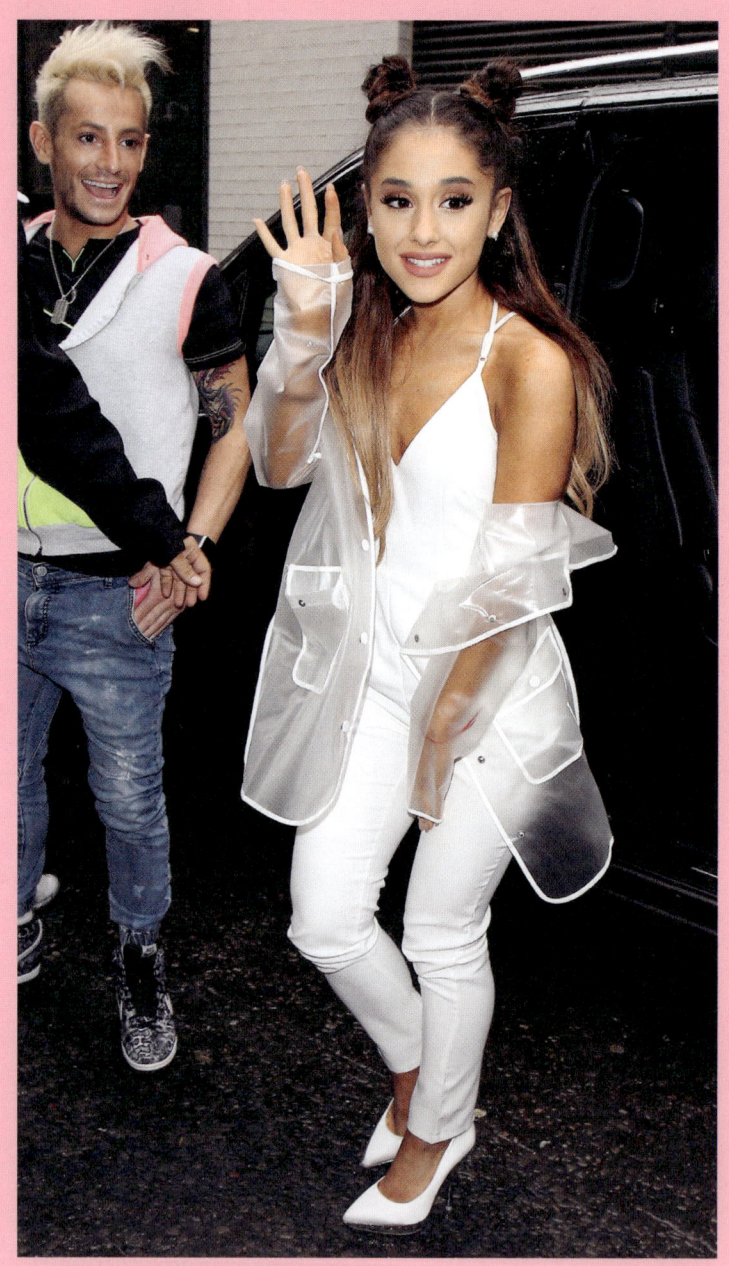

"Grande's got a not-so-secret weapon in all this: showstopping talent."

BILLBOARD

The lingerie in the 'Dangerous Woman' video was also a further move to take "baby steps in expressing my sexuality in my imagery," she told *Cosmopolitan* in March 2017. "I'm still a giving, loving person – that's not lessened by the fact that I showed my booty in a music video. I'm a good person – and I have a cute booty. It's a horrible situation that we're dealing with right now as women. I feel bad for girls who go to school with a short skirt and are told that they're asking for it just because they like [to show] their legs."

The cover of the album firmly communicated this new attitude. No longer the Nickelodeon-child-star persona, nor even the girlish teen star with cat ears, Ariana was now an empowered woman in a latex bunny mask, which she called her "black latex Super Bunny within!" As she told *Billboard* in May 2016, "Whenever I doubt myself or question choices I know in my gut are right – because other people are telling me other things – I'm like, 'What would that bad bitch Super Bunny do?' She helps me call the shots."

She felt the pressure to show a maturity and authenticity beyond her child stardom days, but with her petite stature, young looks and an open love of Super Bunny and Harry Potter, the sexiness could sometimes feel jarring. As *Billboard* wrote: "All the animal-themed, Lolita-meets-S&M gear don't exactly help... But Grande's got a not-so-secret weapon in all this: showstopping talent."

At the American Music Awards in November 2016 in Alexander McQueen tailored trousers and I.D. Sarrieri bustier.

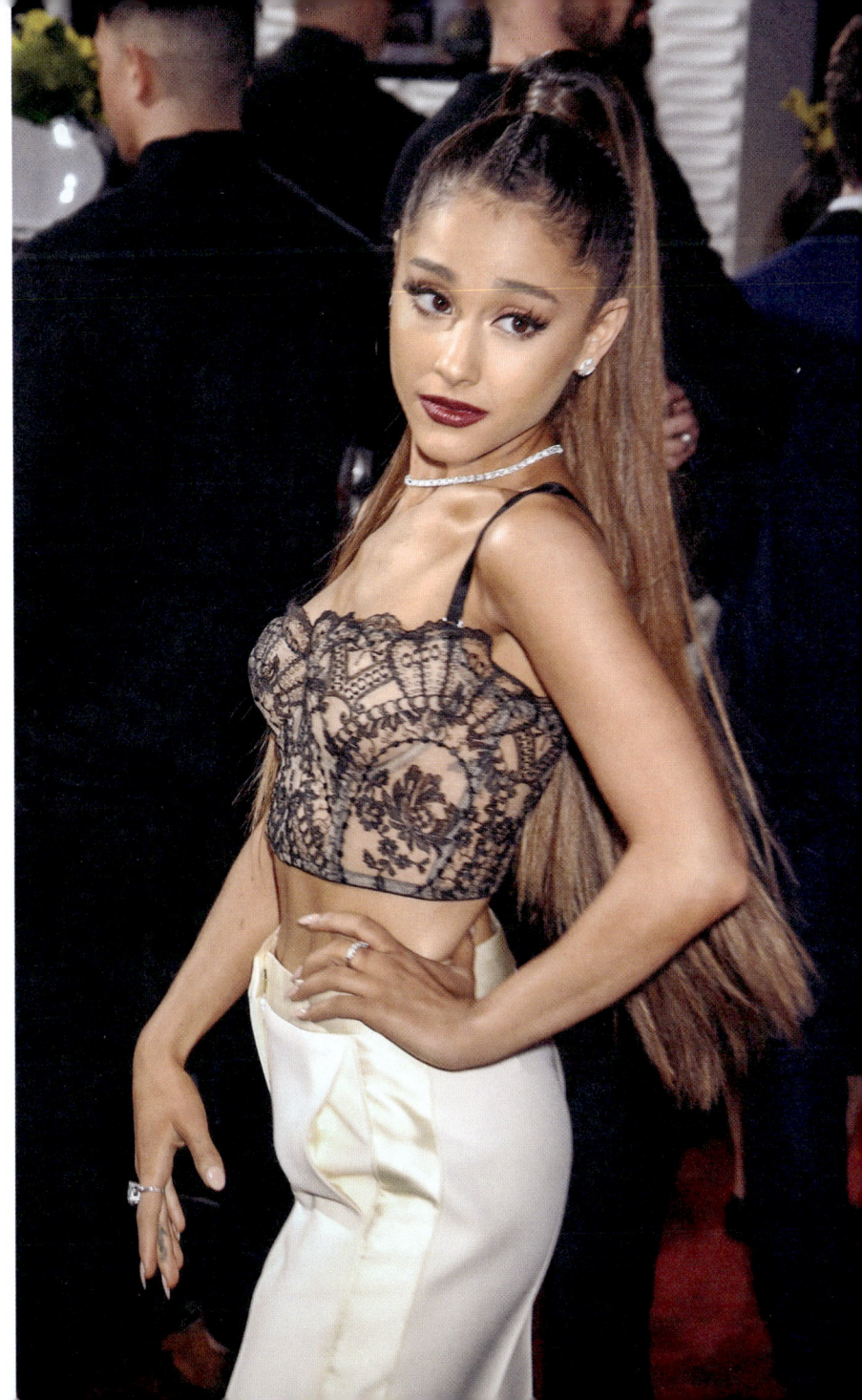

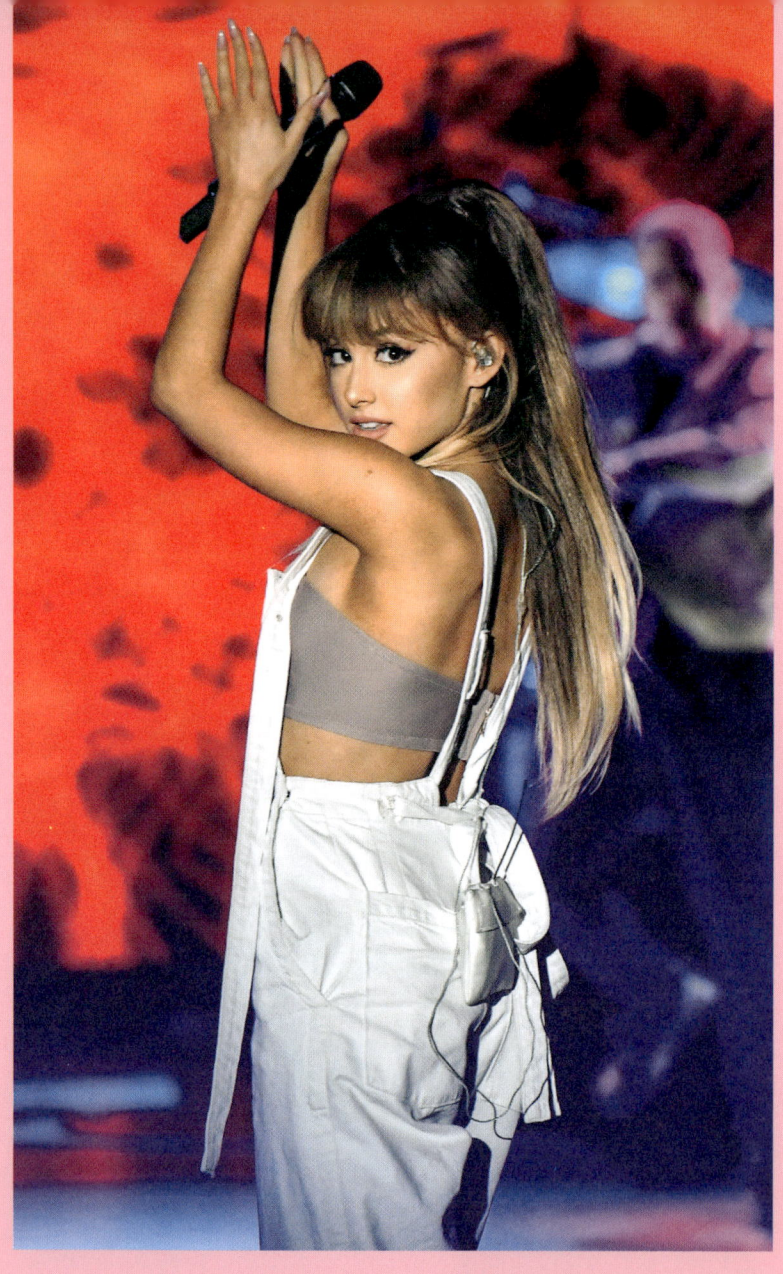

Performing onstage at Macy's Presents Fashion's
Front Row in September 2016.

Law Roach, a Chicago southside native who moved to LA and became stylist to the actress and singer Zendaya, helped smooth out the transition in swapping cute for edgier streetwear and replacing high street brands with couture by Vera Wang, Alexander Wang and Donatella Versace. As he reached out to a variety of designers, including up-and-coming labels like Michael Ngo, he had one major requirement: "We've only worked with people that I knew were fans of her and her music. I wanted them to have a bit of emotion when approaching the clothes. What's their interpretation of Ariana? And if you look, they all were completely different."

He took the flattering silhouette of high-waisted bodysuits and minidresses and then added a unique twist by combining streetwear with haute couture.

Ariana's image had also shifted in the minds of the public over the last year when a number of controversies had painted her as "difficult". There were stories about how protective she was of her image, that photographers were instructed not to shoot her right side and that she had approval of every shot. With reports that she allegedly had a bad attitude toward her fans during meet-and-greets, she was fast becoming a diva in the minds of the press and public although she insisted, "Celine Dion is a diva, thank you. But if you want to call me a bitch, that's not accurate. Because it's just not in my nature."

She later told Apple Music 1 host Zane Lowe in May 2020 that being called a "diva" made her want to step away from interviews and stop expressing herself.

"It's like, when men express their opinions, or defend themselves, or are directing something and making notes on something, they're brilliant, and they're geniuses," she said. "And yet, it's just so not the same thing with women, which I hope we can work on fixing."

And then there was "Doughnut-gate". In July 2015 Ariana was with new boyfriend and backup dancer Ricky Alvarez at a doughnut shop in California when she was caught on the surveillance tape secretly licking one of the products that had been left out on a tray and declaring she hated America. She took to social media to apologize and explain it was a reaction to childhood obesity, and that she was upset about "how freely we as Americans eat and consume things without giving any thought to the consequences" – but there was still a backlash.

As host and musical guest on *Saturday Night Live* in March 2016, dressed in an elegant black Noam Hanoch jumpsuit teamed with Giuseppe Zanotti platform heels, she used the monologue to own her controversies as she performed a jazzy showtune to ask what her next scandal would be. To further rehabilitate herself, she also took part in a skit where she demonstrated her uncanny mimicry of other stars, a skill she had been honing since she was a child.

OPPOSITE At the TIME100 Gala in April 2016 in a black tulle confection by Christian Siriano.

OVERLEAF Ariana performing 'Side to Side' with Nicki Minaj at the 2016 MTV Video Music Awards.

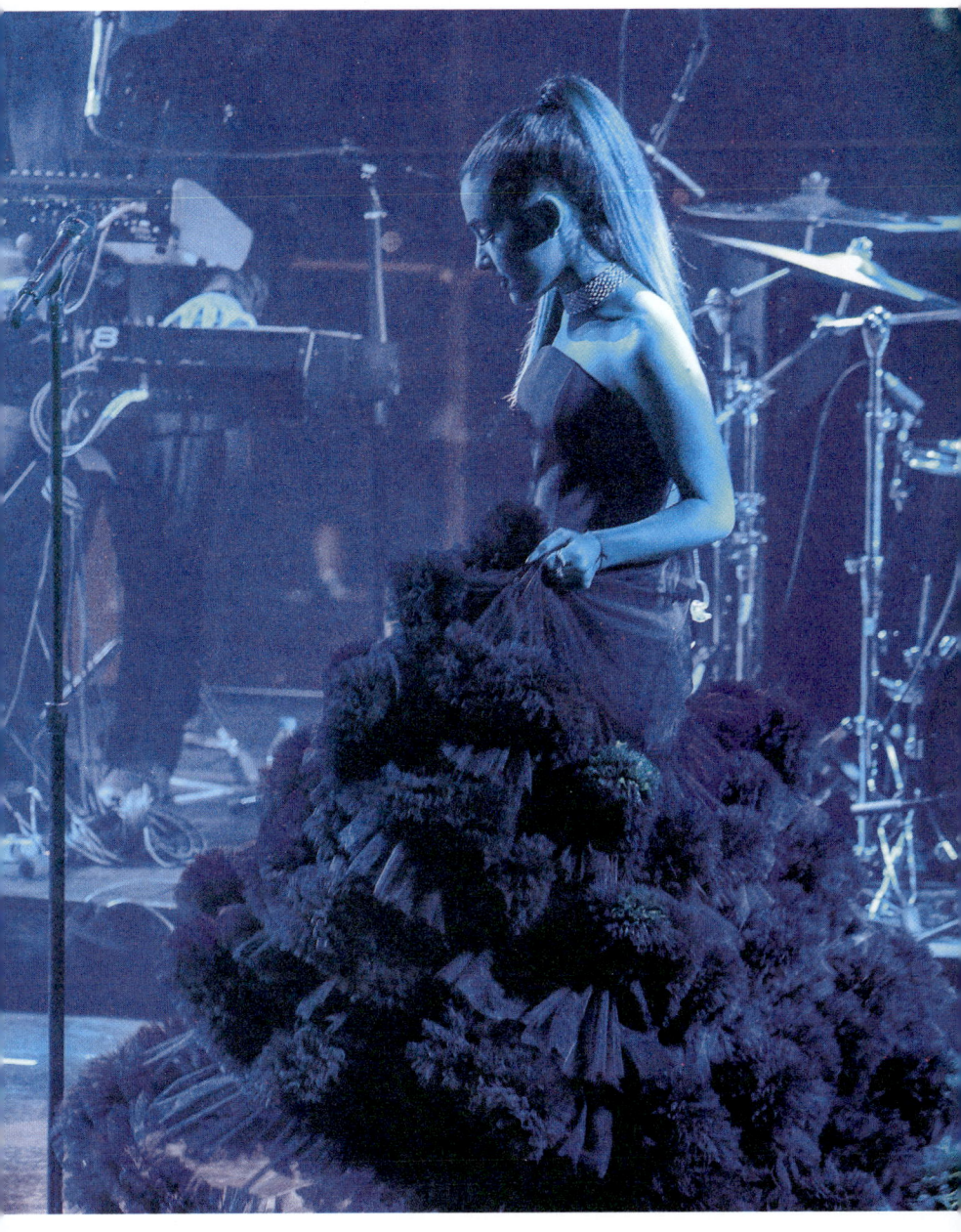

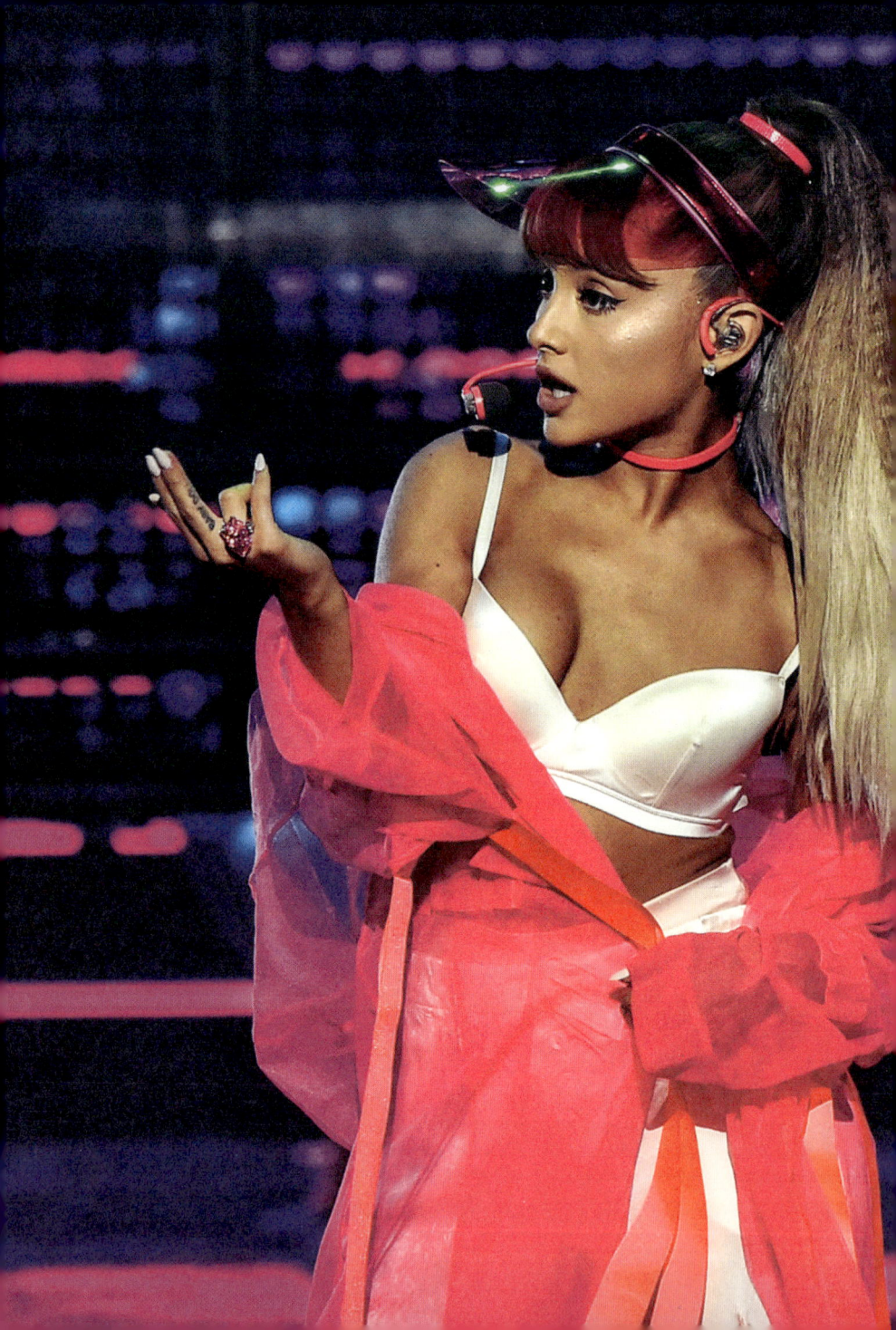

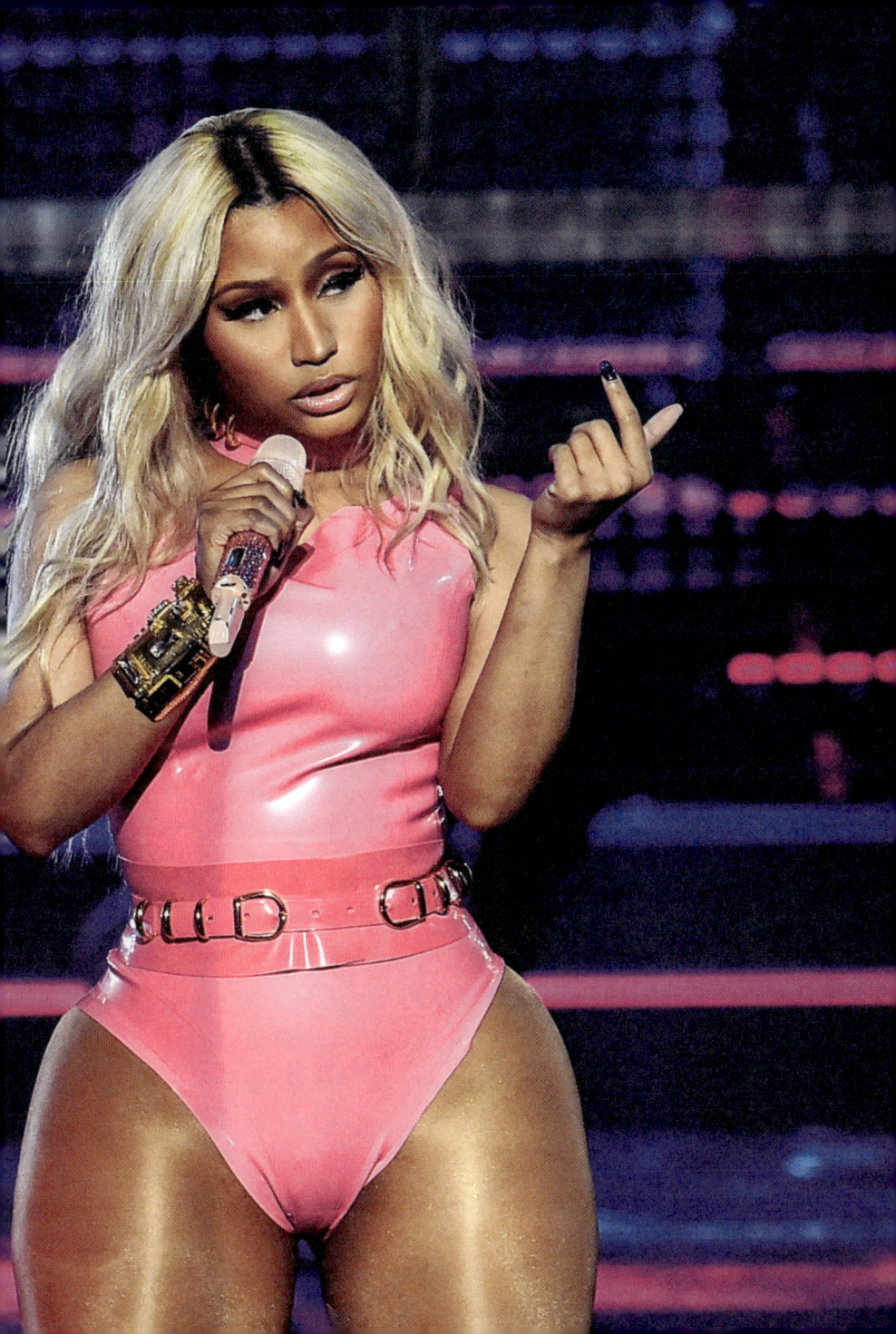

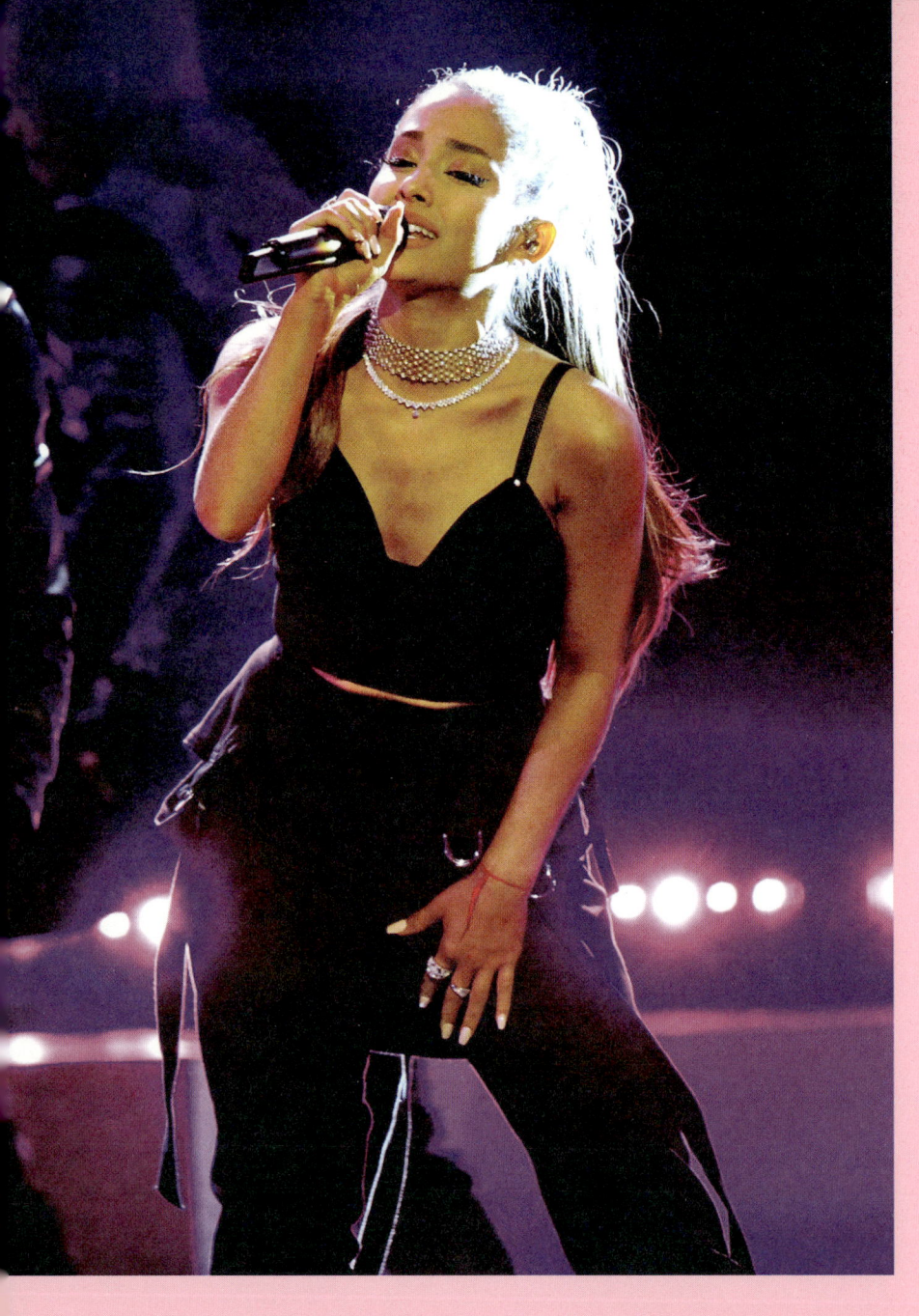

When she was the cover star of *Billboard* magazine in May 2016, her stylist Law Roach helped her play up to her diva reputation. Wrapped in just a white towel, and with another around her hair, Ariana rocked Chanel vintage round sunglasses, an H. Stern "Fireworks" necklace and red lips, every inch the Beverly Hills star.

She wore the same necklace to the TIME100 Gala in April 2016 to complement her black Christian Siriano gown from the Autumn/Winter 2016 collection and with its ruffled skirt constructed from yards of tulle, it played up to her love of princess aesthetics.

She further promoted the album with an acoustic performance of 'Dangerous Woman' at the 2016 MTV Movie Awards, dressed like Marilyn in hot pink, and at the *Billboard* Music Awards, where she performed 'Into You' in a black crop top, cargo pants and her high ponytail – it was sophisticated, edgy and powerful.

At the MTV Video Music Awards in September 2016 Ariana arrived on the red carpet in a similarly dramatic look, of black Alexander Wang pants and a lacy, off-the-shoulder top, and with an updated ponytail, this time streaked with golden highlights and cut with a fringe. She and Nicki Minaj performed the third single from the album, 'Side to Side', rocking the neon outfits of the music video, as styled by Law Roach. This would be a dominant aesthetic for the singer going forward.

Performing 'Dangerous Woman' and 'Into You' at the 2016 *Billboard* Music Awards, mixing the H.Stern "Fireworks" necklace with street style.

"We've only worked with people that I knew were *fans* of her and her music. I wanted them to have a bit of *emotion* when approaching the clothes."

LAW ROACH

In Alexander Wang on the red carpet at the MTV Video Music Awards in August 2016.

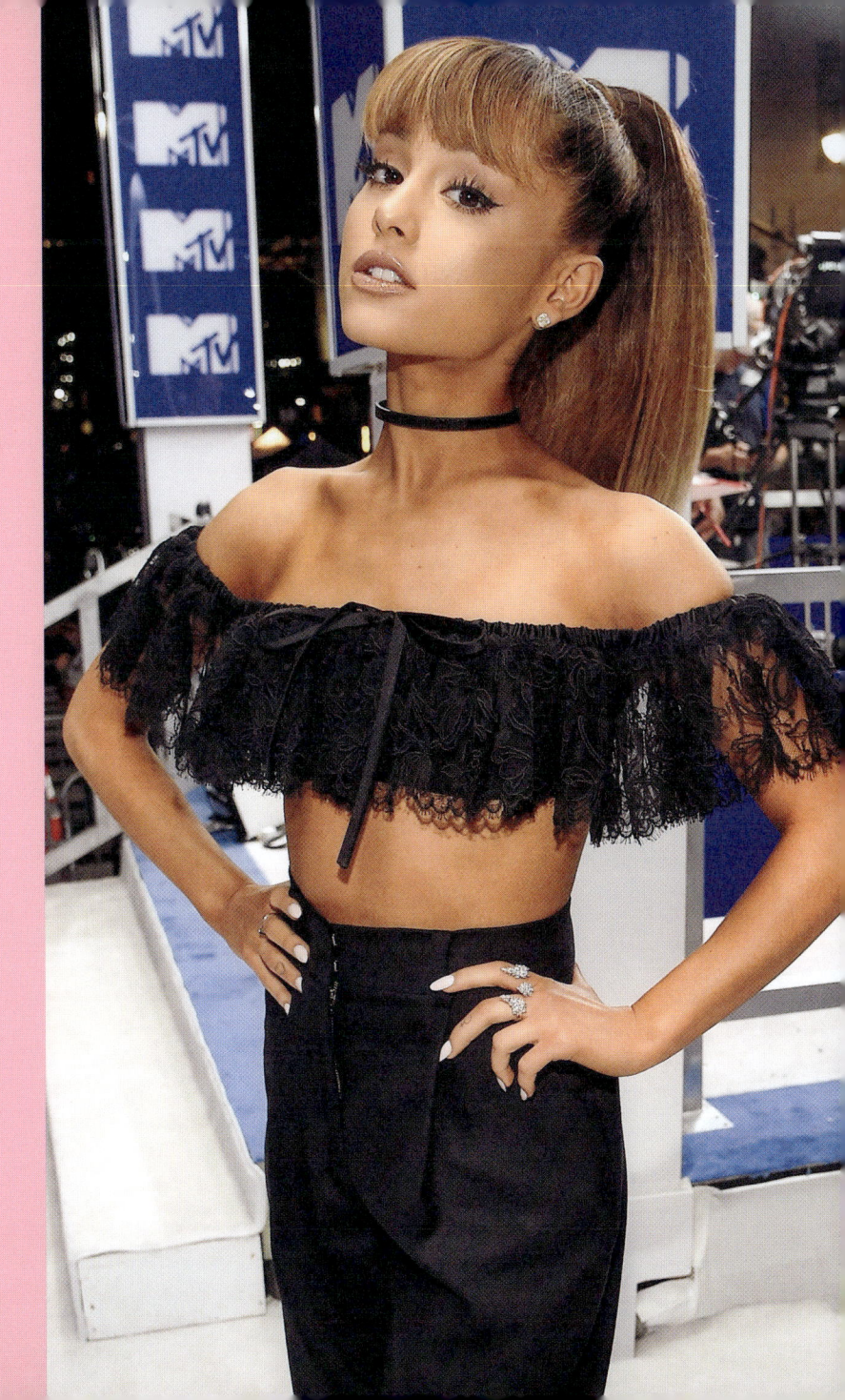

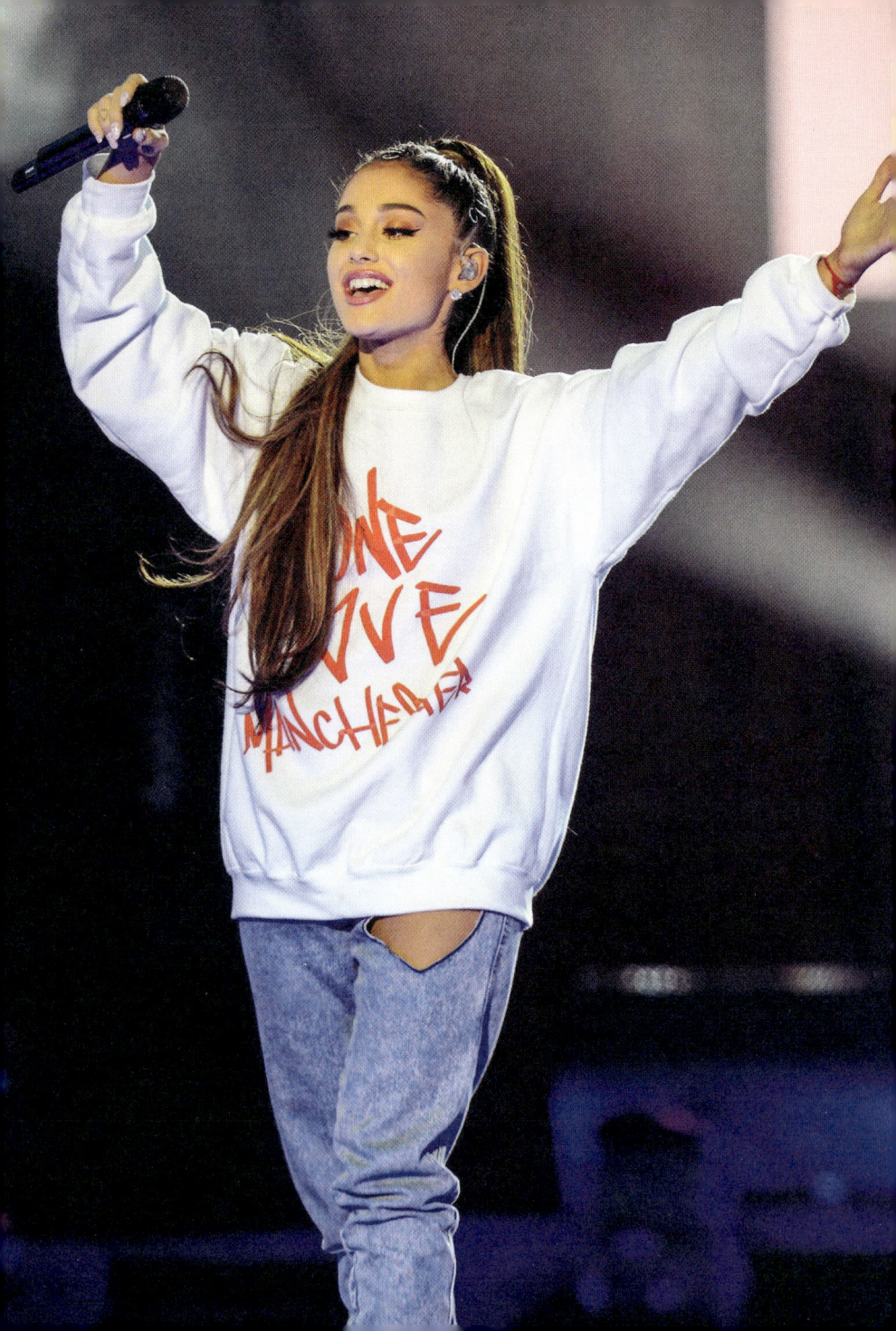

In November 2016 at the American Music Awards, Ariana was named Artist of the Year, and at the GRAMMYs in 2017, *Dangerous Woman* was nominated for Best Pop Vocal Album. After announcing her global Dangerous Woman tour in September 2016, it kicked off in Phoenix, Arizona, in February 2017.

In a moment of unimaginable horror, during the final minutes of her Manchester concert on 22 May 2017, a suicide bomber exploded their device in the arena, resulting in 22 fatalities and many more injured. Ariana's initial instinct was to immediately fly back to the States, but with the cataclysmic impact on her young fans and their parents, she was desperate to do something to help. She returned to Manchester to meet the injured, and with a sense of urgency, hurriedly organized a benefit concert, One Love Manchester. Recruiting guest stars including Coldplay, Justin Bieber and Miley Cyrus, she raised $25 million for the Red Cross and brought an entire city, and country, together after such a shocking event. Dressed simply in a One Love sweater, jeans and heels, Ariana performed her "dirtiest songs" at the request of the mother of one of the victims, given the speculation she was targeted because of her racy image. But the most powerful moment was Ariana singing 'Somewhere Over the Rainbow' as she delivered a healing message of love and unity.

Bringing a message of hope to the One Love Manchester benefit concert on 4 June 2017.

Sweetener

In April 2018 Ariana revealed the cover of her first single since the trauma of the Manchester terrorist attack and what was striking was the newly white-blonde hair worn in a low ponytail and the rainbow prism cast over one eye.

Since her stirring performance at One Love Manchester, she had limited her public appearances to focus on activism. She performed at A Concert for Charlottesville in Virginia in November 2017 after the city was rocked by neo-Nazi violence and in March 2018 she headlined March For Our Lives, the anti-gun violence rally, in Washington D.C., following the mass high school shooting in Parkland, Florida. Now using her voice to call for unity and change, she wore a pared-back uniform of slogan sweaters and pants so as not to distract from the cause.

"This generation, they're standing up and they're not going to take no for an answer," she declared in an interview with *The Fader*, and she was eager to do what she could to support them.

Headlining the anti-gun violence rally March for Our Lives, in Washington D.C. in March 2018.

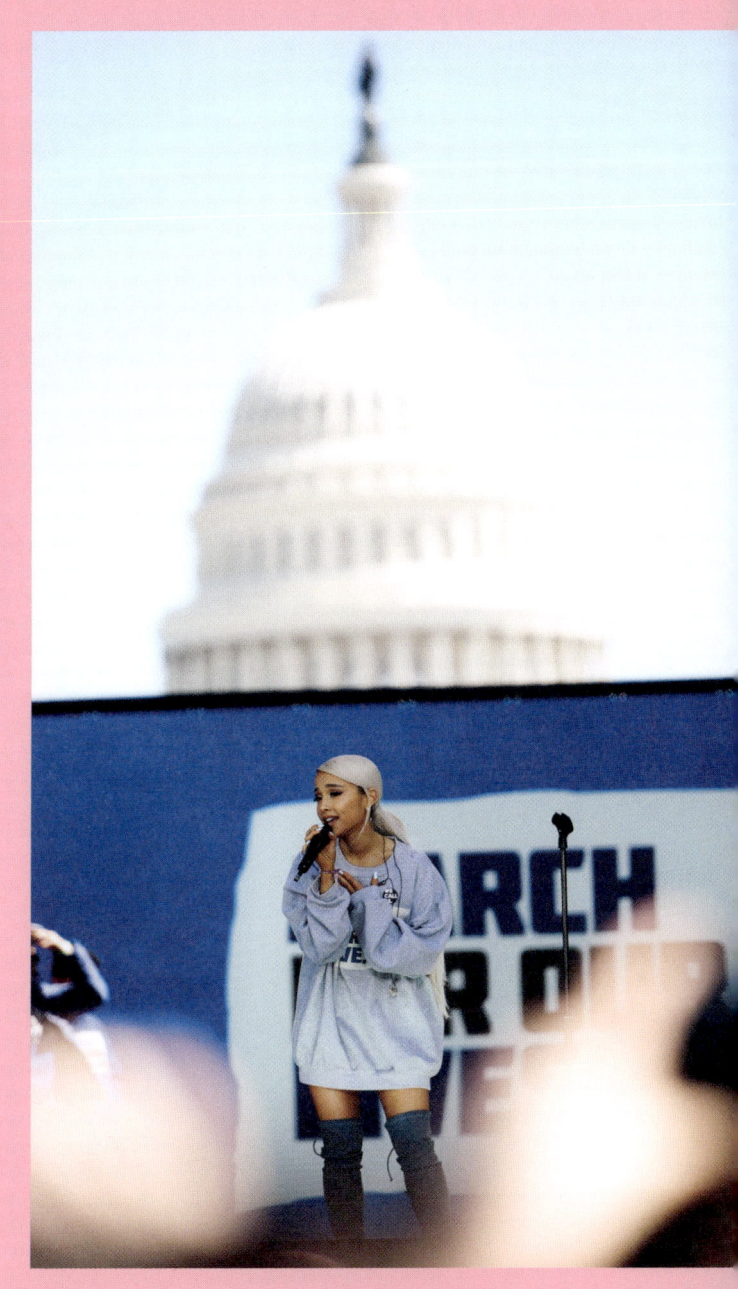

"*This generation,* they're standing up and *they're not going to take* no for an answer."

ARIANA GRANDE

After a four-month social media hiatus, she released her new single 'No Tears Left to Cry', which was a surprisingly upbeat dance tune that celebrated recovery and topped the iTunes charts in 85 countries. She debuted the track during her first ever appearance at Coachella Valley Music & Arts Festival in April 2018 as a guest during DJ-songwriter Kygo's set. She had never imagined she would perform at the festival, but the incredible, collective experience was a part of processing the trauma. Her lilac-tinted ponytail, the matching Grayscale lilac sports set, Chanel quilted belt bag and Le Silla "Eva" over-the-knee boots all reflected the new vibe for her latest album, *Sweetener*, which was designed to cast a prism of hope.

Produced with collaborators including Pharrell Williams and Max Martin, Ariana chose a more soulful pop sound to bring a little "escapism and joy to people's lives when they listen to it. That's why nothing is that sad on the album. I really just wanted to keep it beautiful, and free, and light and sweet."

She chose the name *Sweetener*, "because it sounds so youthful and unassuming at first, but when you listen to the music, you understand what it's really about." The album cover, featuring an upside portrait with her white-blonde hair against a muted background, was a representation of how the singer's life felt at the time: "I want it to be a very simple portrait of me ... I bleached my hair platinum blonde for it and stuff too, just so that everything could be like, more light and ethereal feeling. Fresh feeling."

2018 was a year of firsts for Ariana, and she made her debut at the Met Gala in May 2018, in a custom-made Vera Wang gown printed with imagery from the Sistine Chapel. As well as meeting the "Heavenly Bodies" brief for the gala, the theme fitted with the second single from the album, 'God is a Woman'. Released in July, it was accompanied by a music video packed with historical and symbolic references of female empowerment. As she swirls in a galaxy and lies naked in a watercolour pool, it's as if she's being reborn in pastel hues.

Over the summer of 2018 Ariana moved to New York as part of her plan for fun and escapism, and after connecting with *Saturday Night Live* star, comedian and actor Pete Davidson, she embarked on a very public, and intense, love affair. They announced their whirlwind engagement in June and were spotted frequently around Manhattan, with Ariana in her new off-duty look of Yeezy over-the-knee boots, oversized sweaters and mini Chanel or Louis Vuitton purses. To *Vogue* in 2019 she described this time as being "frivolous and fun and insane and highly unrealistic, and I loved him, and I didn't know him." They appeared on the red carpet together at the MTV Video Music Awards, with Ariana dressed like a warrior cyborg in a metallic Venus Prototype latex chrome bustier and over-the-knee boots. She took to the stage to perform 'God is a Woman' and then again to collect her award for Best Pop for 'No Tears Left to Cry'.

Ariana's custom-made Vera Wang gown for the Met Gala in 2018 printed with imagery of the Sistine Chapel.

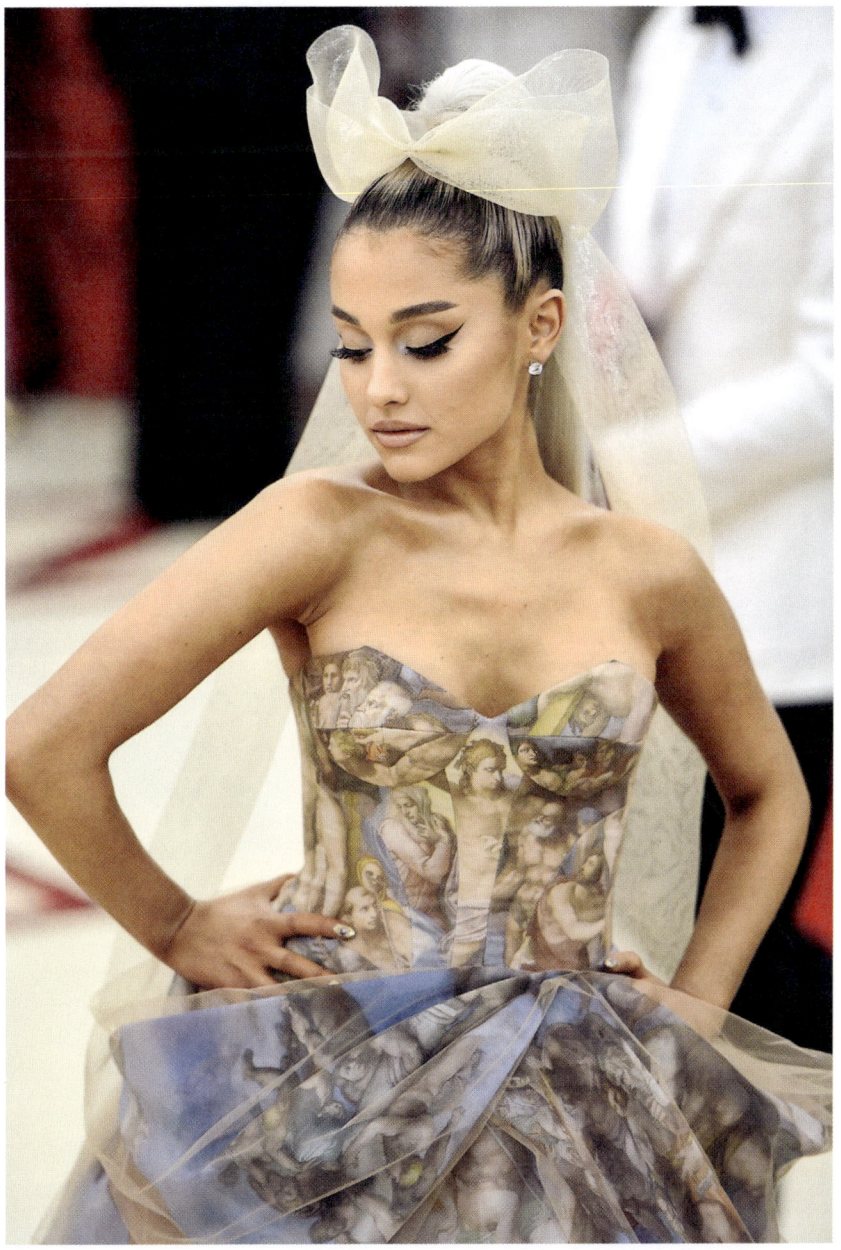

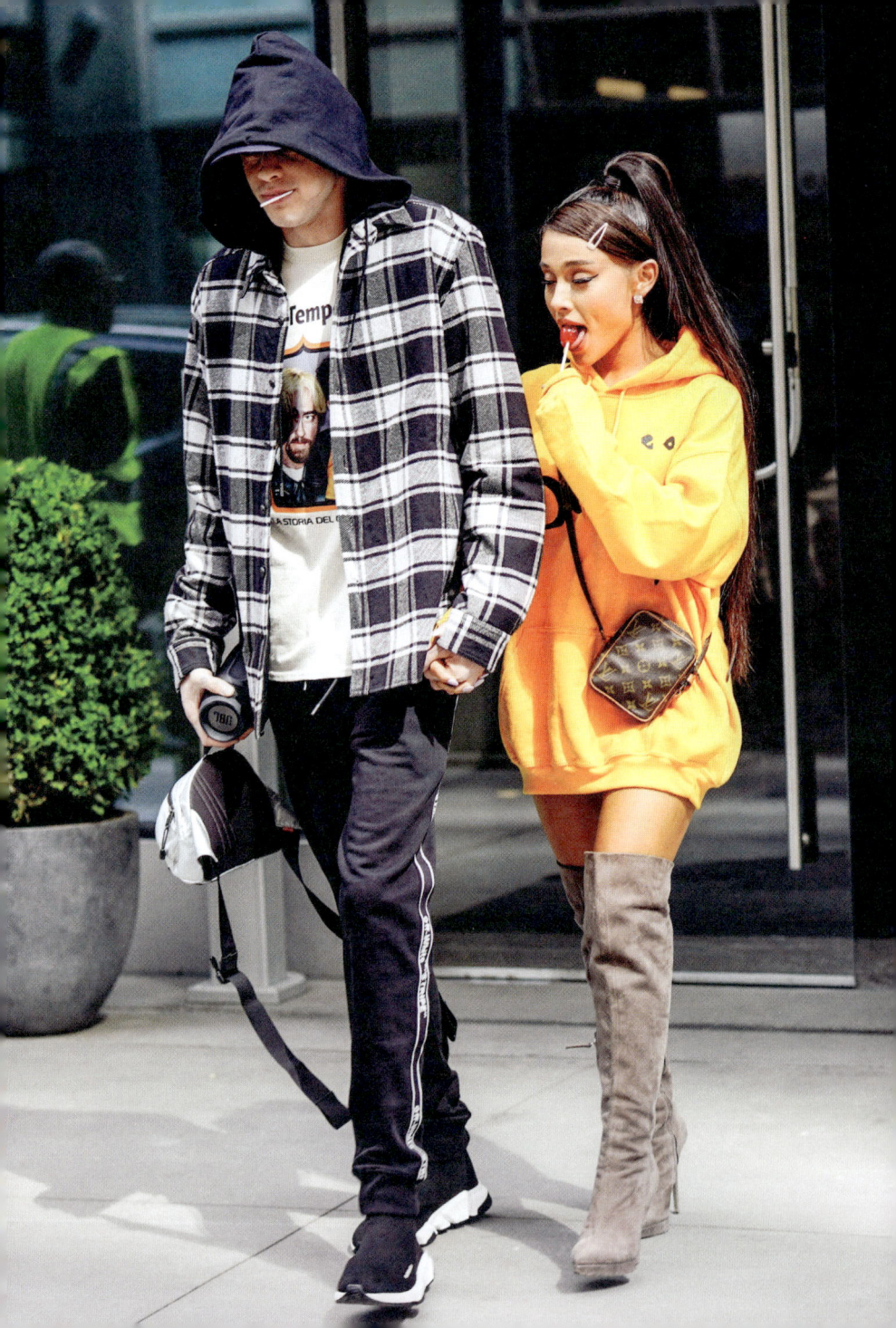

To showcase the album, the Sweetener Sessions was a series of intimate concerts in New York, Chicago and Los Angeles, for which she wore a pared-back costume of lilac Sweetener sweatshirt and her go-to Yeezy suede taupe boots. In London she recorded a special performance for the BBC, where she upped the glamour in a frothy black fairytale gown, with a skirt so enveloping that she joked to host Davina McCall, "I feel like this dress is going to eat me."

Just a few days after recording *Ariana at the BBC* in early September, news broke that her ex-boyfriend and close friend Mac Miller had died of a drug overdose. She went into mourning, and with a broken engagement to Pete Davidson piling on the trauma, she retreated from the spotlight to concentrate on recovery.

In November 2018 she emerged to send a tweet to the world: "remember when i was like hey i have no tears left to cry and the universe was like HAAAAAAAAA bitch u thought." It was a sign that she was ready to enter into her most successful creative and commercial period yet.

Ariana stepping out with Pete Davidson in Manhattan in June 2018, in her favorite sweater and Yeezy boots combination.

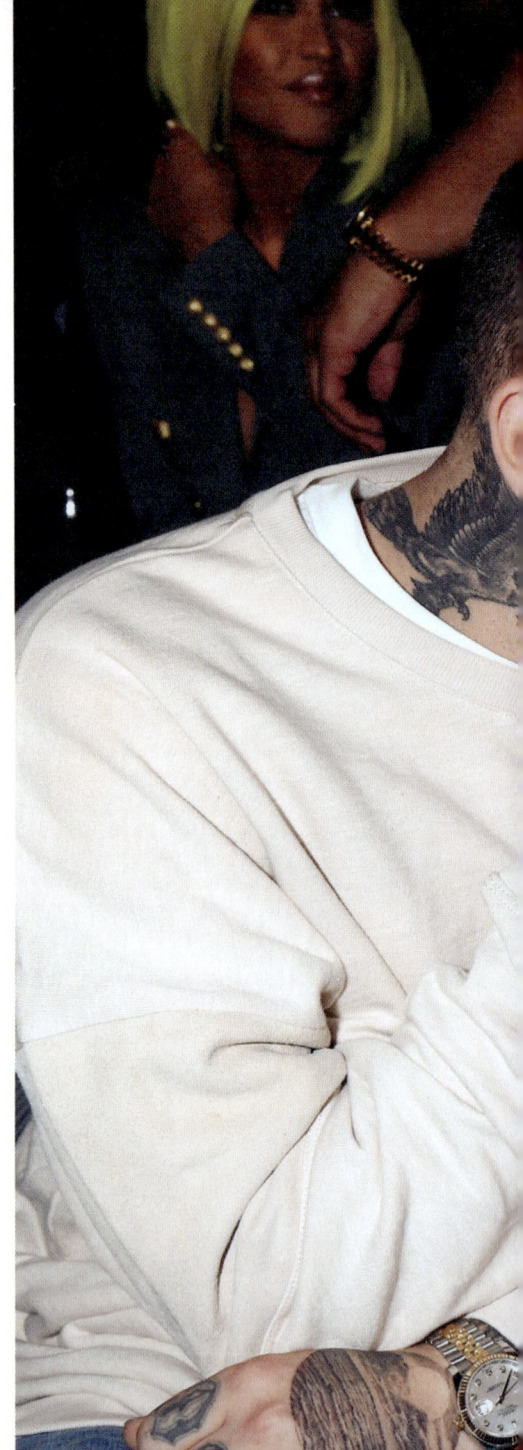

Ariana was devastated when
ex-boyfriend and close friend
Mac Miller died in September
2018. Seen here at the 2016
MTV Video Music Awards.

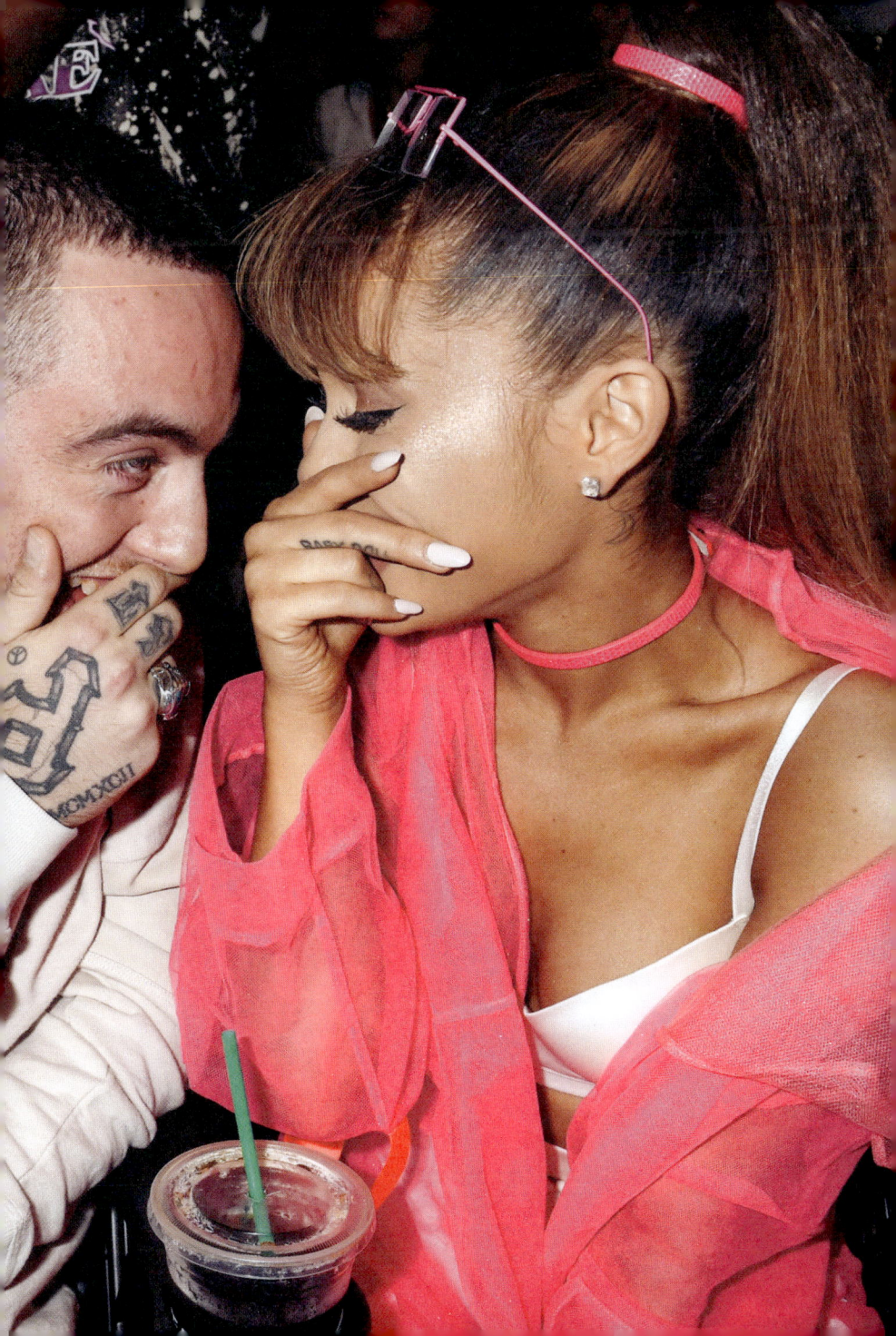

Thank u, next

In November 2018, when Ariana released the surprise new single 'thank u, next', it not only topped the *Billboard* Hot 100, but became an instant cultural touchpoint as a positive ode to moving on from past relationships. The music video, which became the most-watched on YouTube in the 24 hours after its release, was a feast for rom-com fans as she channelled a number of noughties heroines – from *Mean Girls* in a pale pink Pringle Scotland cardigan and suede leather miniskirt, to *Legally Blonde*, *13 Going on 30* and *Bring it On* (in a custom-made cheerleader outfit).

She also announced that a new album, *thank u, next,* would be coming soon. Written and recorded in a champagne-fuelled fever of creativity over the course of two weeks in October with producer Tommy Brown and songwriter Victoria Monét, Ariana told *Vogue* that she barely remembered the process because she was "so drunk" and "so sad". With its trap beats and soulful R&B, it reflected on her broken engagement to Pete Davidson, the death of Mac Miller and her new appreciation of taking time to love herself, rather than giving her all to her relationships.

In a lilac Christian Siriano bustier minidress to accept the Woman of the Year Award at the 2018 *Billboard* Women in Music event.

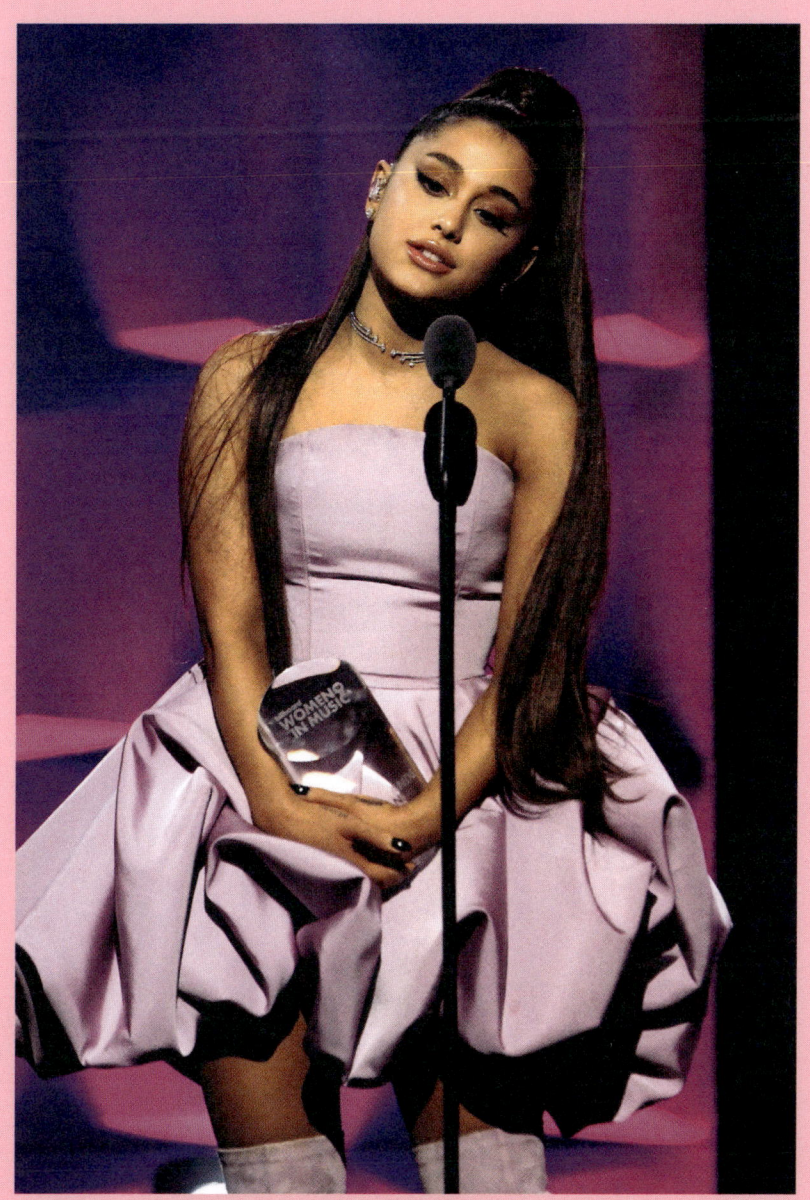

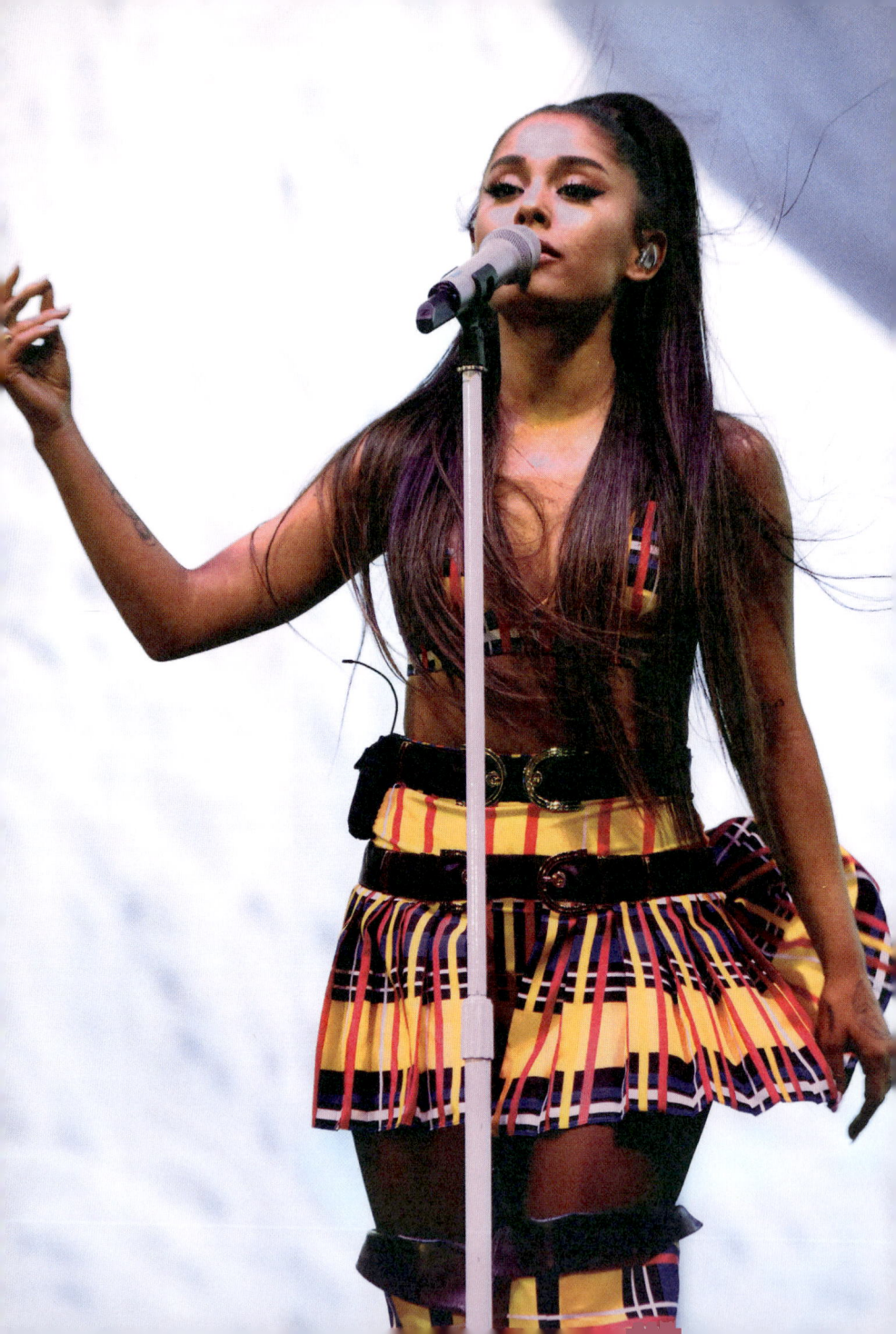

By the end of 2018 she was not only Spotify's most-streamed female artist of the year, but also named *Billboard*'s Woman of the Year, where she described in her acceptance speech that it had been one of "the best years of my career and like the worst of my life". She arrived at the ceremony in a lilac confection, a puffball strapless dress and over-the-knee boots, similar to her pastel lampshade dresses, but instead of the Regina George blonde hair of the 'thank u, next' video, she was back to being a brunette.

She released the single '7 Rings' in January 2019 and it debuted at the top of the charts of the *Billboard* Hot 100. With its riff on *The Sound of Music*'s 'My Favorite Things', and references to *Breakfast at Tiffany's*, it was a celebration of the joys of female friendship. Ariana said it was inspired by a "challenging fall day in New York" when she and her friends went to Tiffany's together: "You know how when you're waiting at Tiffany's they give you lots of champagne? They got us very tipsy, so we bought seven engagement rings, and when I got back to the studio, I gave everybody a friendship ring."

When the album was released on 8 February 2019 it also topped the charts, going straight to No. 1 on the *Billboard* 200, and with the most streams of an album by a female artist in a week, breaking her own record for *Sweetener*, released just six months prior. Ariana was now a pop phenomenon and much of the appeal was the deeply insightful lyrics that fed the desire for gossip around her personal life.

Performing 'thank u, next' at Coachella in a plaid miniskirt and crop top by Versace.

"Strong, feminine, futuristic, cosmic"

LEROY BENNETT

Backstage at the opening night of the Sweetener tour in Albany, New York, in her orange Michael Ngo stage outfit, 18 March 2019.

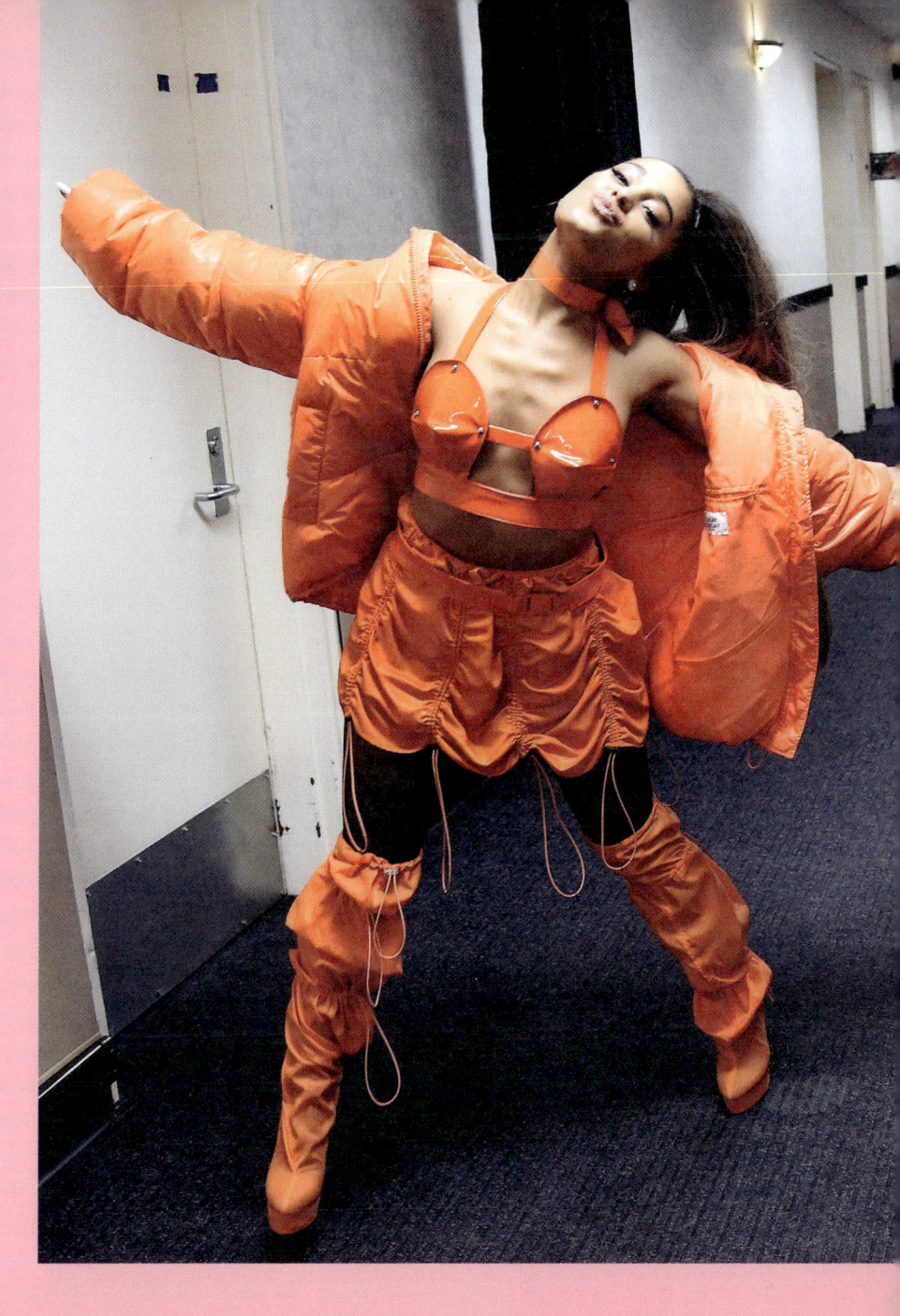

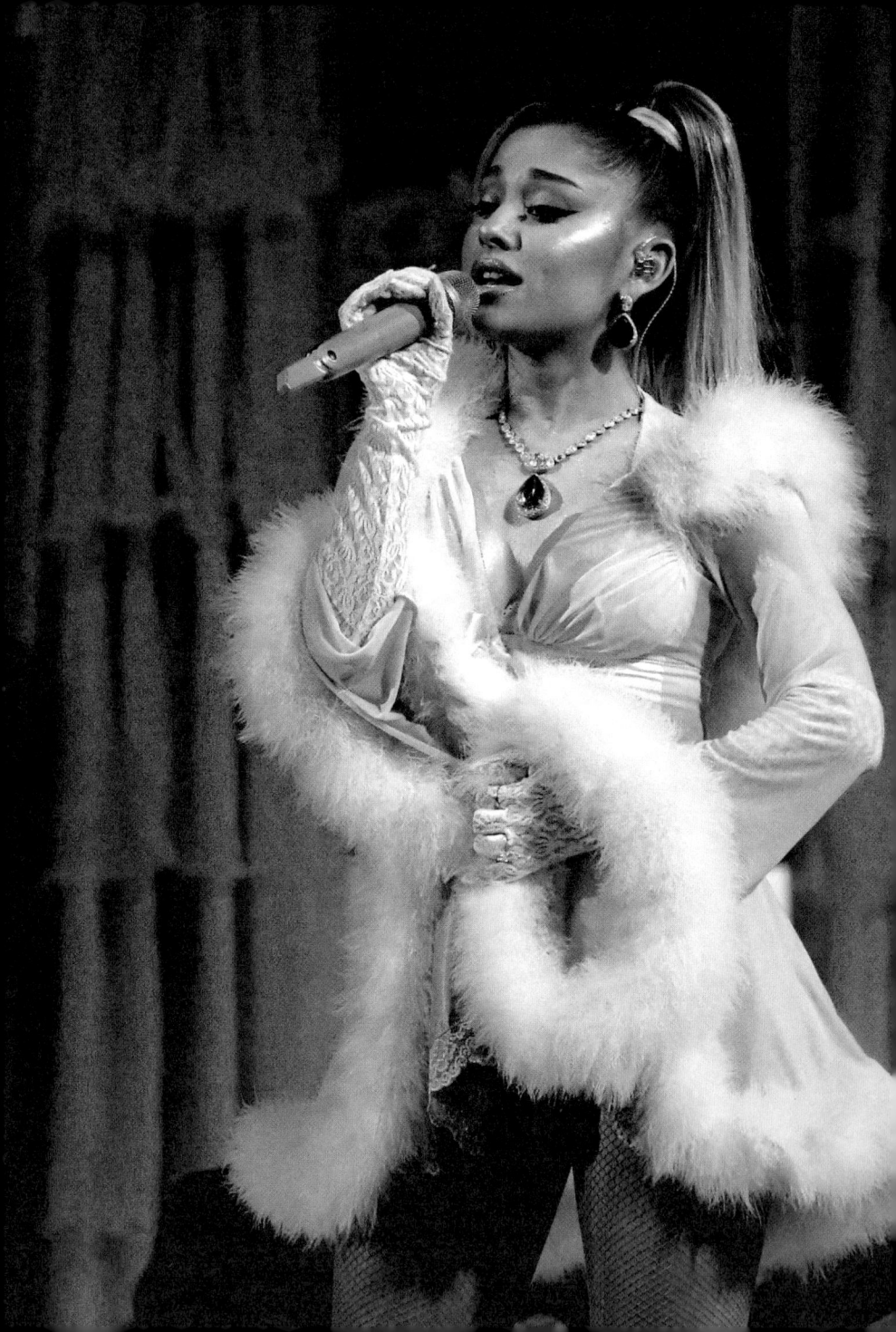

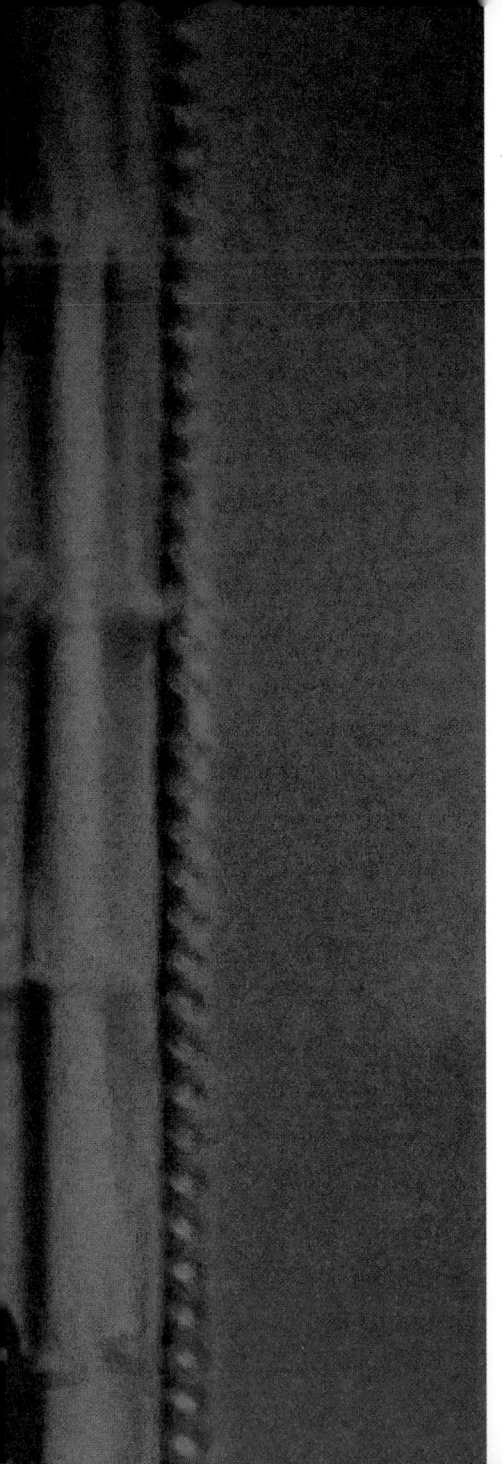

Performing 'thank u, next'
at the Grammy Awards
in January 2020.

In March she embarked on The Sweetener world tour, which combined both the music from *Sweetener* and *thank u, next* and took her across North America and Europe from March to December 2019. With costumes custom-made by Versace and Michael Ngo, she was now a fierce warrior princess in bondage-inspired two-pieces and sportswear.

She returned to Coachella in April 2019, this time as the first female to ever headline the festival, wearing variations of the Sweetener world tour look, and where she shared the stage with guest performers NSYNC, Nicki Minaj and Mase. Her stage manager, LeRoy Bennett of Seven Design Works, described the set as a "strong, feminine, futuristic, cosmic world".

This powerful femininity was showcased at the Grammys in February 2020 when she arrived in a whirl of tulle, her ombre hair tied back in a high ponytail, and with multiple costume changes, all orchestrated by Law Roach.

For the next six months, as the pandemic gripped the world, Ariana's public appearances would be limited. There were collaborations with Justin Bieber for 'Stuck With U', with Lady Gaga on 'Rain on Me' and an appearance at the 2020 MTV Video Music Awards, where she won four awards, including Song of the Year, Best Cinematography and Best Collaboration for 'Rain on Me', and Best Music Video from Home for 'Stuck with U'. Styled in a purple snakeskin Howie B minidress and mask for her performance with Lady Gaga, and with her hair in double pigtails, it was as if she was from the Manga comic *Sailor Moon*. But with a new album on the way, she was also preparing to unveil another shift in style.

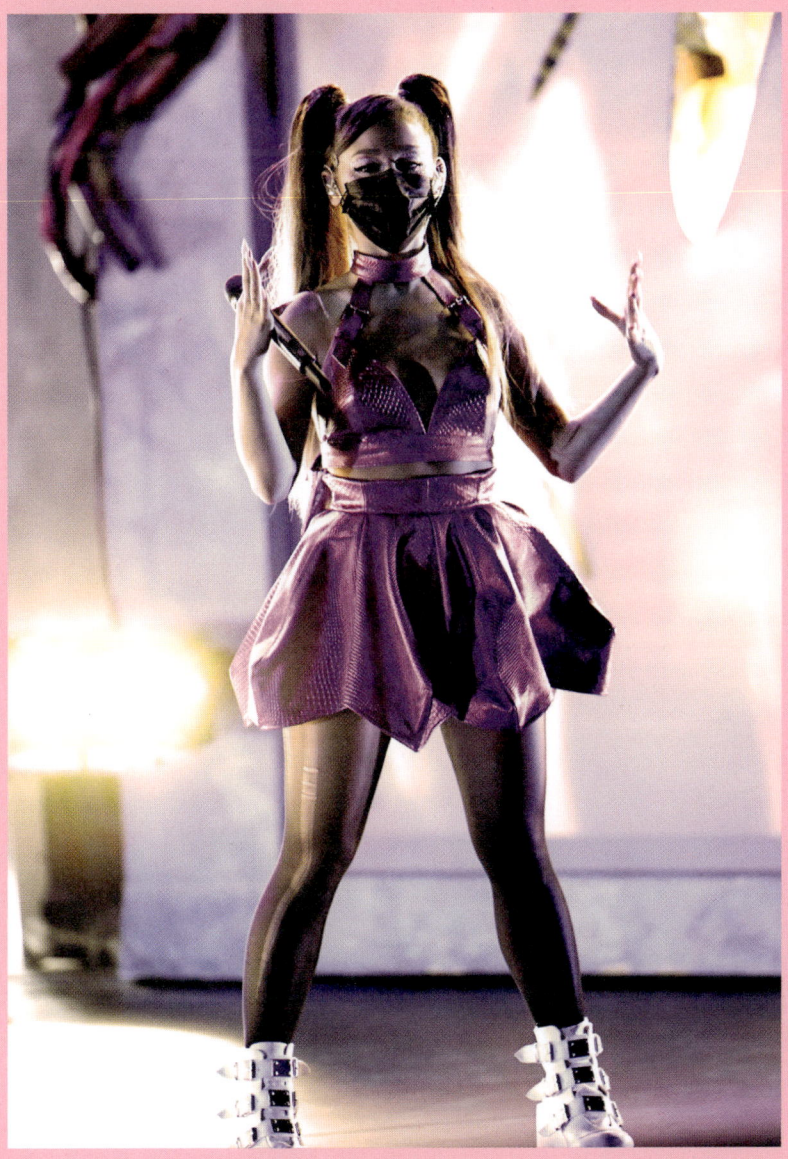

Ariana teamed up with Lady Gaga to perform 'Rain on Me' at the 2020 MTV Video Music Awards, when the Covid pandemic meant wearing a face mask.

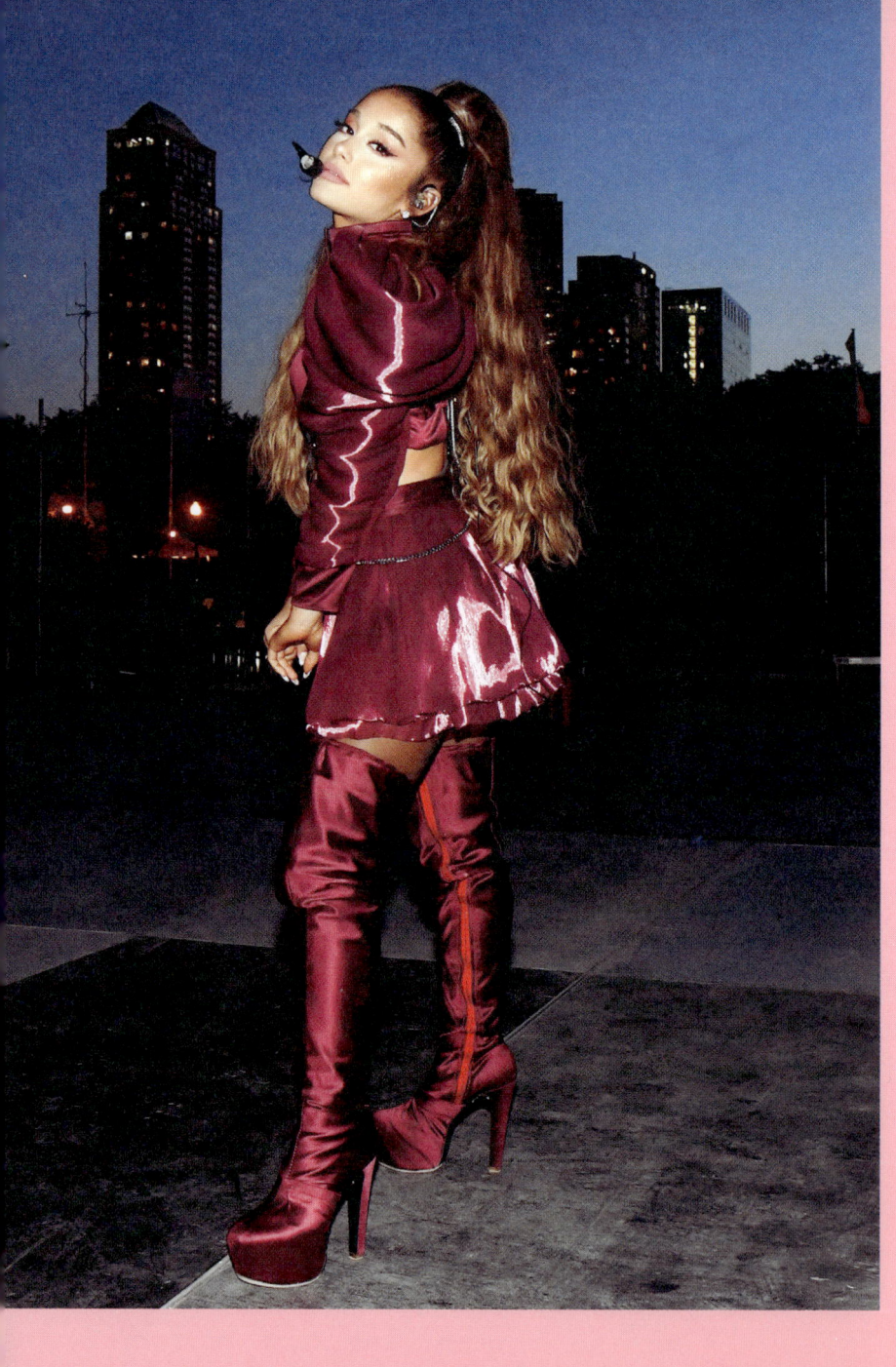

Positions

In 2020, when Ariana teamed up with a new stylist, Mimi Cuttrell, she shook off the lampshade tunics and streetwear and chose a sleeker vintage and designer-led look for a new decade and a new album. *Positions*, released in October, evolved during the long, uncertain months of lockdown, which she had spent quarantining with a new boyfriend, real estate businessman Dalton Gomez, who she met on the job, while she was looking for a house to purchase.

She had overcome tragedy and was now in a blissful period of optimism, and the escapist 90s soul and pop was a perfect confection for the uncertainty of the Covid-19 era. It was almost a throwback to her debut album, *Yours Truly*, combined with the 60s futurism of *My Everything*, and with the confessional aspect of *thank u, next* tapping into her own experiences.

"I've always sort of gravitated towards the 50s and 60s and 70s for glamour references," she said in an interview with *Allure* in October 2021. "I've always pictured myself in a different time period. I've always wanted to wear that makeup, wear that hair, wear those outfits, be those performers."

At Lollapalooza in Chicago on 4 August 2019 in her Michael Ngo-designed burgundy costume from the Sweetener tour.

In the tongue-in-cheek music video for the first single, 'Positions', Ariana plays an American president whose powerful Jackie Kennedy femininity is shaking up the White House. Just as she sang that God is a Woman, now she was bringing female empowerment to the top of the US government.

To shape the look of the music video, Mimi Cuttrell took her signature silhouette of sweet minidresses, but added an early 60s twist with Gucci knit minidresses and pillbox hats, Mugler corset tops and Lanvin button-up capes.

With the double entendre lyrics, Ariana suggests she is capable of being both a domestic goddess and a work powerhouse, and as well as meeting with her all-female cabinet (which includes mom Joan and her friend Victoria Monét, the singer-songwriter), she signs bills into the law, takes to the podium to deliver a media briefing in shift dress and pearls, struts across the lawn in a houndstooth PINKO coat and pillbox hat, and makes pizza in Paco Rabanne broderie anglaise shorts, Dion Lee lace corset and Gucci platforms. This was a nod to the pizzas she sent to early voters in Florida as they waited in line to cast their ballot for the 2020 presidential election.

The lyrically and mathematically suggestive follow-up single '34 + 35' was released as a remix with rappers Doja Cat and Megan Thee Stallion. In the music video she dresses up as lab technician in white leather coat and then as an Austin Powers "fembot" dancing in a fluffy négligée and Le Silla "Prince" platform sandals. On release on 30 October, *Positions*, her sixth album, went straight to No. 1 in the *Billboard* 200.

"*I've always sort of gravitated towards the 50s and 60s and 70s for glamour references. I've always pictured myself in a different time period.*"

ARIANA GRANDE

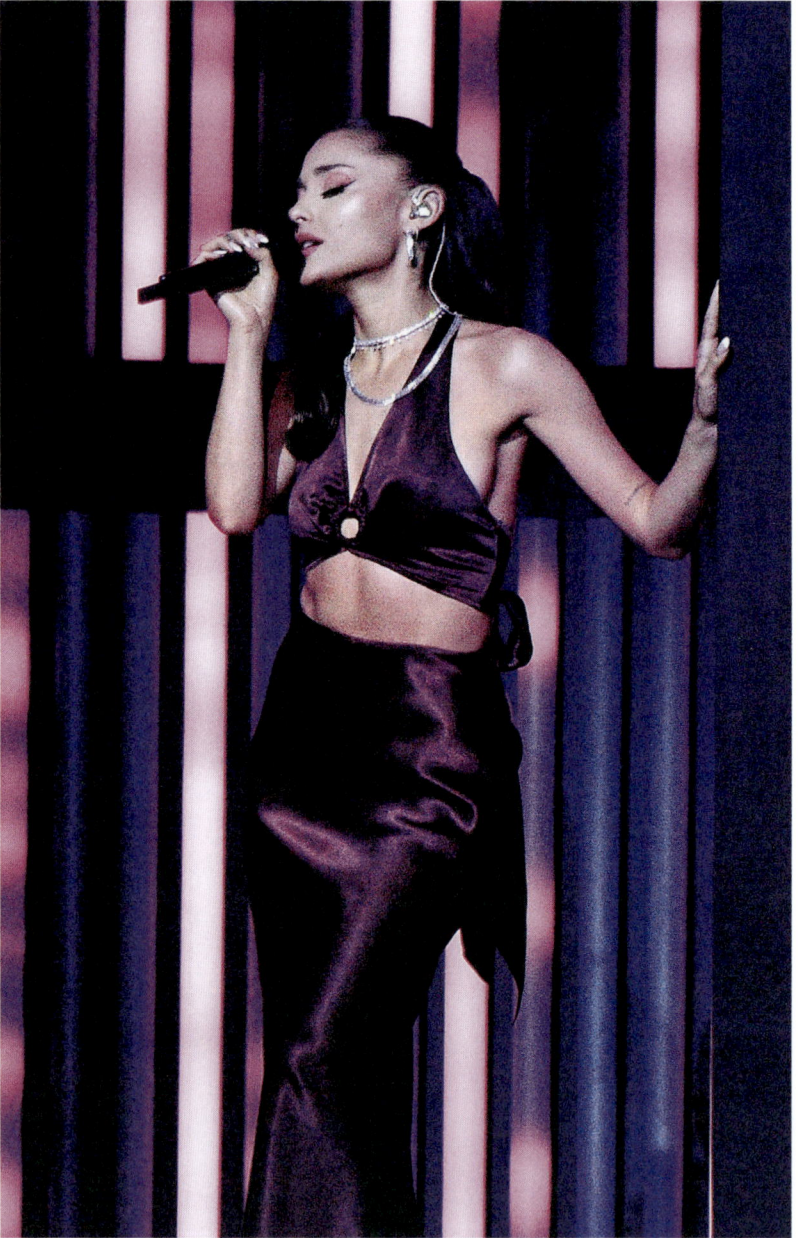

Ariana and Dalton announced their engagement in December 2020 and married in a secret, intimate ceremony on 15 May 2021 at her Montecito home. In photos shared on Instagram, she revealed her custom-made Vera Wang empire-waist wedding gown with a dipped back and hand-pleated bubble veil.

For her first appearance after the wedding, she attended the iHeartRadio Music Awards in May 2021 to perform 'Save Your Tears' with The Weeknd, sleek in a plum-coloured silk halterneck and skirt from Rat & Boa. *Women's Wear Daily* noted, her "midriff-baring silky number is sexy and extremely flattering on her. Purple silk screams mother-of-the bride, but her cool attitude turns it into fashion star."

Taking a break from music to explore what she described as "new versions of storytelling", Ariana had a role in Netflix's comedy/sci-fi *Don't Look Up* (2021) and after signing as a judge on the TV show *The Voice*, which aired in September 2021, she was hailed by *Vogue* for delivering "epic fashion moments" while she explored fresh designers like Miss Sohee, Ulyana Sergeenko and Ivan Young, as well as vintage finds from Versace and Gucci.

Another favourite label of Ariana's was the Italian streetwear brand GCDS, choosing the mermaid-inspired scallop shell-bra and skirt with white blazer for her virtual appearance on *The Tonight Show Starring Jimmy Fallon* in November 2021. By the end of that year she was ready to take a break from pop to return to her musical theatre roots.

On stage at the iHeartRadio Music awards in 2021, she wore a silky plum-coloured halterneck and skirt by British brand Rat & Boa, to perform 'Save Your Tears' with The Weeknd.

"I've always pictured myself in a different time period.

I've always wanted to wear that makeup, *wear that* hair, *wear those* outfits, *be those performers."*

ARIANA GRANDE

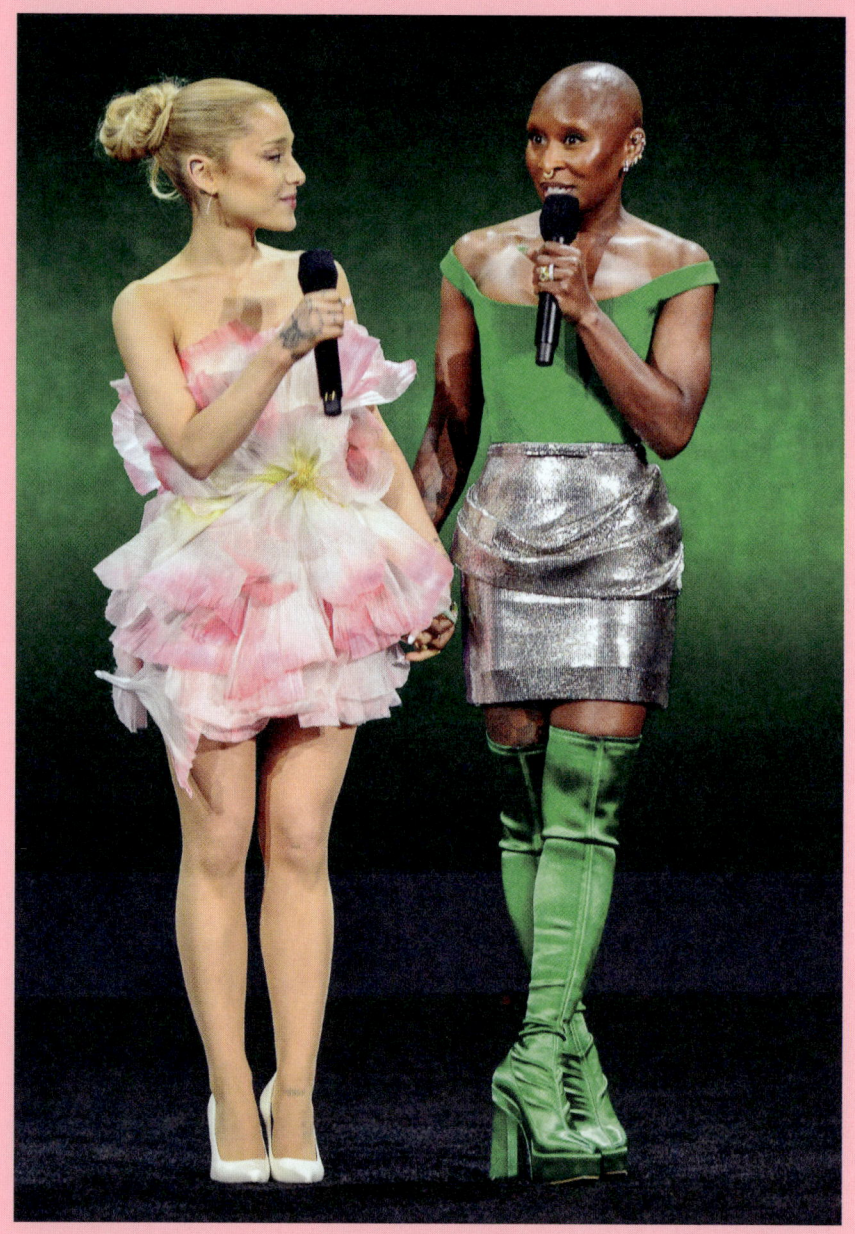

Wicked and *Eternal Sunshine*

After learning that there was a casting call for the film version of the Broadway phenomenon *Wicked*, Ariana went into "full preparation mode" to win what she considered her dream role, that of Glinda, the good witch. She prepped for six months, taking voice and acting lessons every day while working on *The Voice*, to convince the director, Jon M. Chu, that she would be perfect for the role.

She described her casting opposite Cynthia Erivo as Elphaba, the Wicked Witch of the West, as the "most incredible gift of my entire life", and from the beginning of 2022 she dedicated her time to filming in England, with no plans for new music or public appearances. Now that she was focusing on rehearsals, her wardrobe shifted to that of a theatre star devoted to perfecting those music numbers, opting for Miu Miu ballet shoes over skyscraper heels and a vintage Margiela duvet coat from 1996 rather than a hoodie. She even posted a photo on Instagram in October 2022 of herself and Cynthia Erivo, both wearing Miu Miu ballet flats during rehearsals – with Ariana in pink and Cynthia in black with green leggings to suit their opposing characters.

Wearing Oscar de la Renta to promote *Wicked* at CinemaCon in Las Vegas, April 2024 with co-star Cynthia Erivo.

British *Vogue* in November 2022 highlighted Ariana's transformation into #balletcore, an early 2020s TikTok trend for choosing a ballerina palette, dancers' sweaters and crossover tops. Her Instagram posts revealed that she had now abandoned the fake tan and dyed her hair blonde to suit the role of Glinda. She favoured muted greys and pinks, and posted images wearing a pair of white satin pumps from Rodarte's Autumn/Winter 2022 collection and the celeb choice of funky footwear – Bottega Veneta's rubber "Puddle" boots.

While she called it "one of the most deeply special and transformative and fulfilling experiences of my creative life in London [from] the past year and a half", production for *Wicked* was forced on hold in August 2023 due to the SAG-AFTRA strike. The actors' union went on a lengthy strike over labour practices and this, combined with support for the Writers Guild of America strike, effectively shut down American film and television production.

There had also been shifts in Ariana's personal life. Just days after it was announced she was separating from Dalton Gomez, news broke that she was now dating her co-star Ethan Slater, who had also recently separated from his wife of four years, Lilly Jay. When Ariana made an appearance at Wimbledon in July 2023, she also revealed a new look. With her blonde hair under a Wimbledon cap, a pair of Tiffany sunglasses and the fake tan ditched, she chose a simple grey sweater and pleated skirt as she sat in the grandstand to watch the finale with *Wicked* co-star Jonathan Bailey and actor Andrew Garfield.

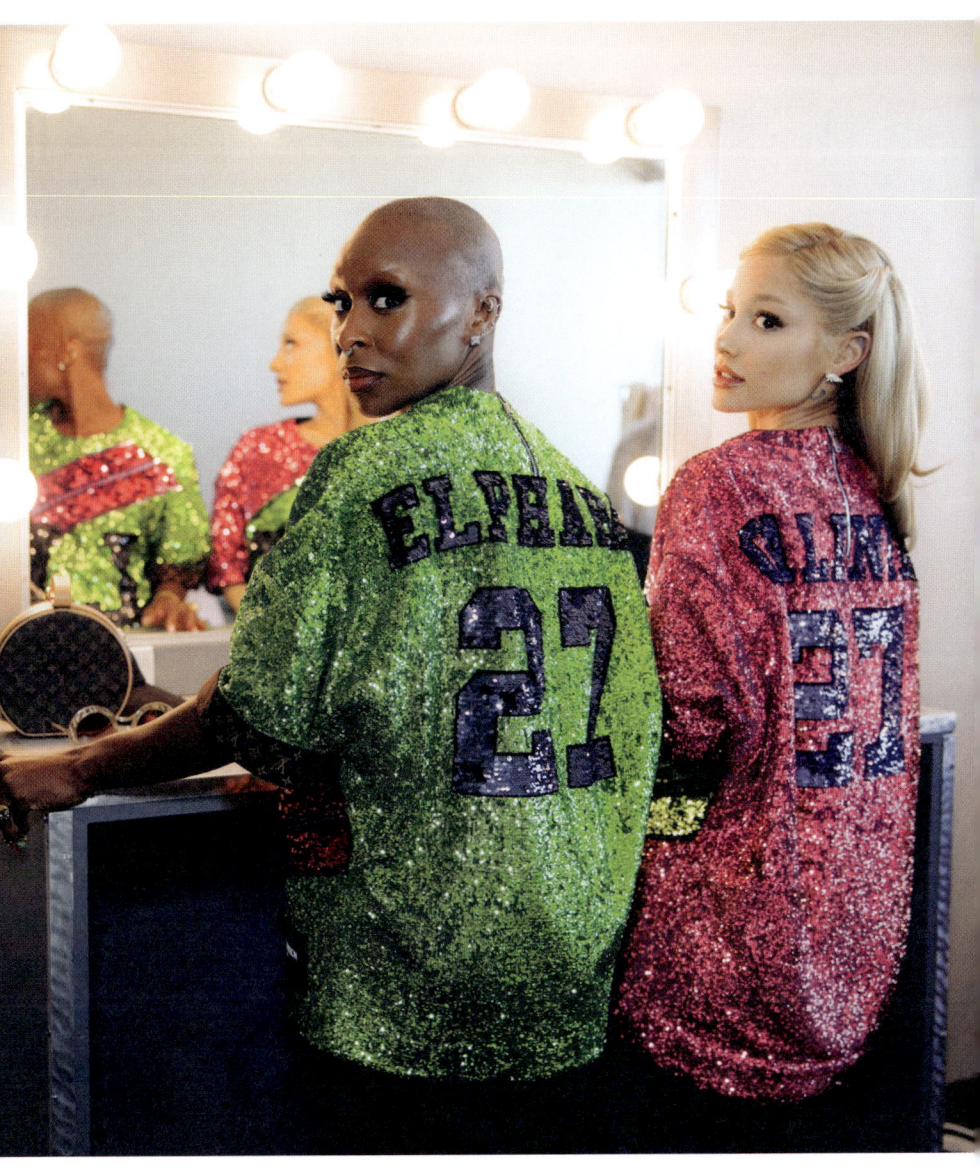

During the publicity tour for the 2024 film *Wicked*, Ariana and Cynthia Erivo were colour-coded to match their characters. Pictured here during the Super Bowl LVIII.

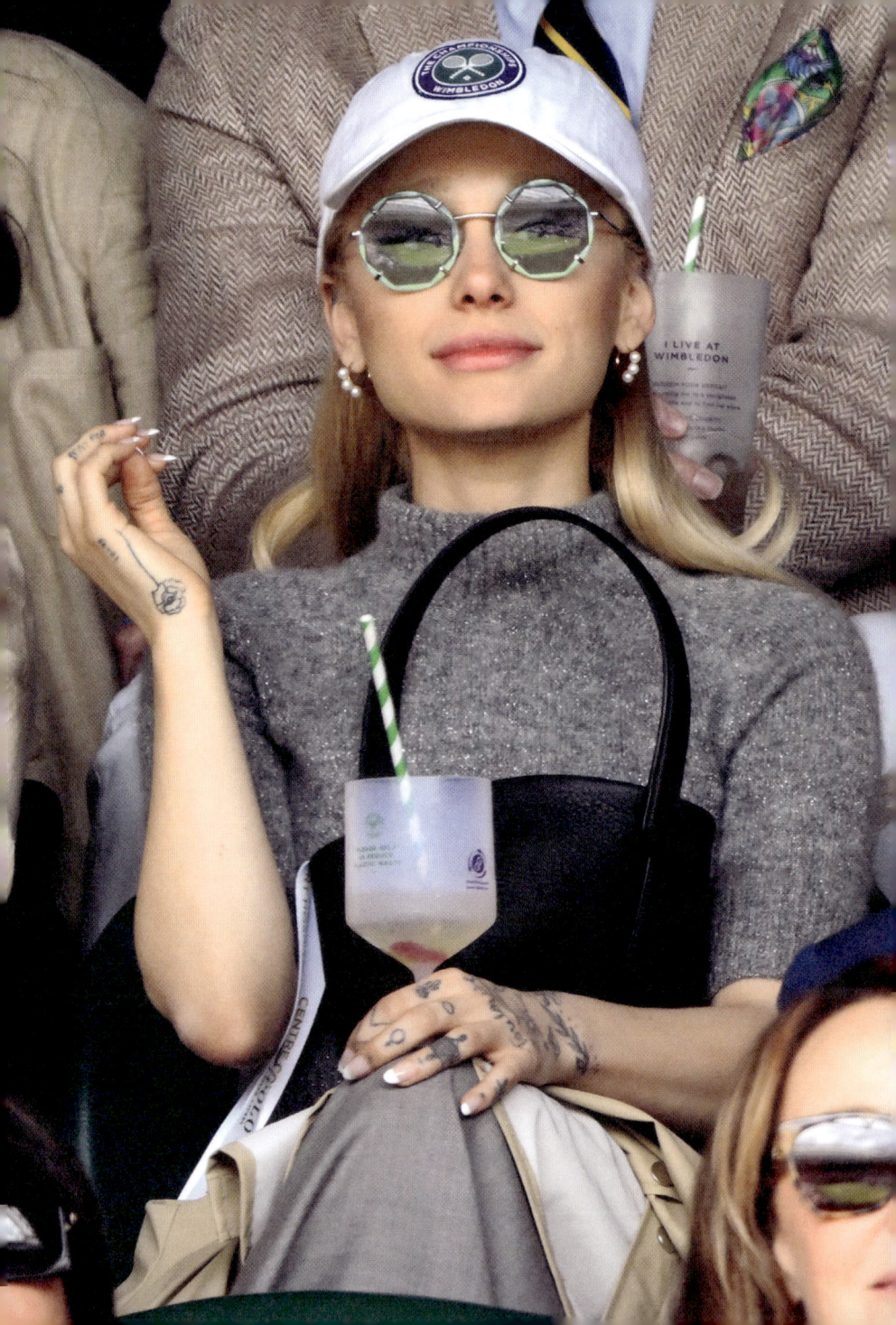

Having been out of the spotlight for much of 2023 as she relocated to the UK to make *Wicked*, Ariana limited her appearances to Wimbledon and the photos she shared on Instagram. Yet she was also coming under unfair criticism about her appearance, where online critics shared their "concerns" on TikTok that she was too thin. She addressed the flurry of comments about her body on her Instagram in April 2023, making the point that "healthy can look different" and that they were "comparing my current body" to "the unhealthiest version of my body" during a period when she had been "on a lot of antidepressants and drinking on them and eating poorly".

She would further address her frustrations at this criticism in the lyrics to her first single in almost three years, 'Yes, And?'. Released in January 2024, it took aim at all the gossip around her love life and the disapproval of her body and her shade of complexion. She was making it clear that her life was her business and she didn't want to hear other negative opinions.

The dance-themed music video, inspired by Paula Abdul's 'Cold Hearted' video from 1989, opened with an audience of critics taking their seats in a warehouse. Ariana emerges onto the floor in a black baker boy cap, which she tosses off, a white criss-cross Rodarte bodysuit with long black sleeves, sleek Alaïa A-line miniskirt, sheer black stockings and a pair of black leather Bloch T-bar dancing shoes.

Watching Carlos Alcaraz vs Novak Djokovic in the Wimbledon 2023 men's final on Centre Court, on 16 July 2023.

Her seventh studio album, *Eternal Sunshine*, was released in March 2024, with its title from one of her favourite films, where Jim Carrey undergoes mind-wiping to get over a breakup. The cover art featured a blonde high-ponytailed Ariana resting her head on the shoulders of her doppelganger. Inspired by the upside-down experiences in her own life, the sumptuous pop, R&B and dance revealed her emotional vulnerability as she shared doubts about her relationships and moving on from divorce to find herself again.

"We're going to have so much fun this year," Ariana wrote on Mimi Cuttrell's Instagram to mark the beginning of 2024, and her fashion choices over the next few months sent commentators into a spin as she embarked on a wardrobe-coded publicity tour for *Wicked*. When she posted an image of herself on Instagram wearing a soft pink Balenciaga gown covered in ribbons and with a bow around the waist, which was from the brand's Autumn/Winter 2023 couture collection, it was both a homage to balletcore and to her role as Glinda.

She performed the second single from the album, 'We Can't Be Friends (Wait for Your Love)', on *Saturday Night Live* on 9 March in yellow Vera Wang bridal couture and on a set that appeared as if from Munchkin land.

The next day she was in Los Angeles to attend the Academy Awards with Cynthia Erivo. Her dramatic Glinda-inspired pink Giambattista Valli gown from the Spring/Summer 2023 couture collection was in contrast to Erivo's dark green Louis Vuitton.

Attending the *Wall Street Journal Magazine*'s Innovator Awards in a corseted lace Vivienne Westwood gown in October 2024.

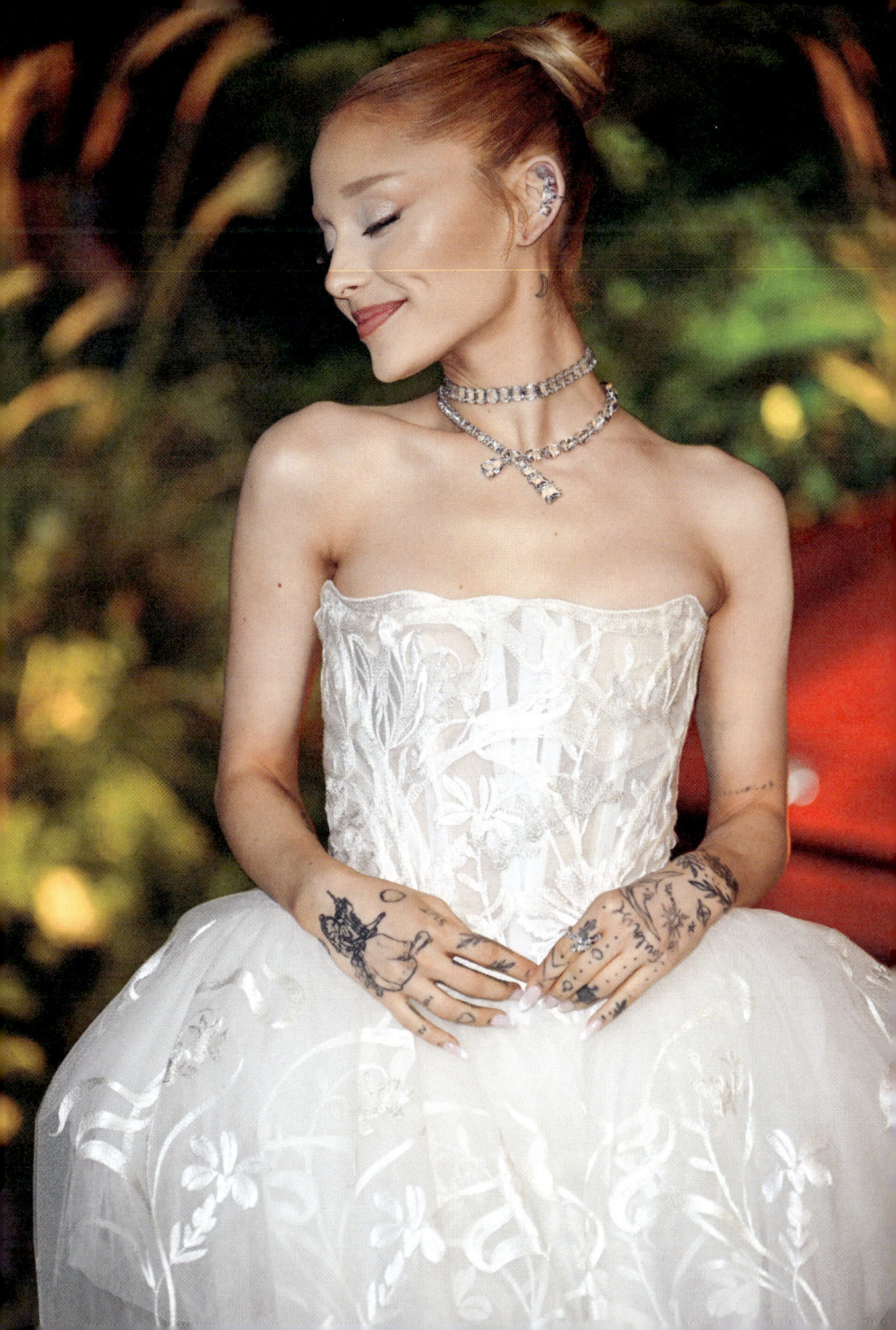

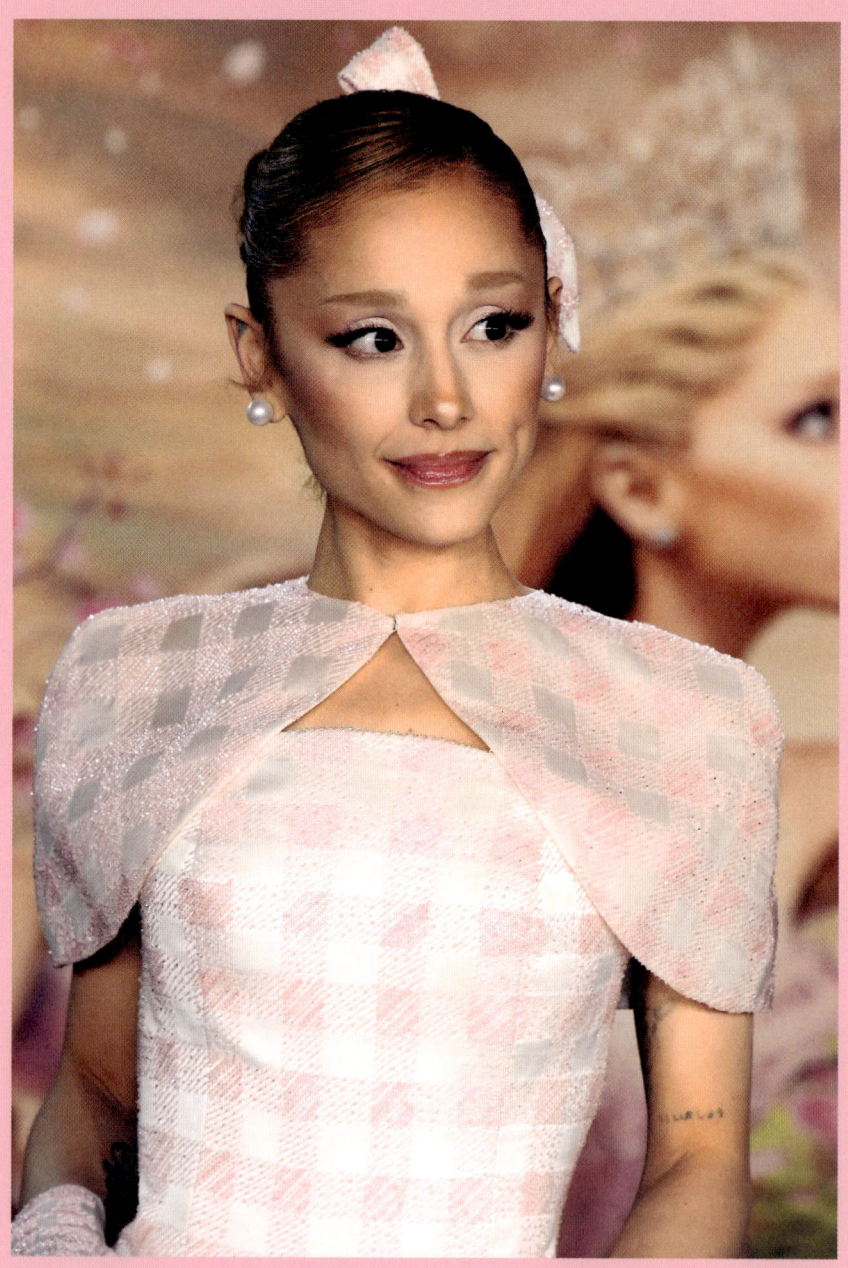

Ariana continued to promote the pale pink palette in the lead-up to the release of *Wicked*. At CinemaCon 2024 in April she appeared as a flower fairy in a pink and white floral minidress from Oscar de la Renta and a ballet pink Versace satin mididress with matching Valentino pumps.

Now that she was back as both pop star and actress, Ariana upped her public appearances, but this time with a stylistic maturity that suited a woman in her thirties who was thriving in her career.

Ariana's gowns for the extended *Wicked* press tour may have been perfect pastel confections embellished with sequins and bows, but there was real designer poise. Mimi Cuttrell orchestrated pink gingham by Thom Browne, a sparkling fairytale of a Vivienne Westwood gown in Sydney, iridescent strapless Versace at the Mexico premiere, and tailored Versace, a ladylike reference to Dior's iconic Bar suit.

For the UK premiere on 18 November, she was as yellow as the Brick Road in diaphanous Ralph Lauren. This nod to an original dress from the Broadway production marked the final stop on the tour. But when Ariana was nominated for an Academy Award for her performance as Glinda, it was a fitting tribute to the *Wicked* Juggernaut.

A pink gingham tribute to Dorothy, designed by Thom Browne, for the *Wicked* premiere in Los Angeles in November 2024.

The Signature

CHAPTER 2

Style

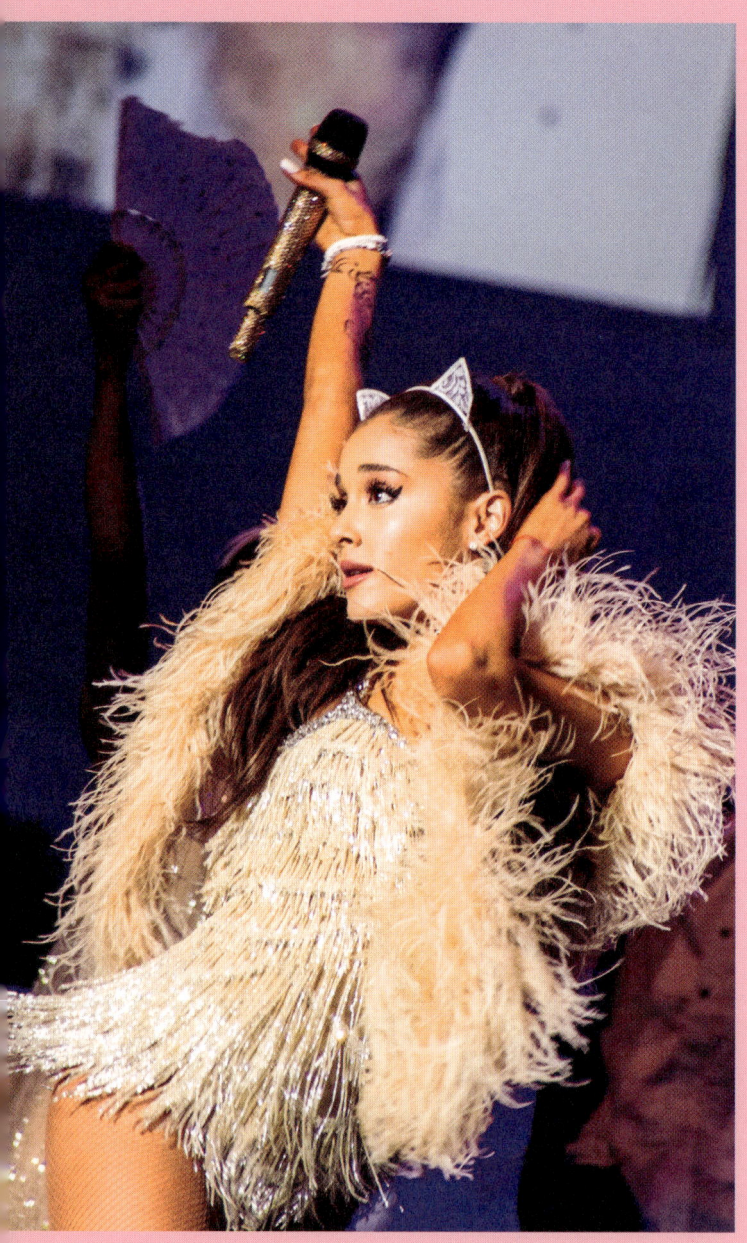

The signature style

While Ariana's style has evolved from cute Disney princess in strapless prom dresses to a Barbarella meets Brigitte Bardot heroine, from oversized streetwear to elegant couture and balletcore, her philosophy has always been to be as authentic to herself as possible: "I think it is important to stay true to who you are and pick things that you really, really love," she told *Miss Vogue* in February 2016.

Throughout her style trajectory, she has embraced the retro with Audrey Hepburn A-line dresses, 60s miniskirts and go-go boot combinations, and the 90s-inspired streetwear.

"She's like an R-rated version of a Disney character, super-vivid," said producer Pharrell Williams. "But she's full of self-awareness. That meta-cognition is part of her personality."

For Ariana, clothes are a form of costume that allow her to play a character, which she described to *Vogue* in 2019 as an "exaggerated version of myself. It protects me. But also I love disrupting it for the sake of my fans and making clear that I'm a person—because that's something I enjoy fighting for."

On the Honeymoon tour in May 2015, in Assago, Italy, in a shimmering fringed leotard and ostrich feathers, designed by Marina Toybina.

"...she's **strong**, *defiant* and isn't afraid to make a **bold statement** about *feminism*, *gender or equality through her music, performance and fashion."*

MICHAEL NGO

Her fans, the Arianators, were first attracted to her pretty sparkles, when her wardrobe choices of skater dresses and the cat and Minnie Mouse ears were accessible and easy to replicate. But as she shook off her kids' TV origins, Ariana wanted to reveal a mature, sensual side, and to keep it fresh and experimental, she supported young streetwear designers from diverse backgrounds.

Michael Ngo, the queer designer who shaped her stage looks for the Dangerous Woman and Sweetener tours, described her as an "uber adorable latex-wearing bunny, spreading her fierceness and fabulousness throughout an urban-pop jungle; she's strong, defiant and isn't afraid to make a bold statement about feminism, gender or equality through her music, performance and fashion."

Key to Ariana's style are the signature elements that are vital to her private and public persona: "You go to her concerts and you see ponytails, bunny ears, and cat ears—all the things that she's done in the past. I don't think there's any other pop star who has that kind of appeal or that same type of devotion," her stylist Law Roach told *Vogue* in July 2019.

At the iHeartRadio Ultimate Pool Party in Miami Beach on 27 June 2014. The 1960s minidress and go-go boots were the dominant look for *My Everything*.

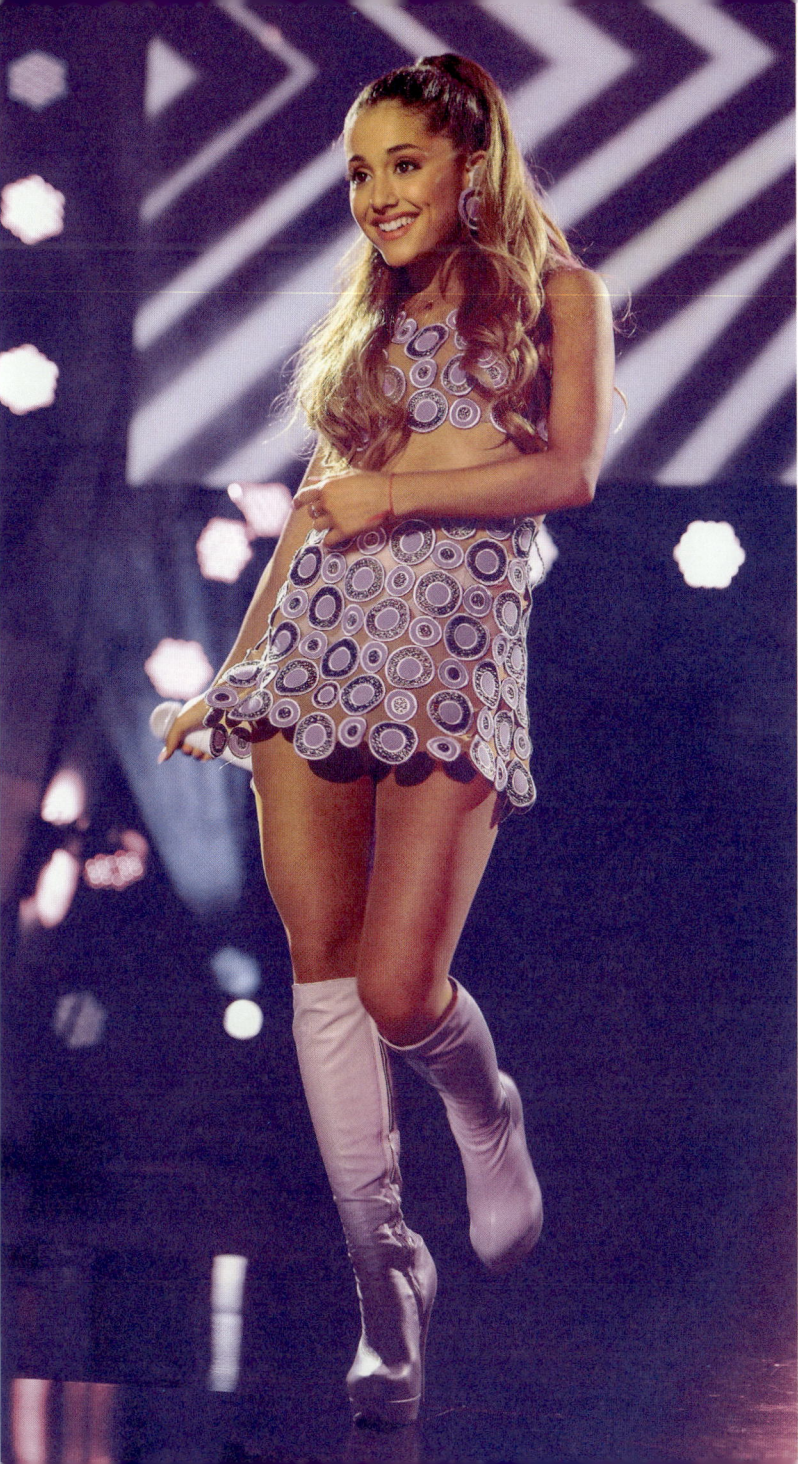

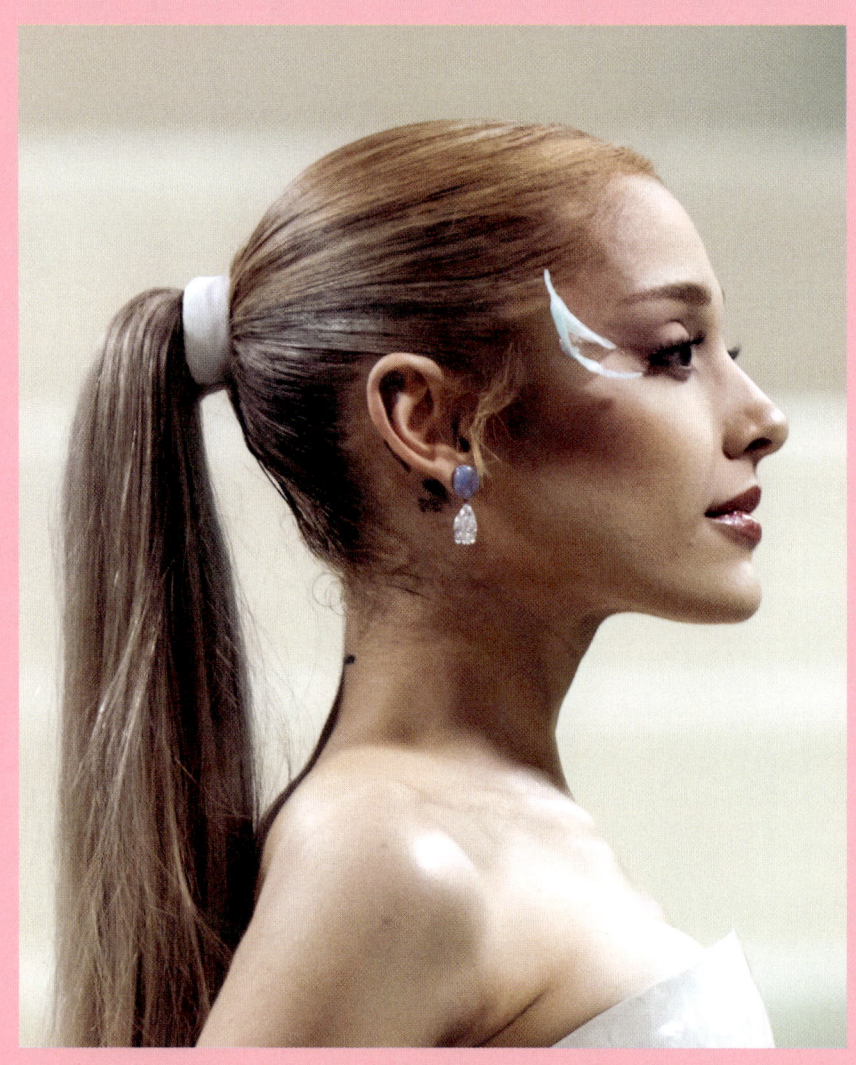

Accessorizing her Loewe gown with a high ponytail at the Met Gala in 2024.

The signature ponytail

Ariana's famed ponytail, described by *Vogue* as the "most scrutinized up-do in history", may have become a signature for practical reasons, but it's also a communication tool as her fans track its height, length and colour as if there are patterns to analyze.

She described her preference for "the high, sleek, dark one. But she takes many forms. Many forms. There are lots of different girls in this sisterhood."

The ponytail came into being in 2013, when the years of bleaching and dying for her character Cat Valentine in *Victorious* took its toll on the condition of her hair. Using wigs and extensions, Ariana began with a half-up style, before transitioning to the full ponytail. While it had initially been a "super easy" means of wearing her hair, this was also the symbol of where her life was at. When the cover of 'No Tears Left to Cry' revealed a low, platinum blonde ponytail, it sparked a frenzy among fans as it visualised her transformation.

"The pony has also gone through an evolution, and I'm proud of that," she told the *The Fader* in 2018. "Old pony? I don't know if she's that girl. But new pony? I like her. I mean, it's like a Victoria's Secret angel without angel wings. It's still her without them, but when she's with them it's like, Ohh, I get it, she's an angel."

"You go to her concerts and you see *ponytails*, *bunny ears*, and *cat ears*—all the things that she's done in the past.

I don't think there's any other pop star who has that kind of appeal or that same type of devotion."

LAW ROACH

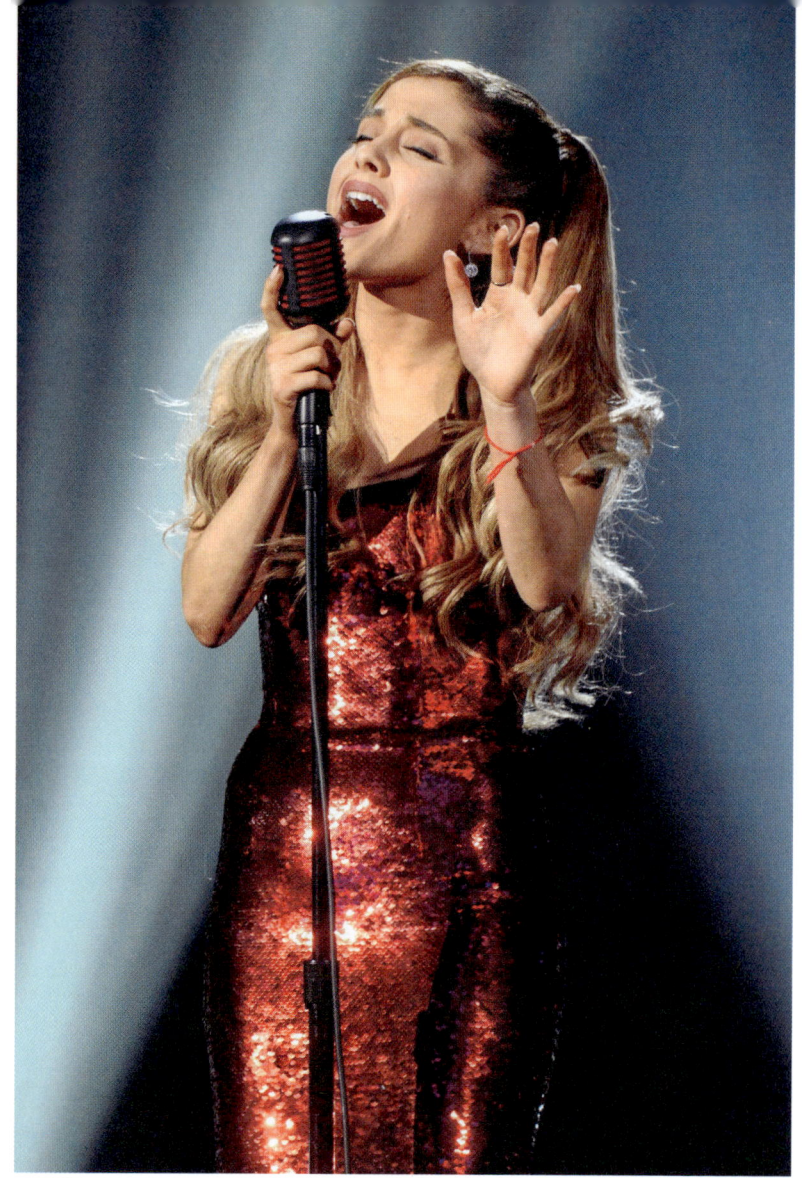

ABOVE The half ponytail worn with a red sequined Dolce & Gabbana gown at the 2013 American Music Awards.

OPPOSITE Onstage at the 2018 iHeartRadio Wango Tango By AT&T, on 2 June 2018.

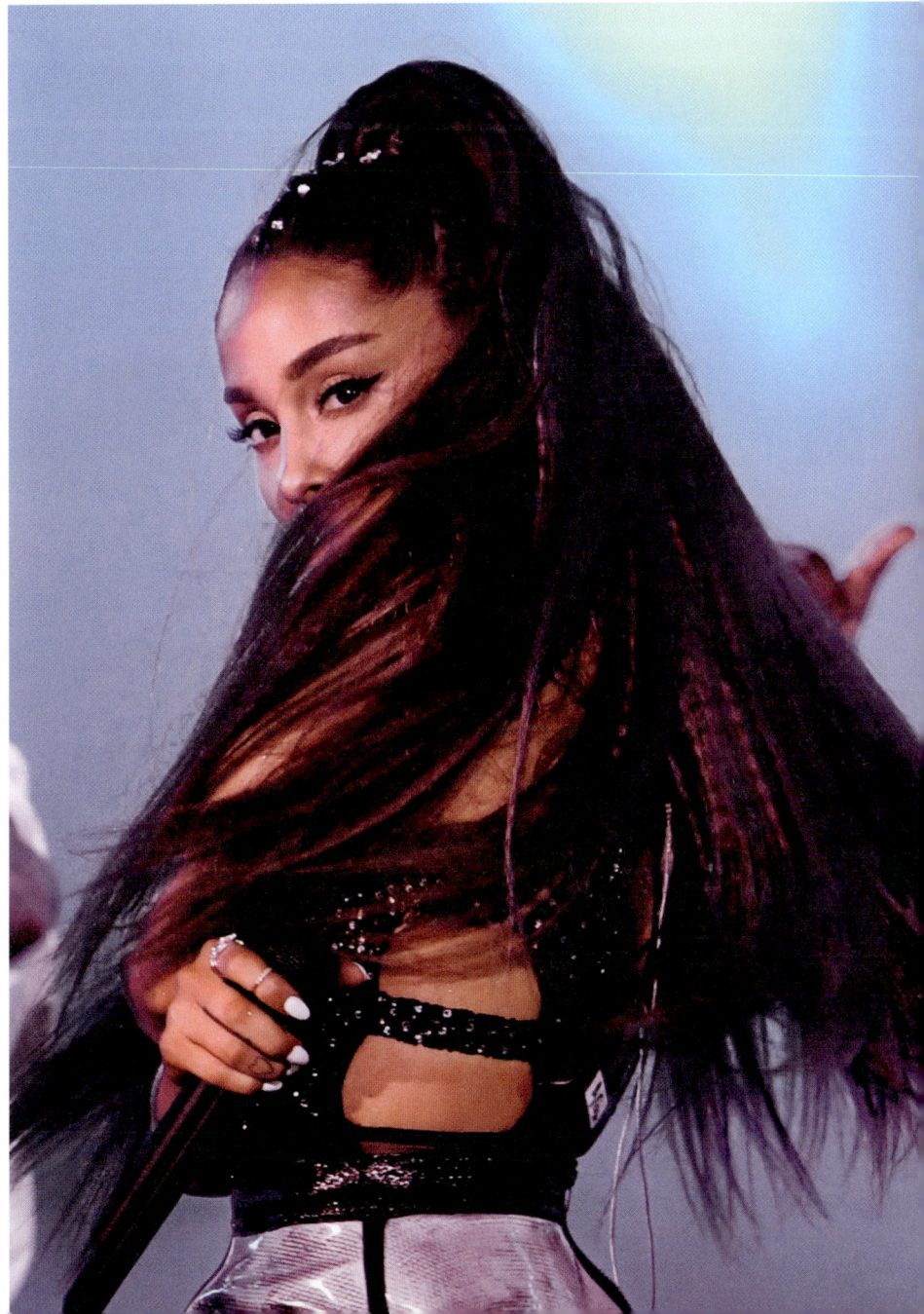

"The *pony* has also gone through an evolution, and *I'm proud of that.*"

ARIANA GRANDE

Promoting tracks from *Dangerous Woman* at the 2016 *Good Morning America* Summer Concert Series in New York City's Central Park.

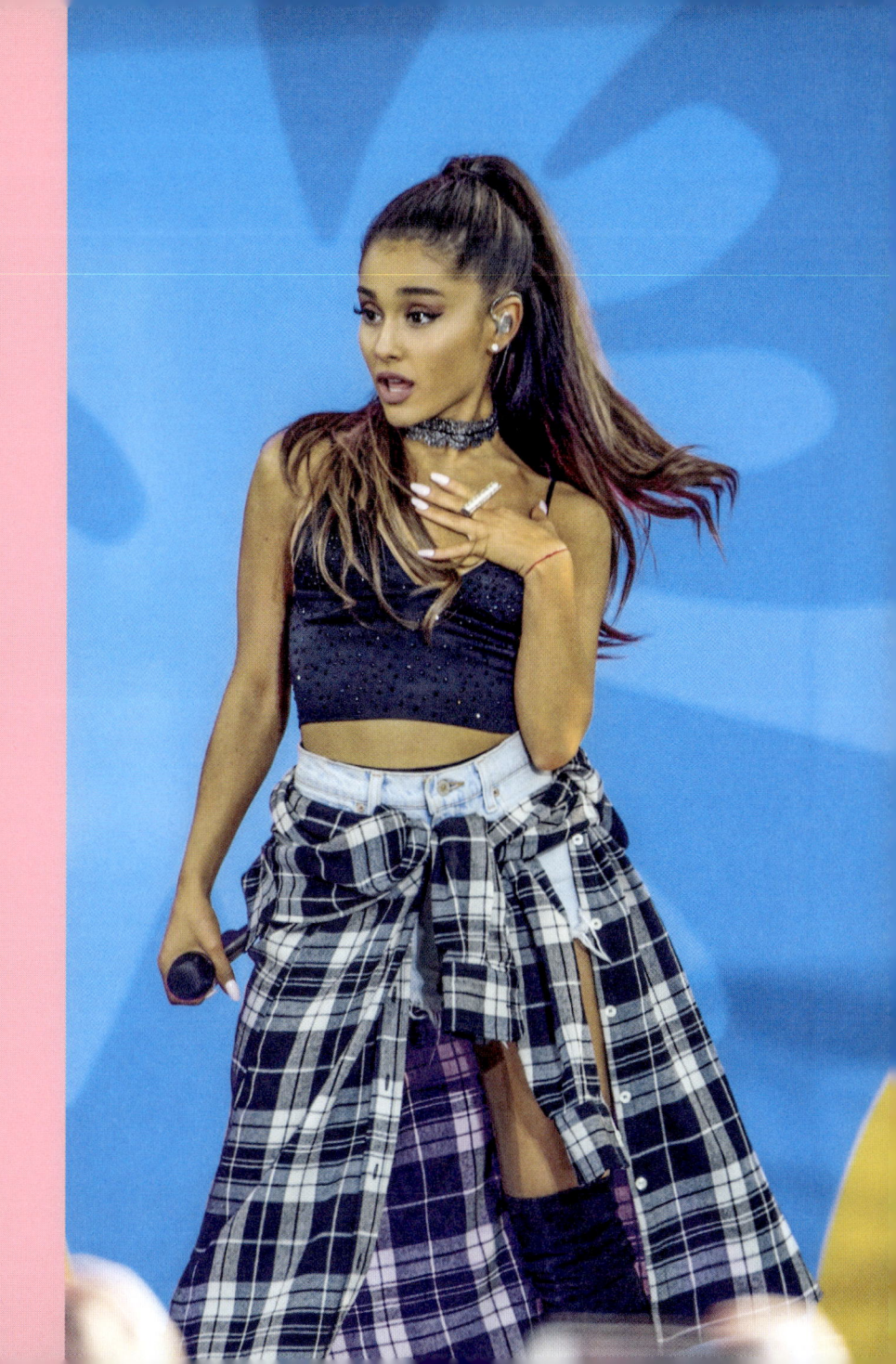

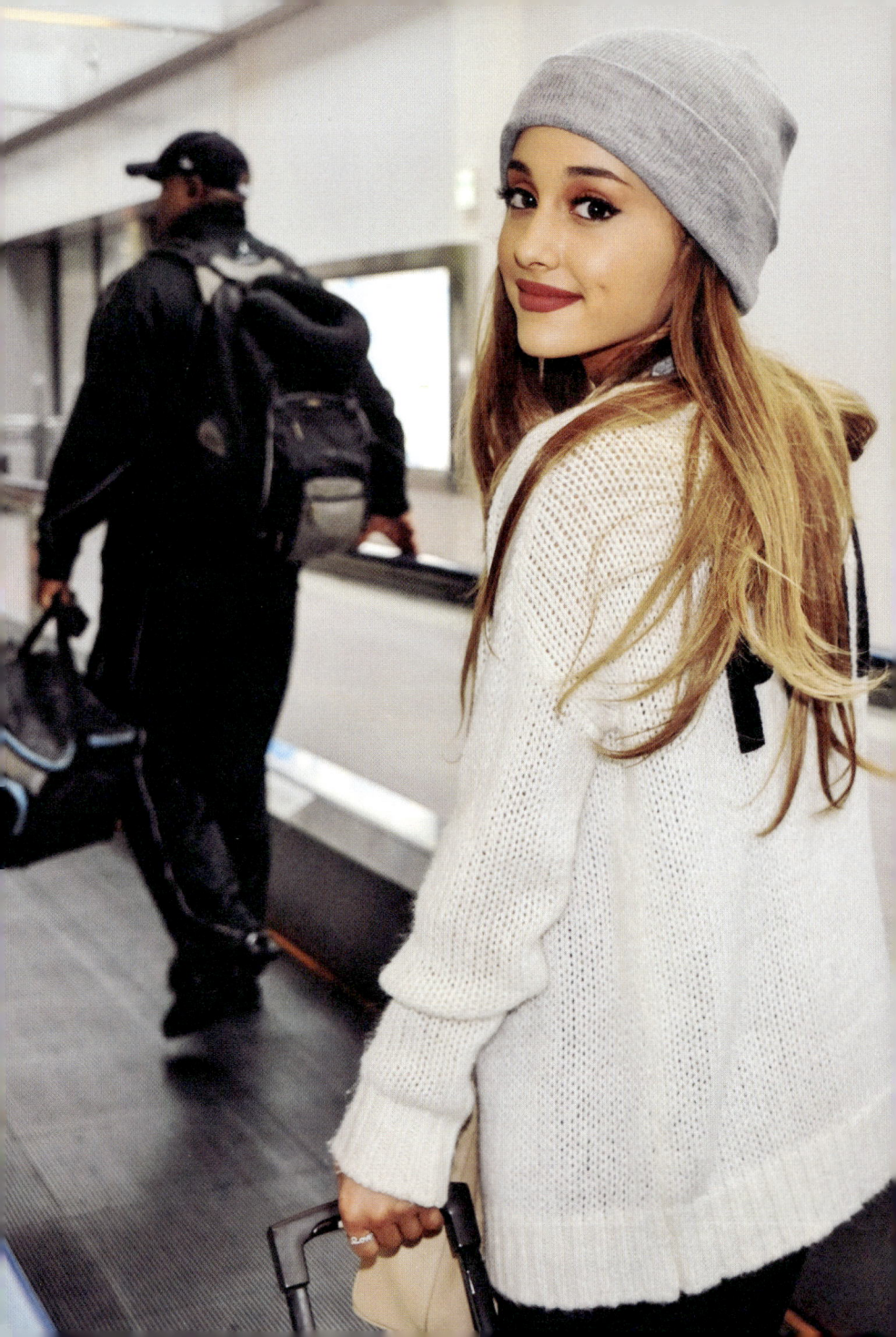

Make-up

From her Maria Callas flicked eyeliner and thick layers of eyelashes to the highlight on her nose, Ariana has developed a make-up style that works for her. She described how her preferred look changes depending on her mood: "If I'm feeling sexy or sassy, I'll do a cat-eye or a really bronze lid with a fluffy lash. Sometimes I don't even wear any makeup; I just wear my lashes and go." A choice trick, she said, is "a pink highlighter on my nose and cheeks."

Ariana's approach to beauty has completely shifted over the years. She was a curly-haired kid on Broadway who dyed her hair cherry red for Nickelodeon. She then transformed into a pop and R&B star with winged eyeliner and accentuated lips, playing up to her love of retro style. She even launched her own brand, r.e.m beauty, for fans to copy her palette.

To meld with Glinda, hairstylist Gabor Kerekes and long-time make-up artist Michael Anthony transformed Ariana's looks to follow a more natural aesthetic. Her ethereal blonde hair matched her skin, and instead of heavy kohl she chose sparkling pink shadow and pale gloss to go with the classic Audrey Hepburn lashes. With a touch of highlighter on the tip of her nose, for a button effect, she described her new appearance as "unrecognisable" from old.

OPPOSITE Ariana dressing for comfort while arriving at Narita Airport, Japan in 2014.

OVERLEAF With mom Joan at the 2024 Stanley Cup Final on 8 June 2024 in Sunrise, Florida.

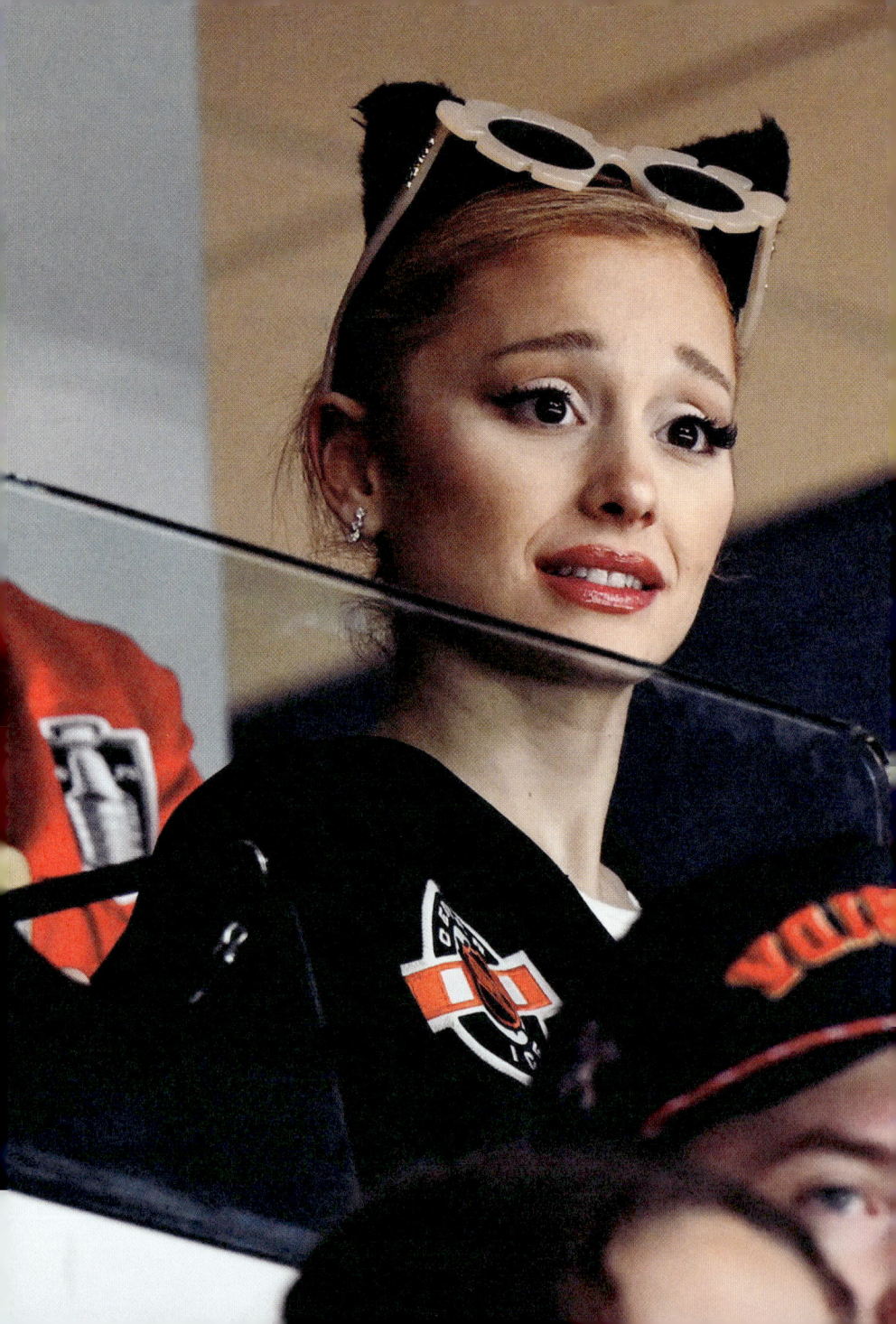

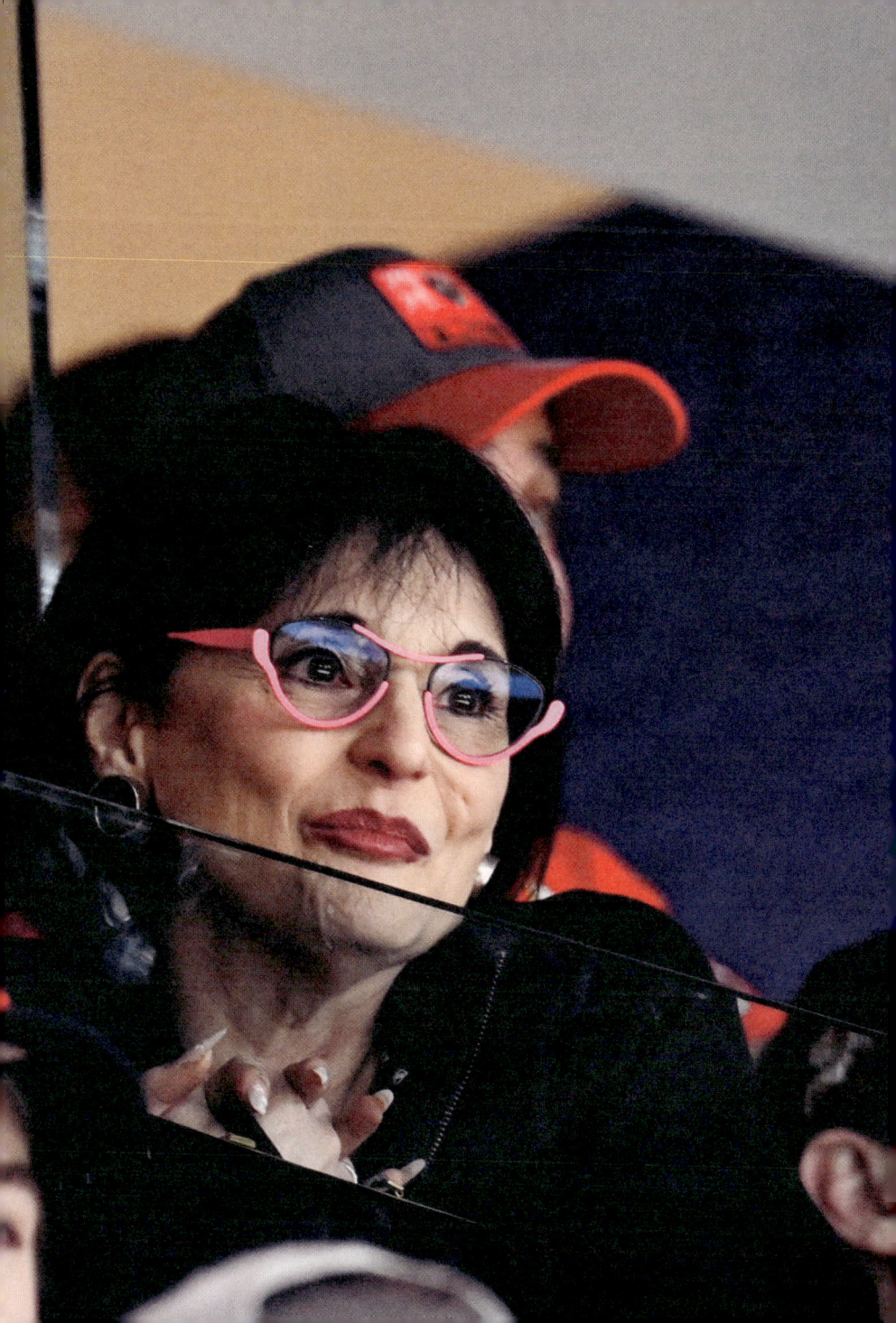

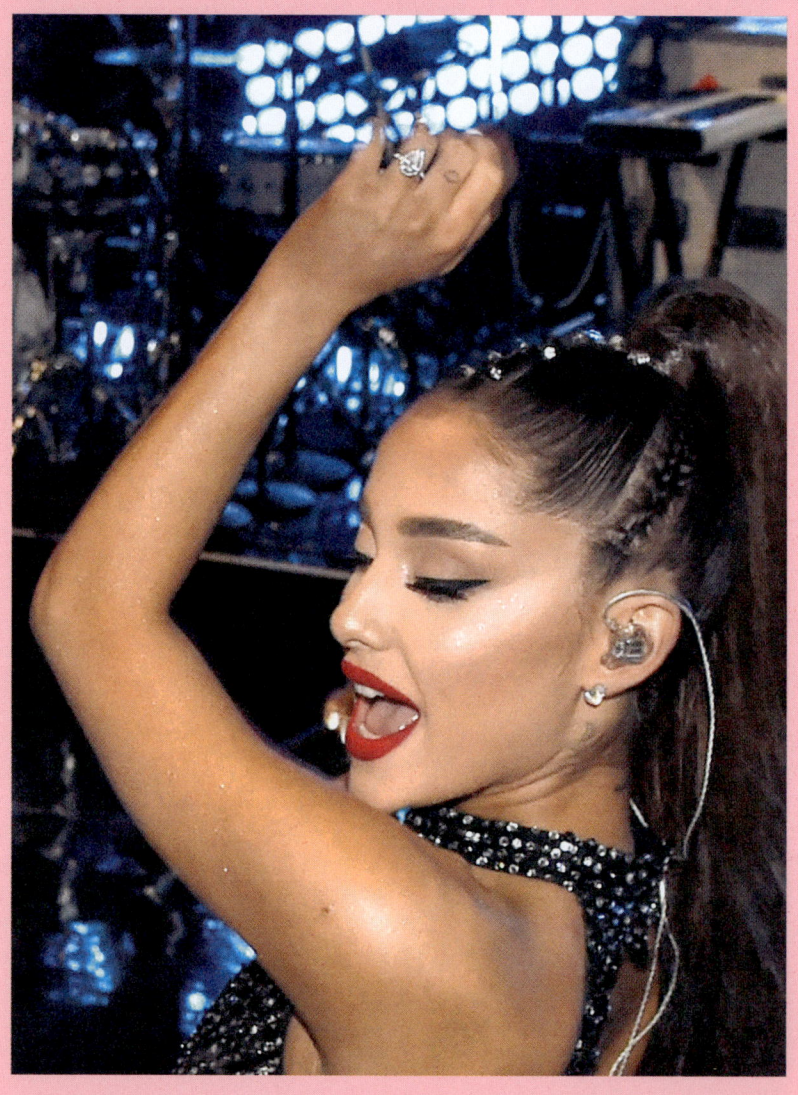

ABOVE Ariana in June 2018, at the iHeartRadio Wango Tango By AT&T.

OPPOSITE Ariana's classic winged eyeliner was inspired by Audrey Hepburn. At the Annual Women in Music event in December 2018.

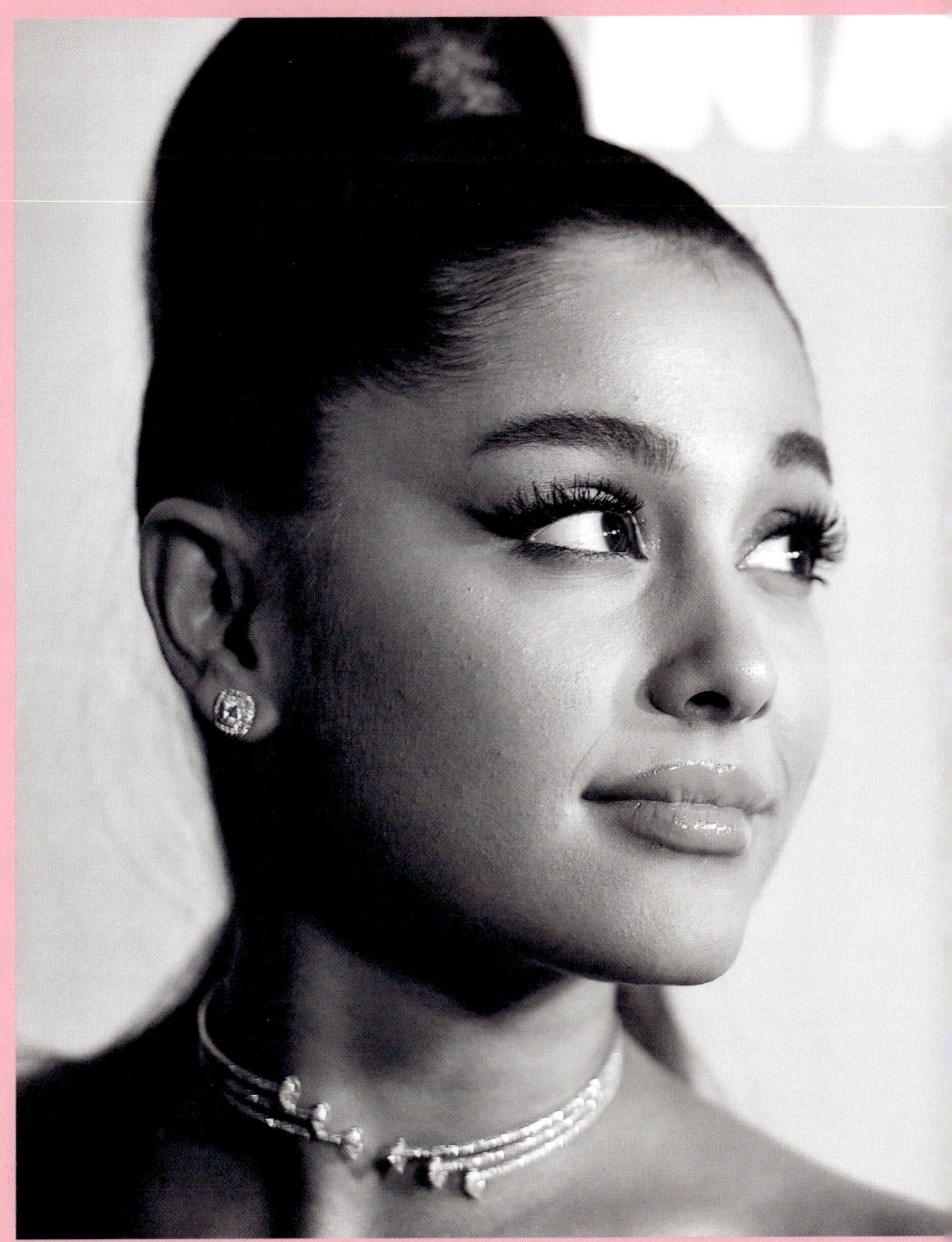

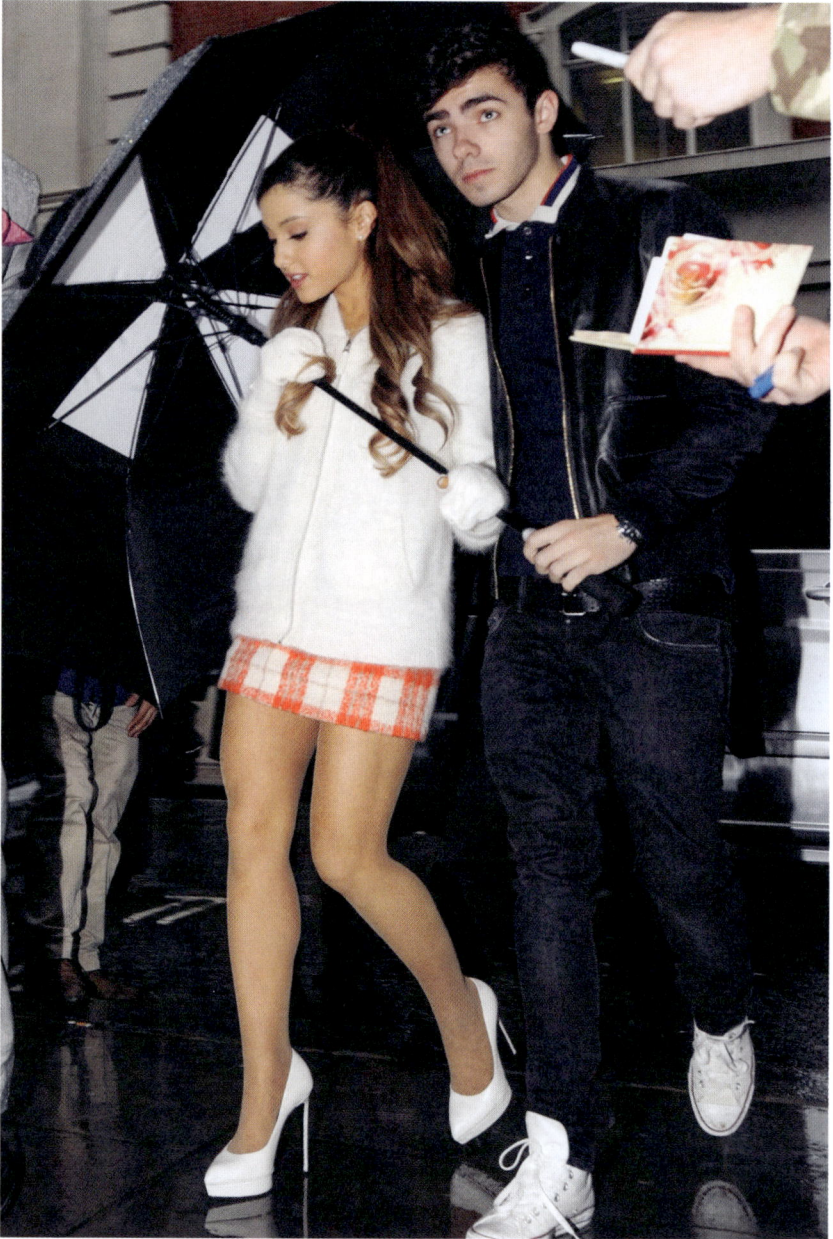

Heels

Along with the ponytail, high heels and platform boots are the key ingredients to Ariana's pop star persona. Like the ponytail, the heels were also selected for practical reasons. The sparrow-like singer is only 5ft tall, and they help boost her stage presence: "If you are as petite as I am, heels really help make an outfit," she declared.

For her early public appearances, she teamed cute dresses with her favourite Saint Laurent cap toe pumps (as worn at the *Billboard* Music Awards in 2013) and the Saint Laurent Tribute pump. As she graduated to over-the-knee boots for *My Everything* and the Honeymoon tour, the choice brand was often Christian Louboutin "Bianca Botta" boots. Rocking a streetwear look in 2018 and 2019, she frequently wore a pair of Yeezy taupe over-the-knee boots, or Le Silla "Eva" boots for performing at Coachella. As she upped the elegance in the 2020s, she teamed Giuseppe Zanotti platforms with Vera Wang couture and then, entering into a balletcore period for *Wicked*, there were the Miu Miu ballet pumps and flats. But she didn't say goodbye to the heels for too long, as she often teamed her Glinda-inspired couture with rose pink Valentino "Nite-Out" satin heels.

Arriving at BBC studios with Nathan Sykes in October 2013, in a Topshop skirt and Saint Laurent heels.

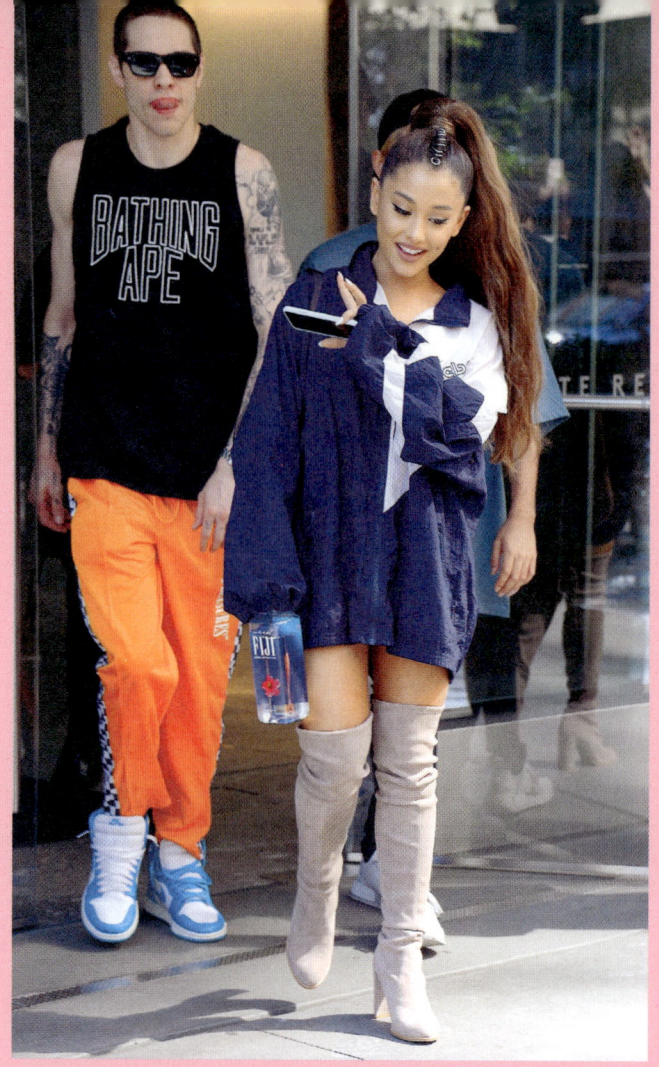

ABOVE Ariana's "summer of 2018" style when dating Pete Davidson,
of taupe Yeezy over-the-knee boots and a baggy sweatshirt.

OPPOSITE Opening night of the Sweetener world tour on
18 March 2019 in Albany, New York. She wears pink platform
heels by Pleaser and Michael Ngo's custom-made costume.

OVERLEAF The platform heels at the 2016 iHeartRadio Music
Festival on 24 September 2016 in Las Vegas, Nevada.

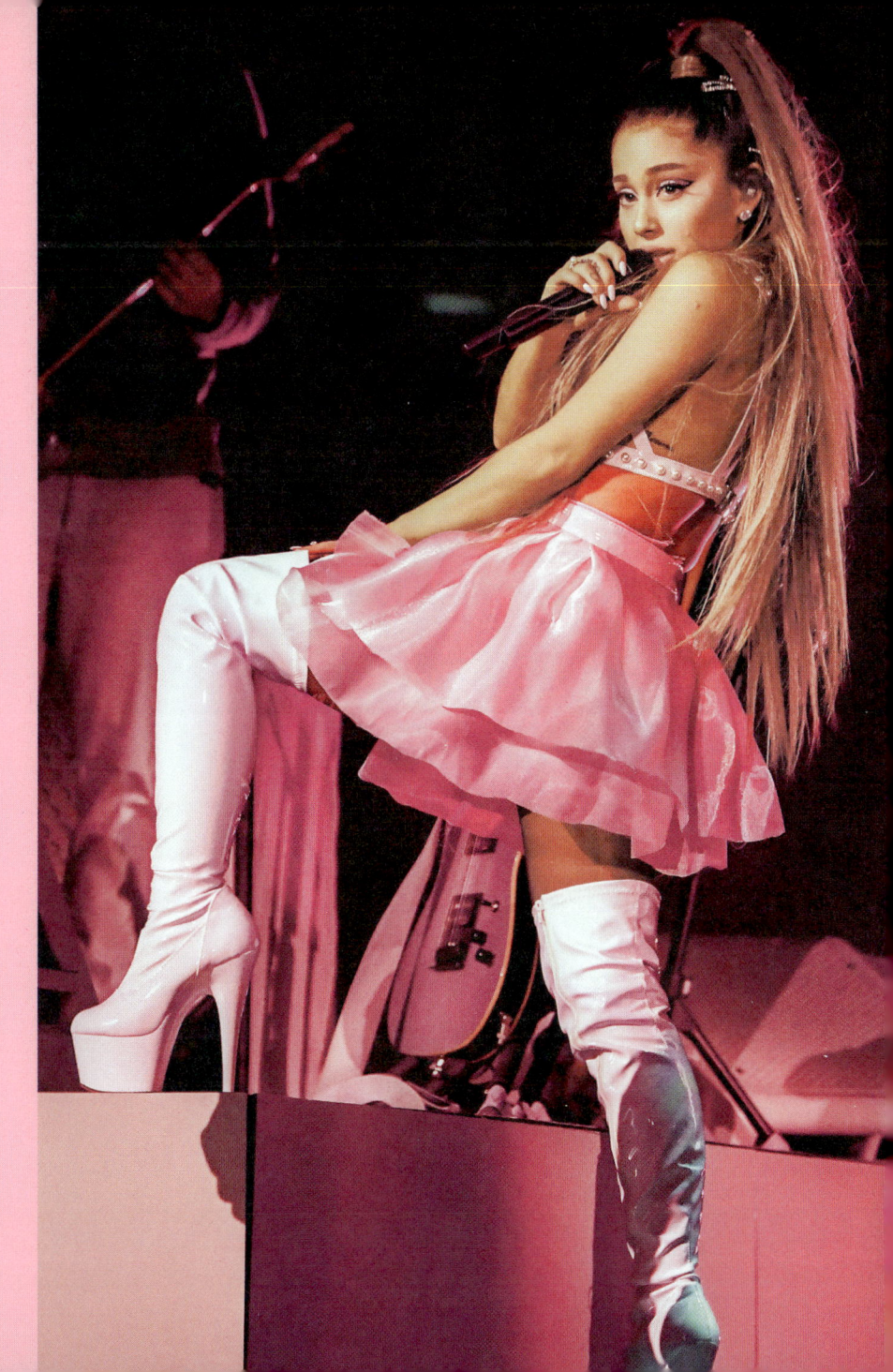

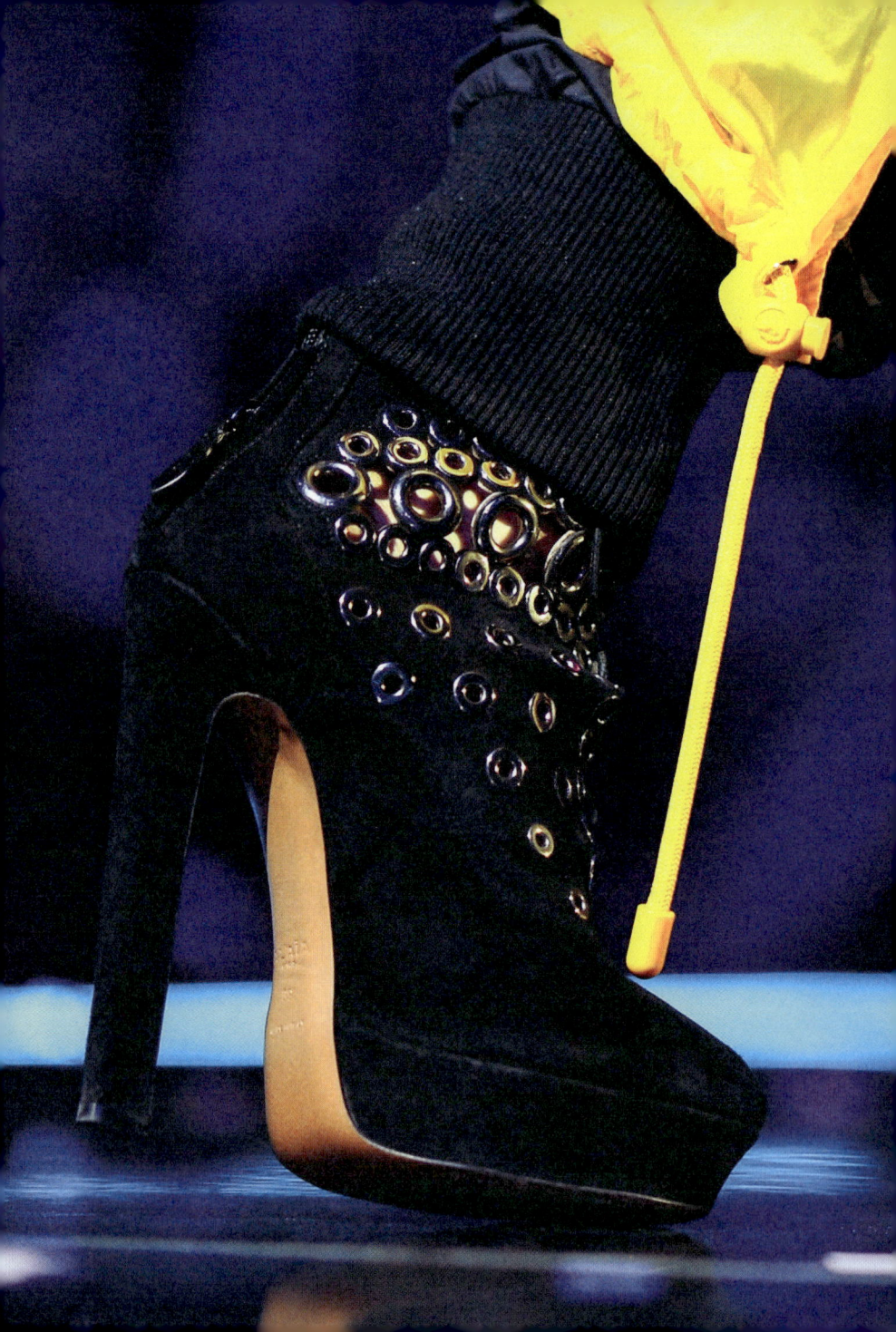

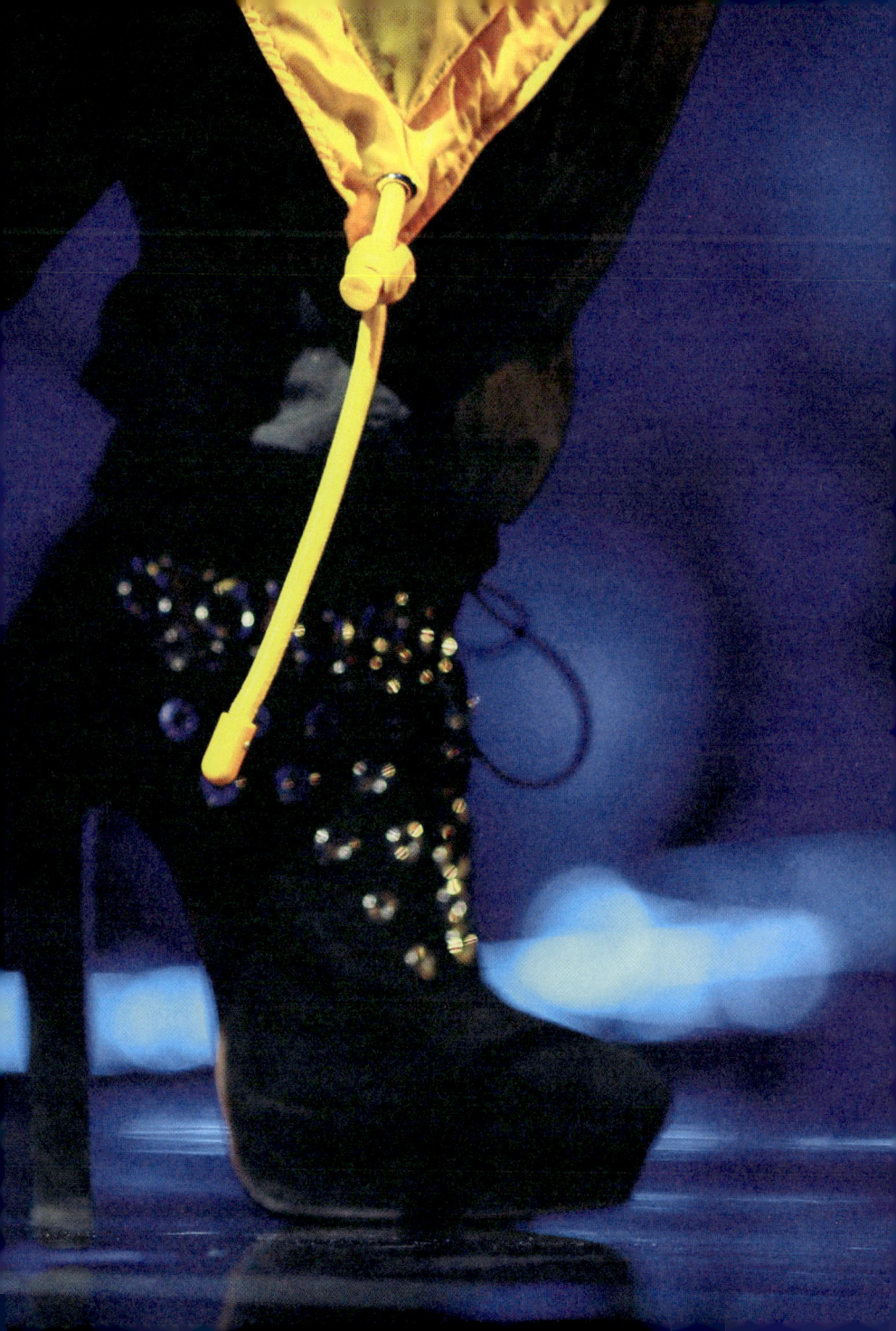

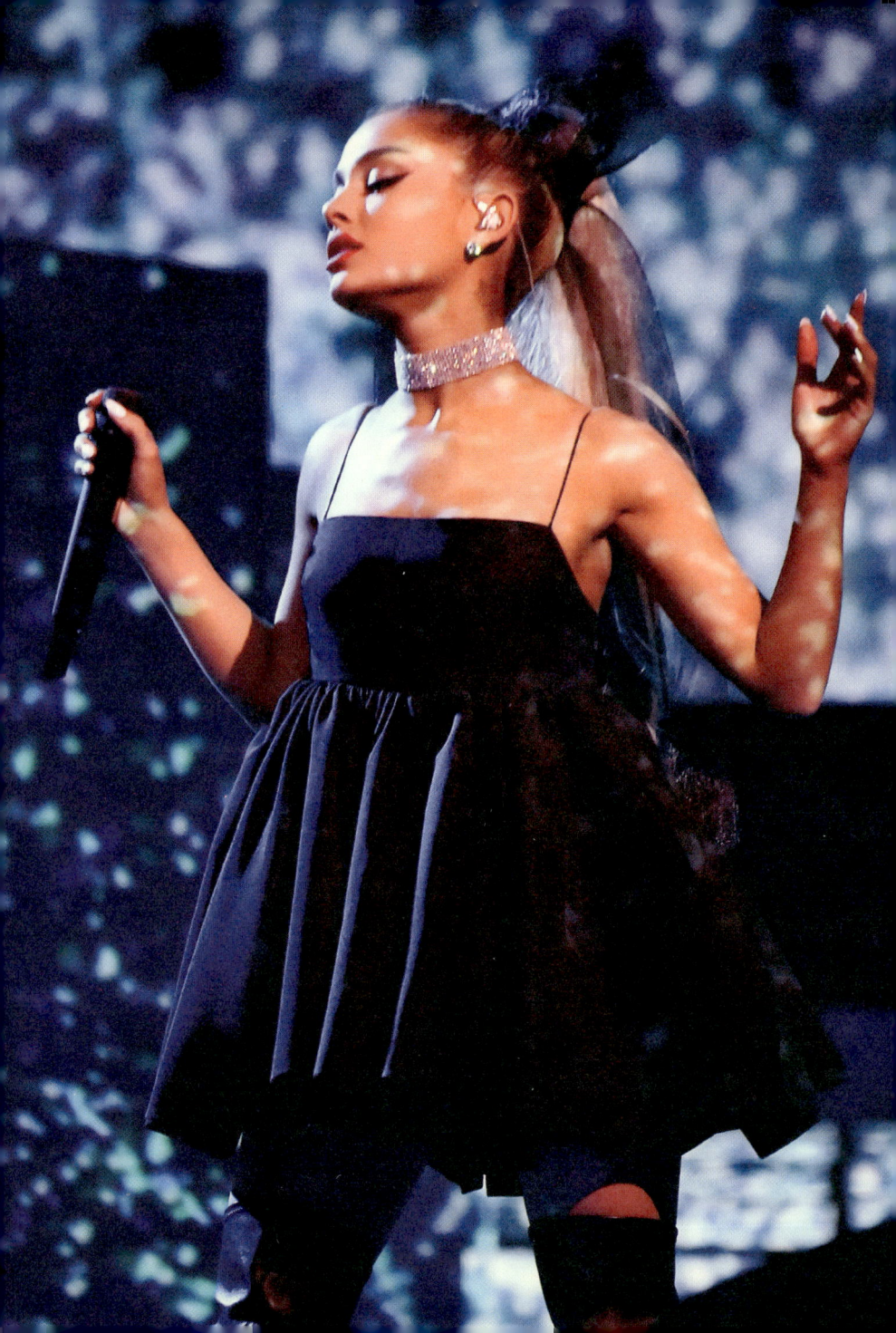

The lampshade tunic

As Ariana recovered from the trauma of a terrorist attack at her Manchester concert and relaunched her image with the 2018 album *Sweetener*, the empire-waisted lampshade tunics were all about sweet escapism.

On *The Tonight Show Starring Jimmy Fallon* on 1 May 2018, she performed tracks in a cute Cecilie Bahnsen "Beverly" peplum satin top, worn with Le Silla "Eva" over-the-knee stiletto boots. And at the *Billboard* Music Awards on 20 May, she chose a lampshade-shaped black dress with over-the-knee boots for a powerful performance of 'No Tears Left to Cry'. While Ariana was criticized for the bubblegum pop gowns worn with thigh-high boots, as if it was too much Lolita, Law Roach described the lampshade dress as "authentic to her, she owns that space and I don't think she should change or try to change to please anybody."

Ariana was also embracing the pastel themes of *Sweetener*, describing one outfit to *Vogue* in 2018 as "serving heather-grey realness". She said, "My fans are obsessed with knowing my favourite colour so this is important: it was lavender, and then it was yellow, but now it's ice blue. Like, ice blue mixed with grey." Lilac, or violet, the shortest wavelength in the colour prism, bends or refracts the most and so this symbolic choice also reflected the change she was going through.

At the 2018 *Billboard* Music Awards in Las Vegas on 20 May 2018 in a Christian Siriano lampshade dress and Casadei boots.

"*[The lampshade dress is]* authentic to her, **she owns that** space and

I don't think she should change or try to change to please anybody."

LAW ROACH

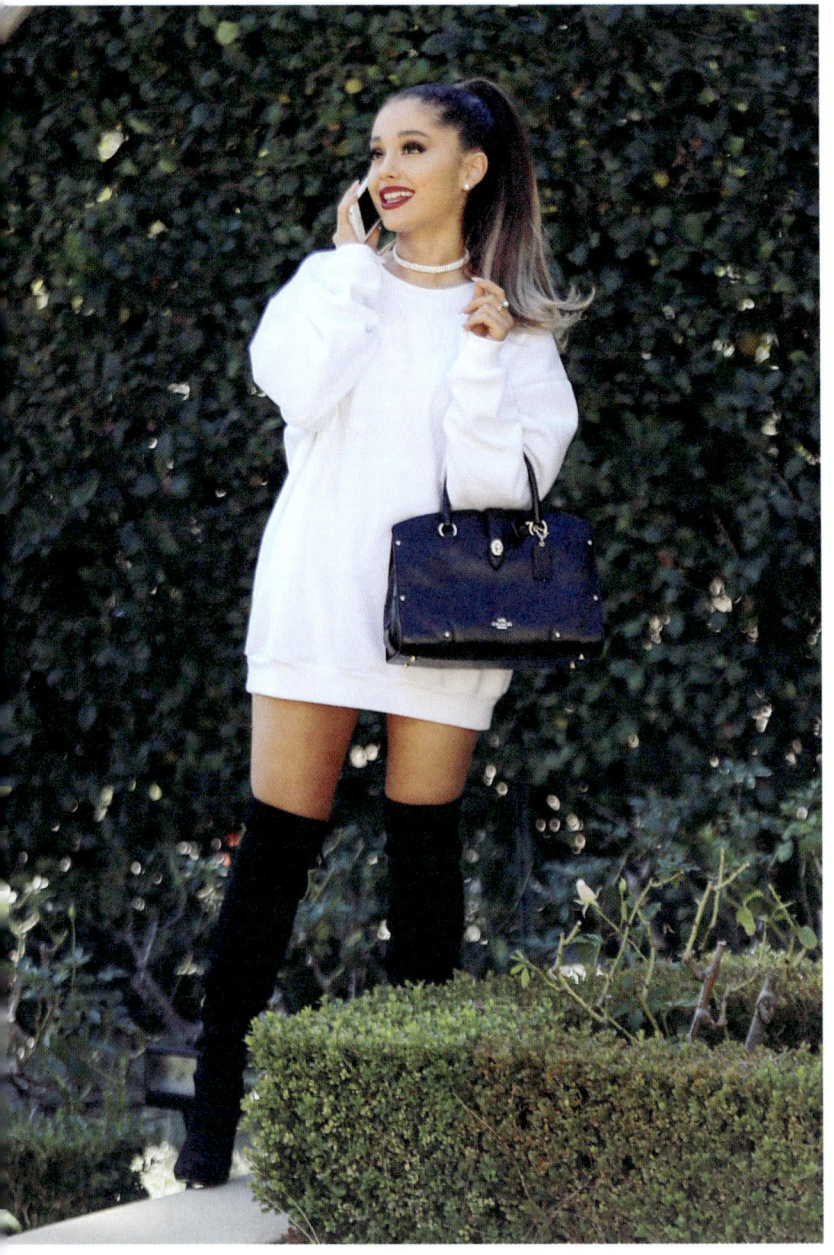

The hoodie

By wearing an oversized hoodie or sweater as a dress, Ariana took a unisex item and imbued it with femininity.

Worn with knee-high boots, and with the sweater stopping halfway up her thigh, it mixed the sensual with streetwear, and given how oversized they were, the effect was as if she had borrowed it from her boyfriend. And sometimes the hoodie would be wrapped around her waist and worn with leggings and a crop top. Favourite labels included Yeezy, Benji and branded versions by Social Club and for her own Sweetener tour, but she would also use them as a means of promoting a cause. By choosing to wear a Manchester One Love hoodie and A Concert for Charlottesville hoodie she was actively showing her support in calling for unity. Given she was the target of a terrorist attack in 2017, Ariana began to shift her wardrobe choices as she used fashion to actively campaign for the issues she cared about.

Ariana in Los Angeles in February 2016, in an American Apparel sweater, Christian Louboutin boots and Coach bag.

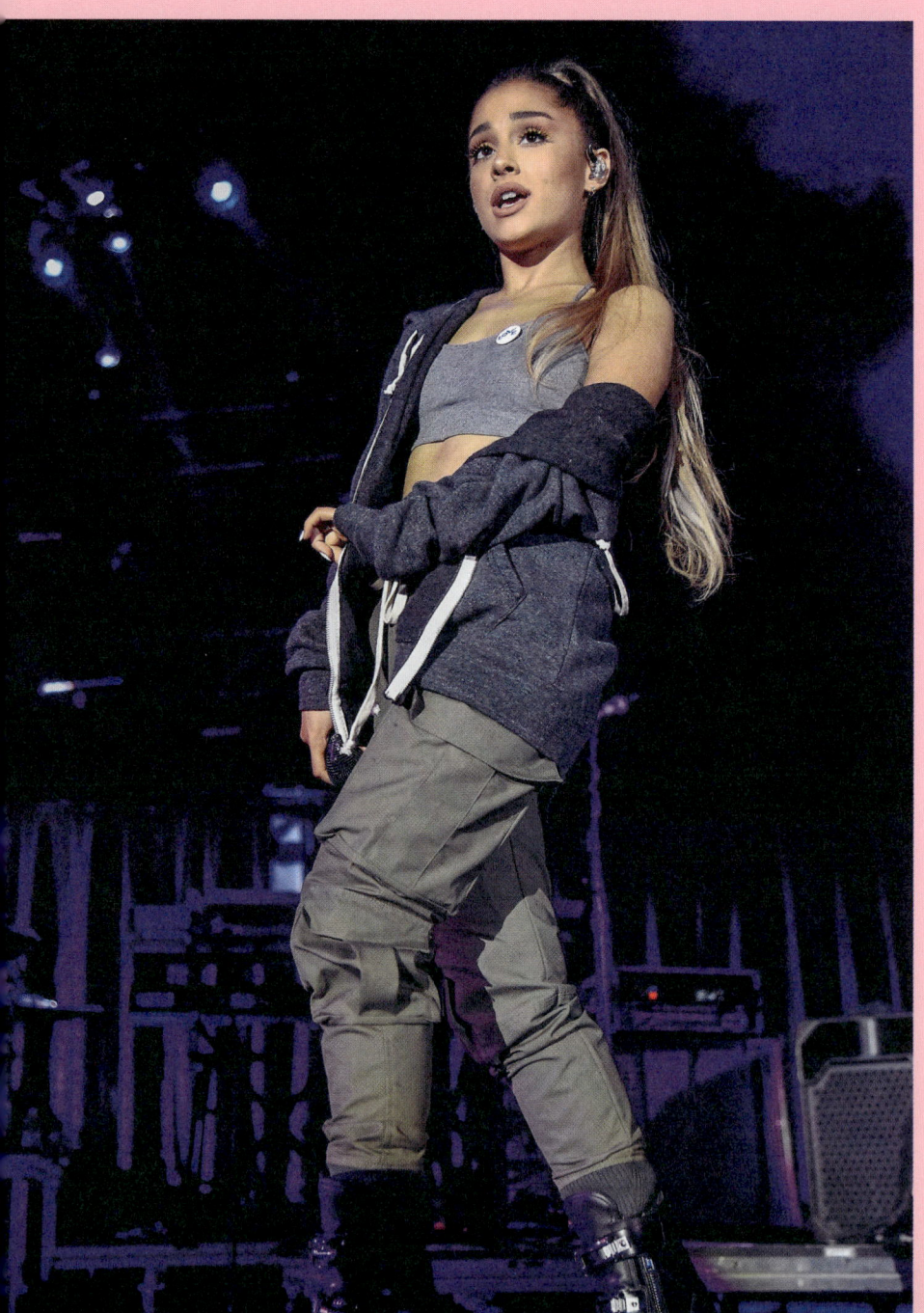

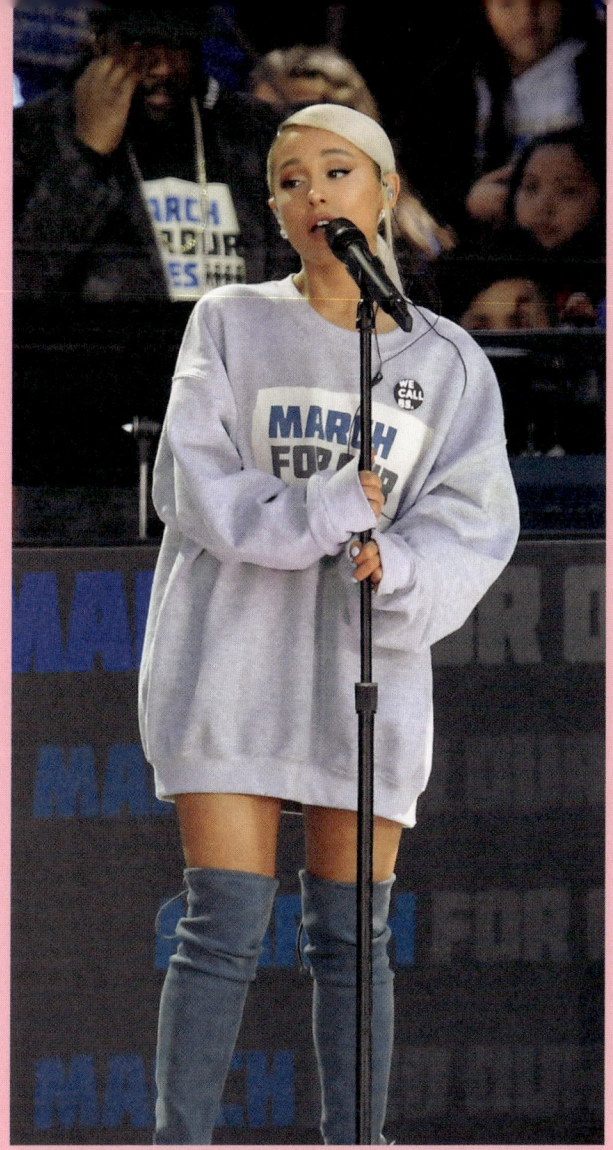

ABOVE Wearing the March for Our Lives sweater at the rally in Washington, D.C. on 24 March 2018, to campaign for gun safety.

OPPOSITE Performing at A Concert for Charlottesville in September 2017, to raise funds for the counter-protesters who were killed and injured at a white supremacist rally.

> "*My fans are obsessed with knowing my* favourite colour *so this is important: it was* lavender, *and then it was* yellow, *but now it's* ice blue. *Like, ice blue mixed with grey.*"

ARIANA GRANDE

A pared down stage look of sweater and boots for The Sweetener Sessions, in Chicago on 22 August 2018.

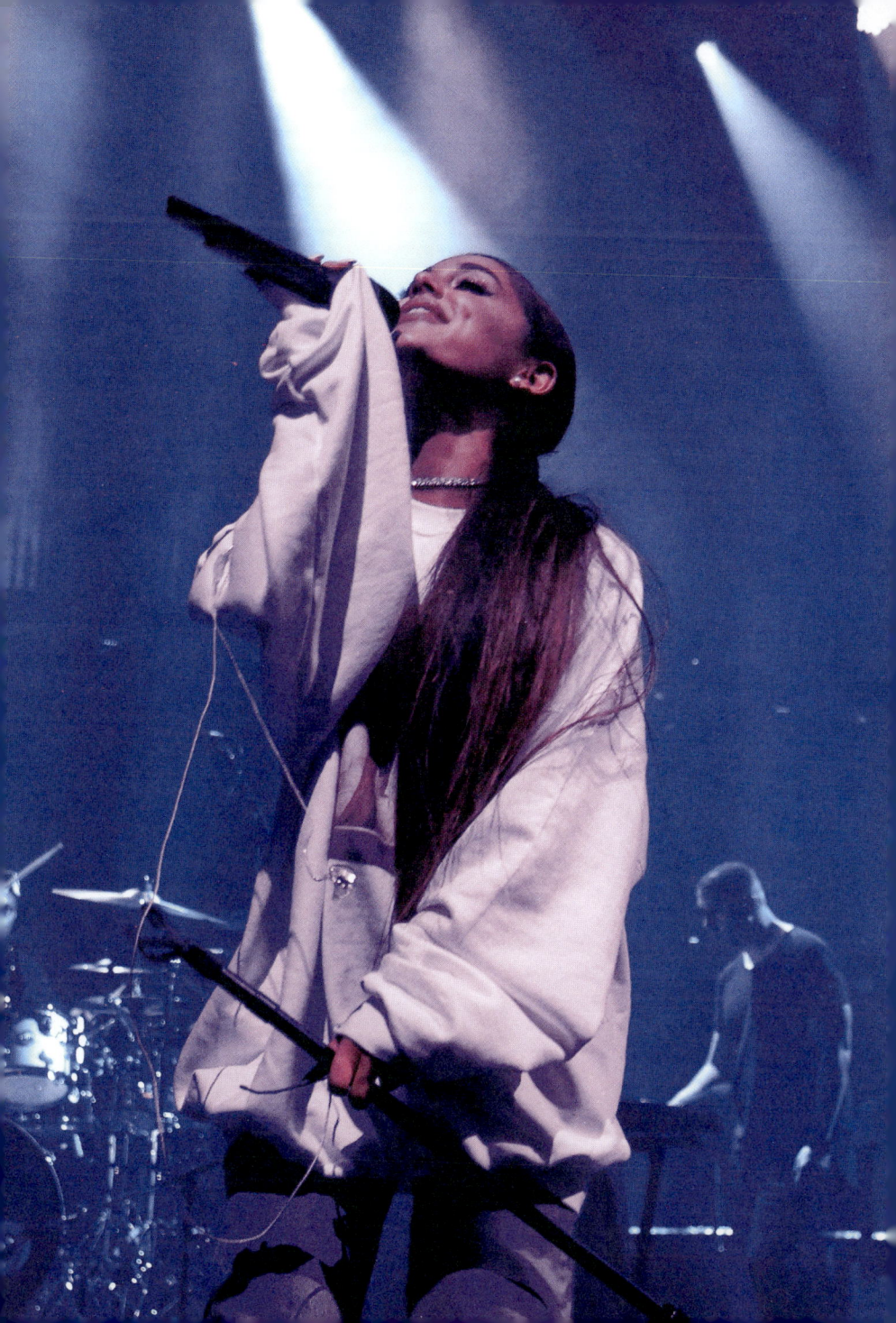

Key

CHAPTER 3

Pieces

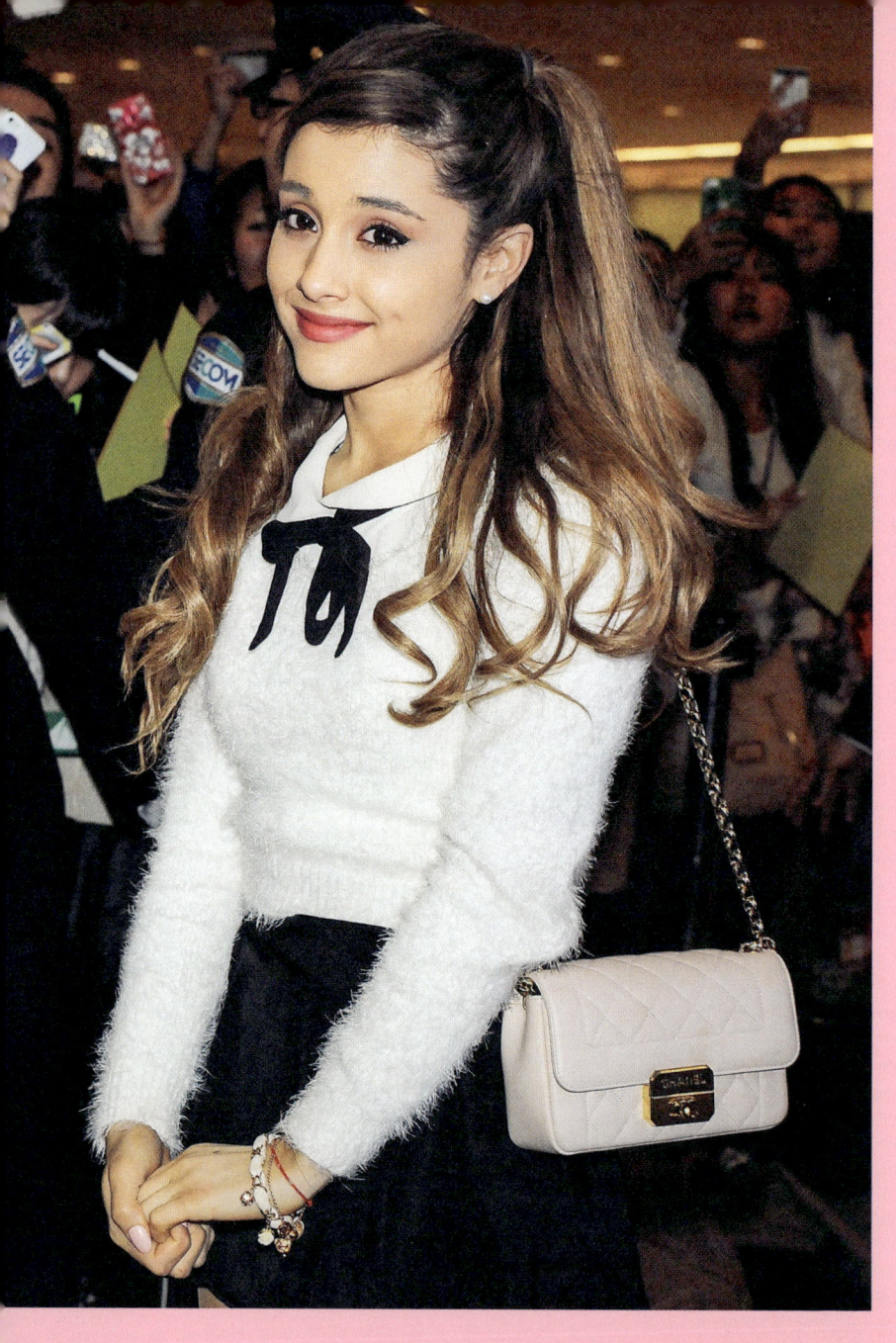

Casual looks

Once describing her relaxed style as "Oversized men's jackets as dresses, thigh boots and generally no pants [trousers]", Ariana used her public "off-duty" appearances to showcase a range of streetstyle hoodies, statement coats and puffer jackets, but when she first emerged as a pop star, she was more into preppy elegance.

During the promotion in 2013, her go-to labels were Topshop and Nasty Gal, affordable brands her fans could emulate, and she was often snapped in a Parisian schoolgirl style of plaid shirts and blouses, with Saint Laurent heels and Chanel purses.

Stepping out in London in October 2013 to visit BBC Studios with boyfriend Nathan Sykes from The Wanted, she teamed her orange and white plaid Topshop skirt with white heels and a white hoodie; in Amsterdam, her white heels and white hoodie were worn with a plaid Nasty Gal cape coat – again, mixing elegance with street style – and in Tokyo, she was Parisienne chic in a Nasty Gal white blouse with black bow, Topshop sweater, black miniskirt, black Saint Laurent heels and Chanel and Louis Vuitton luggage. Her travelling style was also one of comfort and security. Arriving in Tokyo in August 2015, she was wrapped in a Kigu unicorn onesie teamed with Saint Laurent Tribute pumps, while puffer jackets, Keds and Converse were reliably easy for being ushered through customs.

Ariana Grande arriving at Narita International Airport in Japan on 31 December 2013, in a Topshop jumper and Nasty Gal blouse.

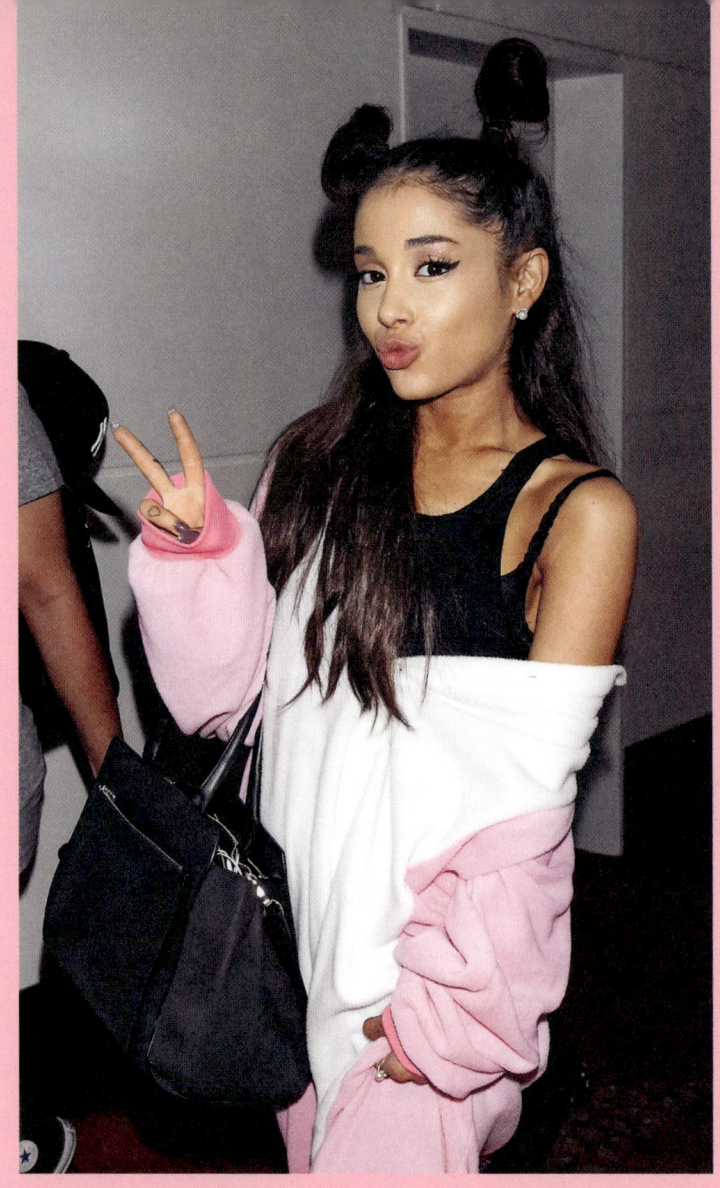

ABOVE Arriving in Tokyo on 13 August 2015
in a onesie for comfort travelling.

OPPOSITE In New York in August 2018, in her customary oversized
sweater, Chanel belt bag, over-the-knee boots and high ponytail.

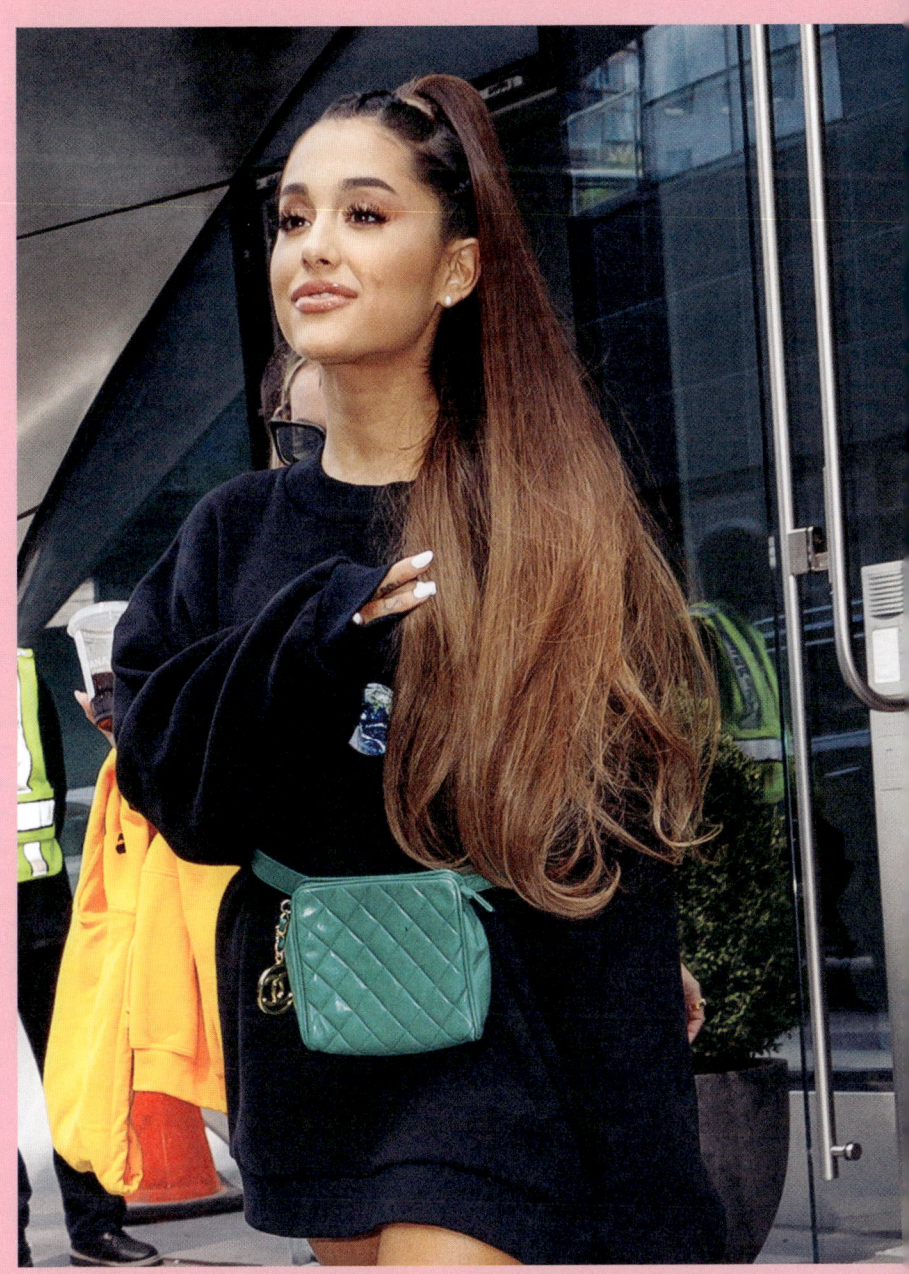

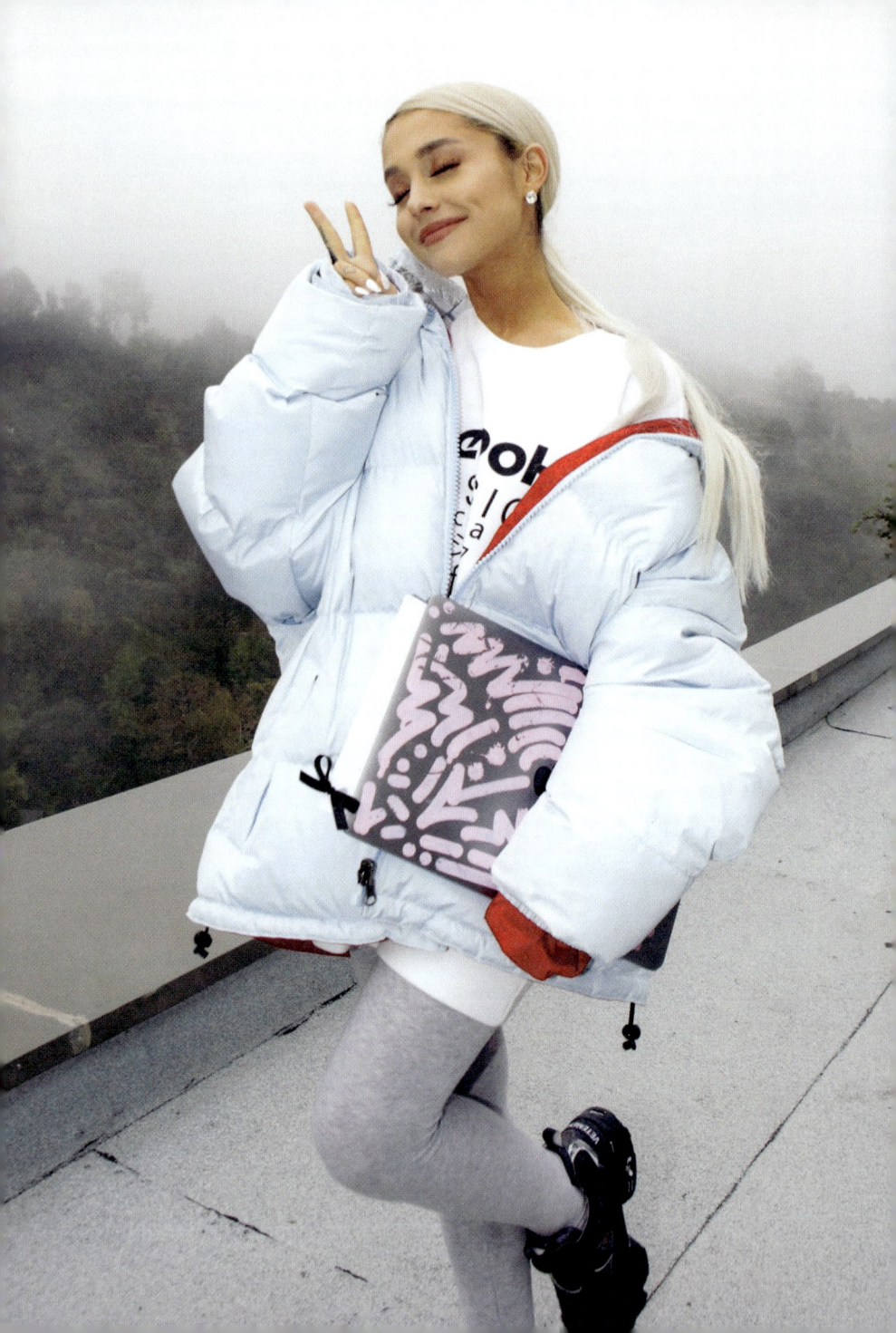

When Ariana teamed up with Law Roach in 2015, he helped her select cutting-edge labels with oodles of street cred, such as Virgil Abloh's men's puffers. Not only did they look more feminine on her small stature, but choosing sportswear was also a means of grounding herself when she was so often dismissed as polished and glitzy. "I probably wouldn't like me if I only knew what the world knows of me, or reads of me, because half of it is bullshit and half of it is true, like videos of me touching my hair and being polished pop star girl, and I'm like, 'Ew. F— you.' I see my shit that I make and I'm like, that's crazy," she joked with podcaster Zach Sang in November 2019.

Her *Sweetener* period would be the peak of Ariana's signature style – the high ponytail, the sweaters and hoodies so big that they were worn as dresses, the flash of thigh between her over-the-knee boots and the Chanel or Louis Vuitton mini-purses.

During their intense relationship, she was spotted around New York with a grungy Pete Davidson. It was a look marked by contrast – luxury streetstyle, provocative boots and oversized casual. At the same time she was making the lampshade tunic her own and this lollipop sweet, streetwear style would be undeniably Ariana in her 2018 era.

Revealing newly platinum blonde hair ahead of the release of *Sweetener* on 10 March 2018 in Los Angeles, California.

"I like to grow with my clients," Law Roach told the *New York Times* in 2019, adding that Ariana "went through so much these last two years: the bombing at the concert, the death of what could have been one of the loves of her life, the breakup with Pete... It's just, she has 148 million people on Instagram alone watching her go through it."

Ariana wasn't seen in public for much of 2022 and as she worked on *Wicked* and was styled by Mimi Cuttrell, streamlined elegance reflected her growth as she went through both a marriage and then a divorce. She served up this new mood at Wimbledon in 2023, in a Ralph Lauren grey turtleneck wool sweater and pleated wool maxiskirt, Tiffany sunglasses and Wimbledon logo cap. Attending the opening night of *Spamalot* on Broadway in New York in November 2023, she chose a Loewe tailored wool coat, black velvet bustier dress and pumps, and with the red lips and low blonde ponytail, this was grown-up elegance personified. It was a new fashion transformation that represented exactly where she was in her life: "The whole point of being on this earth is to change: Life is a process and you're always evolving," she told *The Kit* in 2016.

An oversized Chanel bag, tracksuit and Converse Chuck Taylor All Star sneakers for her arrival at Haneda Airport, Tokyo in June 2016.

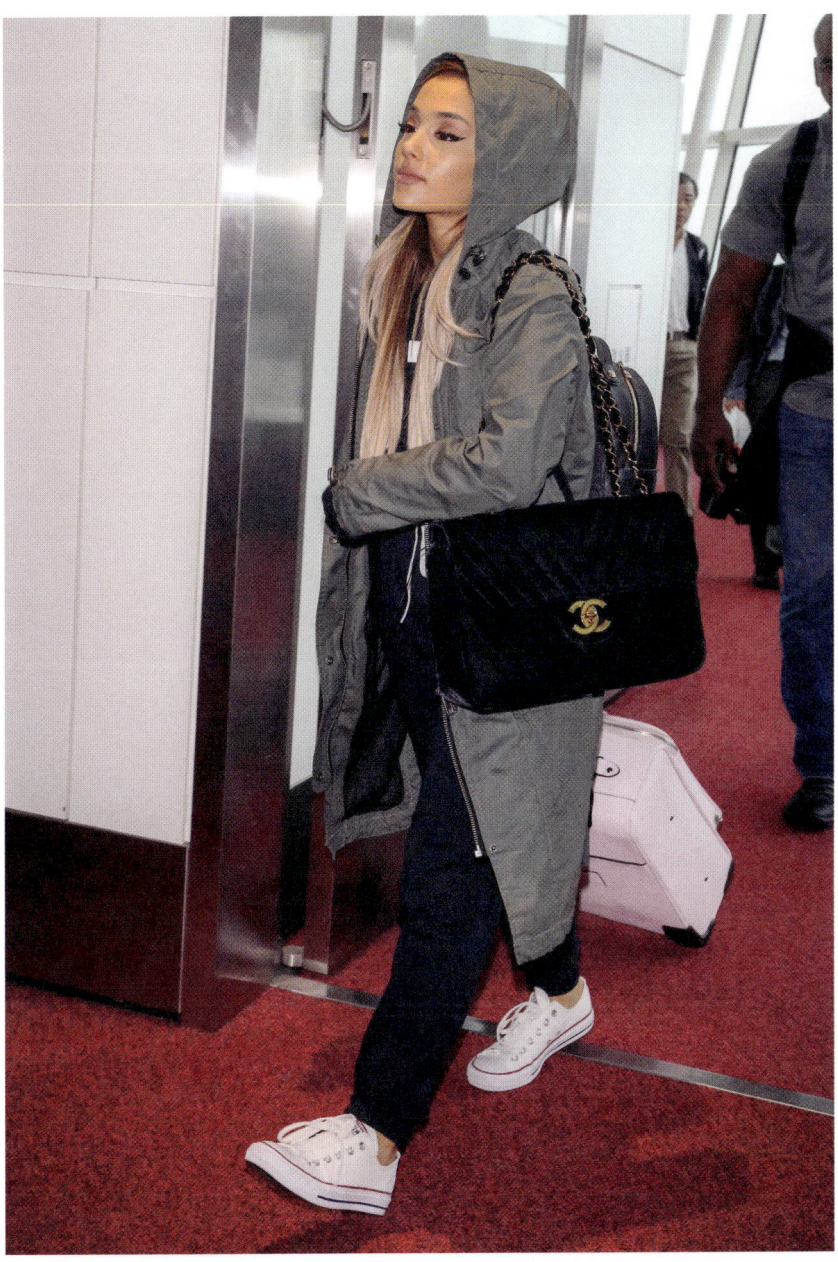

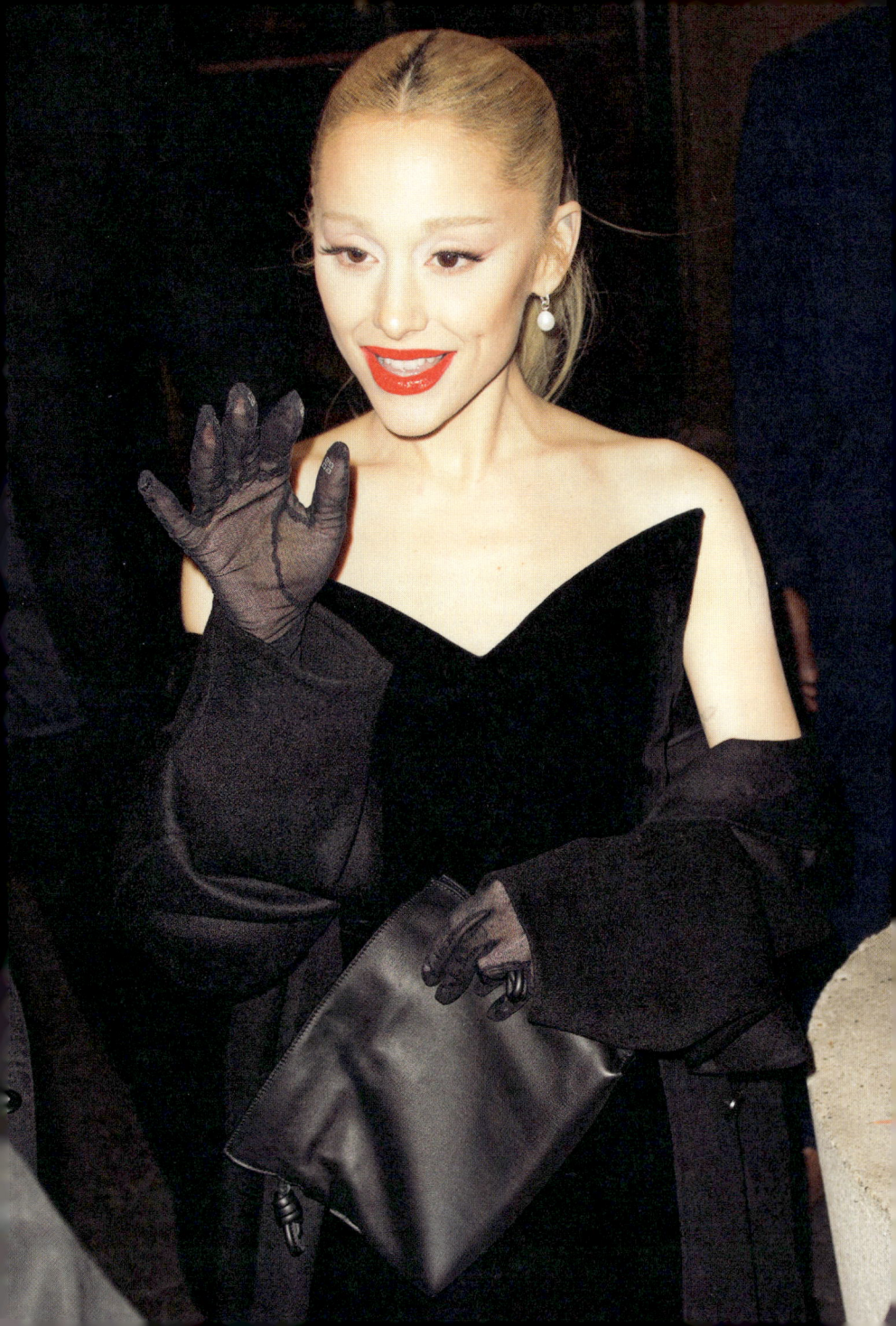

"The whole point of being on this earth is to change: Life is a process and you're always evolving."

ARIANA GRANDE

Exuding sophisticated glamour in a black satin Loewe midi dress for the opening night of *Spamalot* on Broadway in December 2023.

Event dressing

Starting out as a teen star, Ariana followed a template of cute minidresses and heels often selected by herself for her early event appearances, such as the gold Tibi cocktail dress she found online to wear to the Creative Arts Emmy Awards in 2011. As she told interviewer Joslyn Davis outside the venue, "I had a fitting with my stylist and everything, and it didn't work out... I feel like sometimes I have to shop for myself, with my mom, and just do it that way."

The 53rd Grammy Awards in February 2011 marked her first major prestigious event and Ariana arrived on the red carpet with her brother Frankie, wearing a white minidress with tight skirt, draped top and with peep-toe heels. Then there was a Jovani black cocktail dress for her first appearance at the *Billboard* Music Awards in May 2013 and at the 2012 Emmy Awards she broke away from the strapless prom dresses in favour of a long, breezy red gown with crossover halterneck bodice. There were also risks – at the MTV Video Music Awards in August 2014 she took a fashion U-turn with a dominatrix style Moschino resort black bustier and skirt and Tom Ford leather, over-the-knee boots. And with her hair in a dirty-blonde high ponytail, it was a look that channelled Madonna, circa 1985.

On the red carpet at the 2012 Primetime Creative Arts Emmy Awards at Nokia Theatre Los Angeles on 15 September 2012.

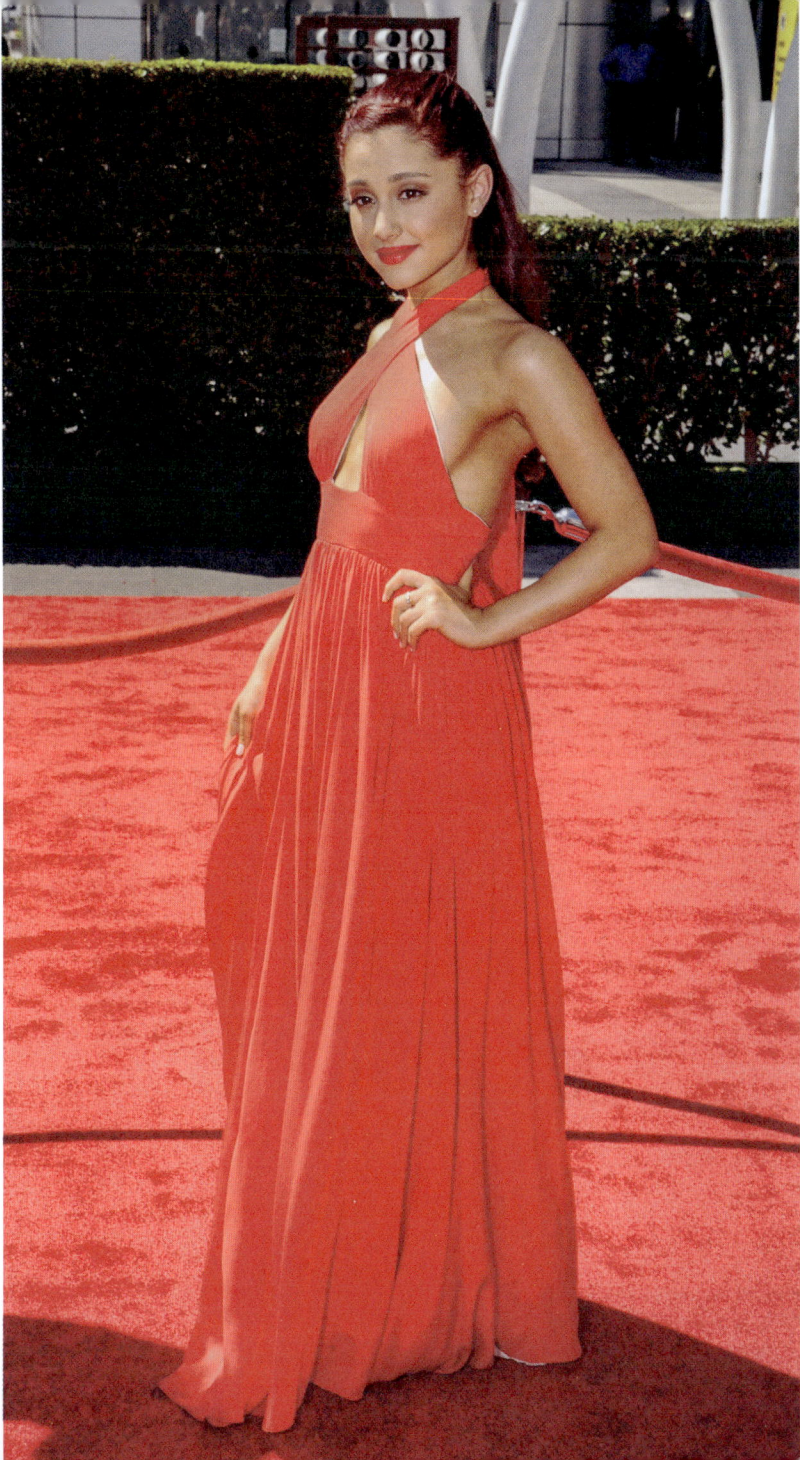

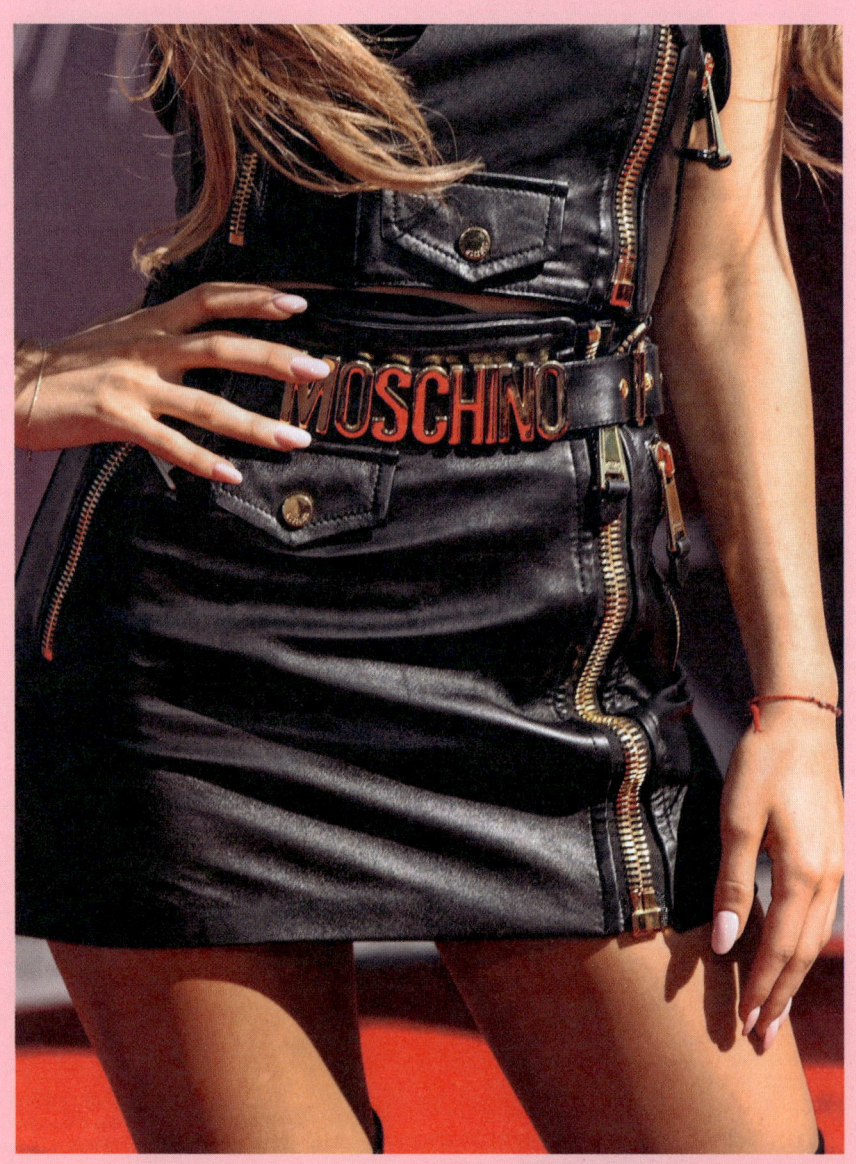

Under Roach's guidance, she transitioned from floral prom dresses to dramatic couture by Versace, Alexander McQueen and Giambattista Valli. At the same time, she wanted to ensure she didn't alienate desire devoted fans and that she remained true to herself, rather than copying catwalk trends. "The girl is authentic," said Roach to *Vogue* in July 2019. "I've never had a conversation with Ariana Grande about wanting to look like or be like someone else."

The first event he styled her for was the American Music Awards in November 2015, where he selected a one-of-a-kind Giambattista Valli couture gown. They gelled during four-hour fittings, where she told jokes and did impressions, and as they tried on clothes for hours and hours, they forged a series of daring red-carpet looks.

Wearing black leather Moschino at
the 2014 MTV Video Music Awards.

"The girl is **authentic,** *I've never had a conversation with* **Ariana Grande**

*about wanting
to look like
or be like
someone else."*

LAW ROACH

The 58th Annual Grammy Awards, February 2016

Arriving at the Grammy Awards in 2016, Ariana wore a fire-engine red Romona Keveza gown, buttoned down the bodice, the back and train.

The sleek gown was a perfect piece of event dressing to indicate a shift in direction for the upcoming *Dangerous Woman* album, but with the dip-dye high ponytail and red satin Giuseppe Zanotti red satin platform heels, it was undeniably Ariana. *Nylon* praised the bold choice of wearing red on a red-carpet, but she "nailed it".

"My new music has a bit of an edge to it and I've been having fun incorporating that into my style," she said. "For the GRAMMYs we really wanted to do something classic with that edge – I loved the Romona Keveza gown I wore! I think it is important to stay true to who you are and pick things that you really, really love."

The red Romona Keveza gown was a signal that Ariana was entering her *Dangerous Woman* era.

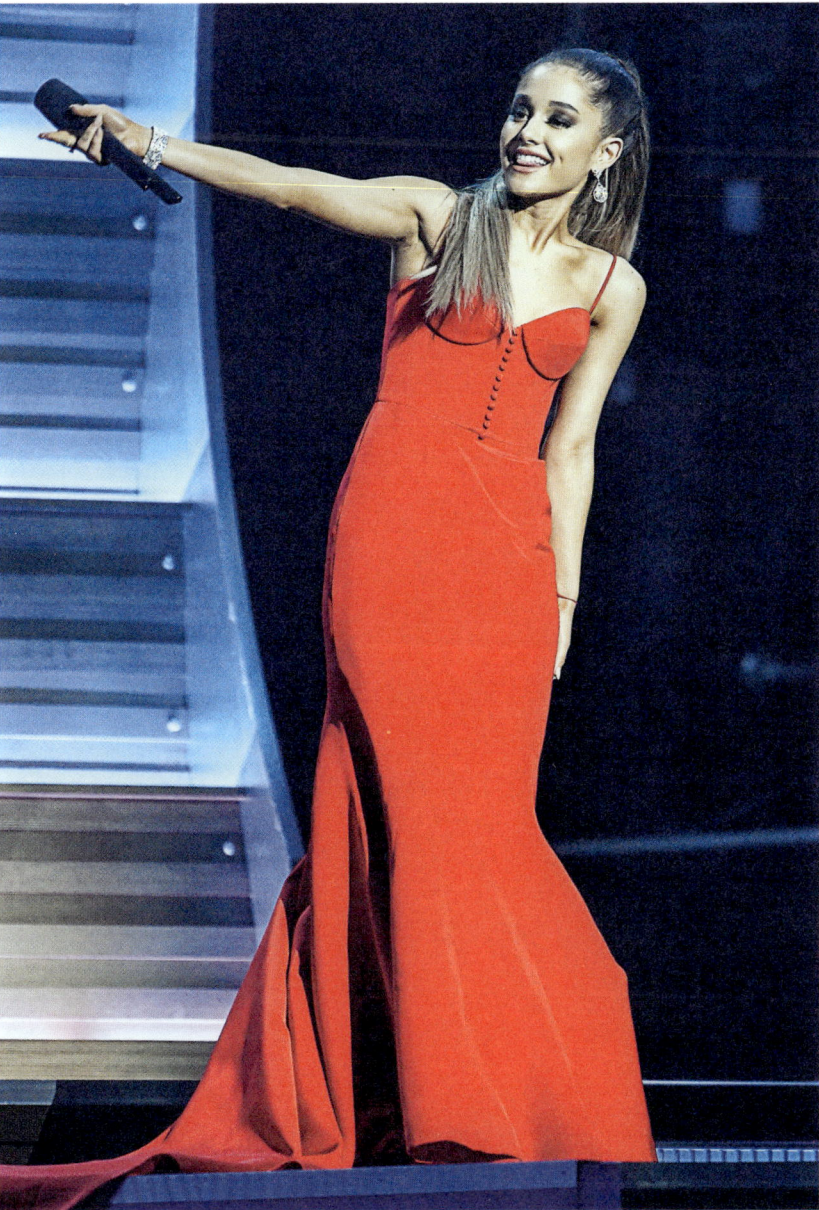

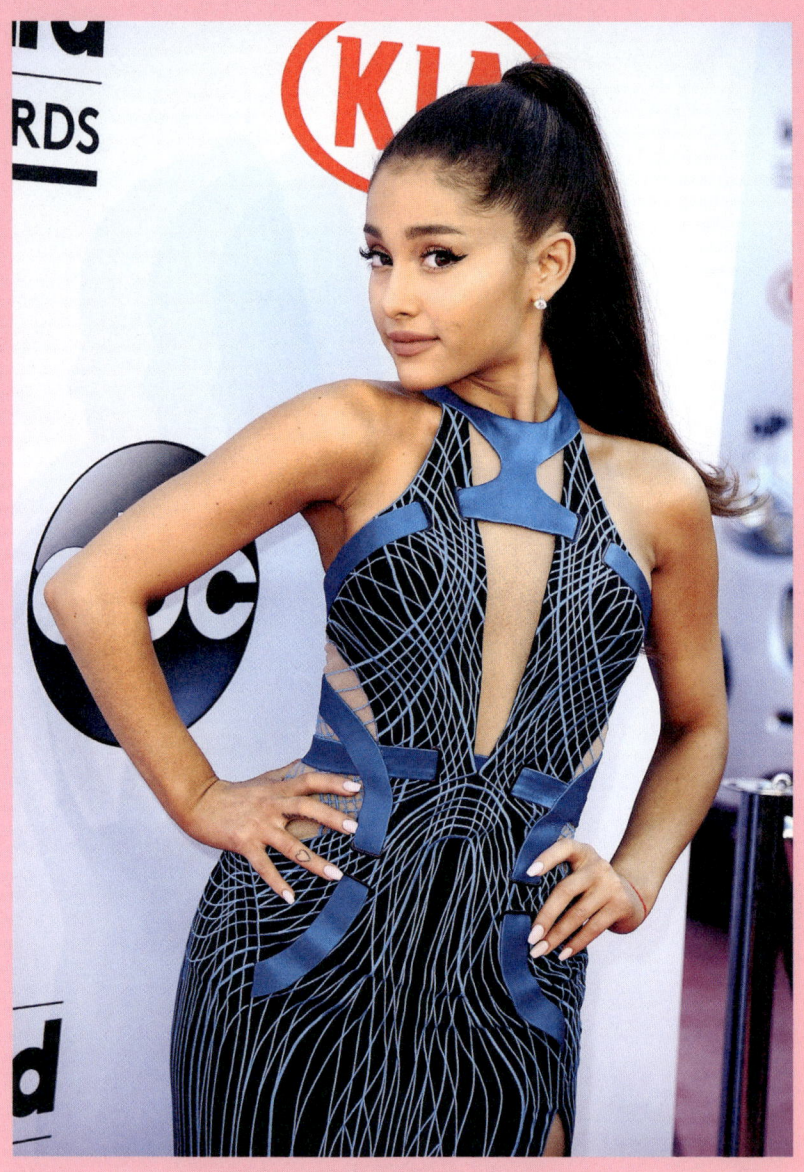

The graphic print Versace gown at the 2016 *Billboard* Music Awards
marked the start of a strong relationship with Donatella Versace.

Billboard Music Awards, May 2016

Ariana had long been a Versace fan and Roach called on Donatella Versace to dress the singer for the *Billboard Music Awards* in May 2016, held in Paradise, Nevada.

As a double nominee, she arrived in a blue graphic print Versace gown with cut-out details, complete with signature ponytail and Giuseppe Zanotti black satin platform pumps. From then on, Ariana would form a close friendship with Donatella, who went on to create looks for the Sweetener world tour.

"This is one of my favourite ever Ariana looks," Law Roach told *Teen Vogue* in June 2016. "She is evolving, and her new music has evolved and so has her look. That's what you get as you grow as an artist and from a young girl into a young woman."

To perform a 'Dangerous Woman' and 'Into You' medley Ariana switched into Alexander McQueen black trousers, crop top and a diamond choker necklace. Chic and powerful, it firmly placed the girlishness of past albums behind her as she performed as a woman in control of her sexuality. It was a similar style to the scalloped crop top and high-waisted black trousers by Jonathan Simkhai that she wore to perform 'Dangerous Woman' on *The Tonight Show Starring Jimmy Fallon* in April 2016.

MTV Movie Awards, April 2016

Law Roach described the hot pink Michael Costello gown with fishtail worn by Ariana to the MTV Movie Awards as "one of my all-time favourites".

Inspired by old Hollywood glamour, and Marilyn Monroe in the iconic film *Gentlemen Prefer Blondes*, she accessorized it with a white Maggie Berry faux fur jacket as she took to the stage to croon 'Dangerous Woman' to a piano accompaniment.

"We got references for how the staging and lighting would be for the performance first, and wanted to do something that fitted the look, so we turned to Marilyn for inspiration," the stylist explained to *Teen Vogue* in 2016.

A tribute to Marilyn Monroe in *Gentlemen Prefer Blondes* at the MTV Movie Awards in 2016.

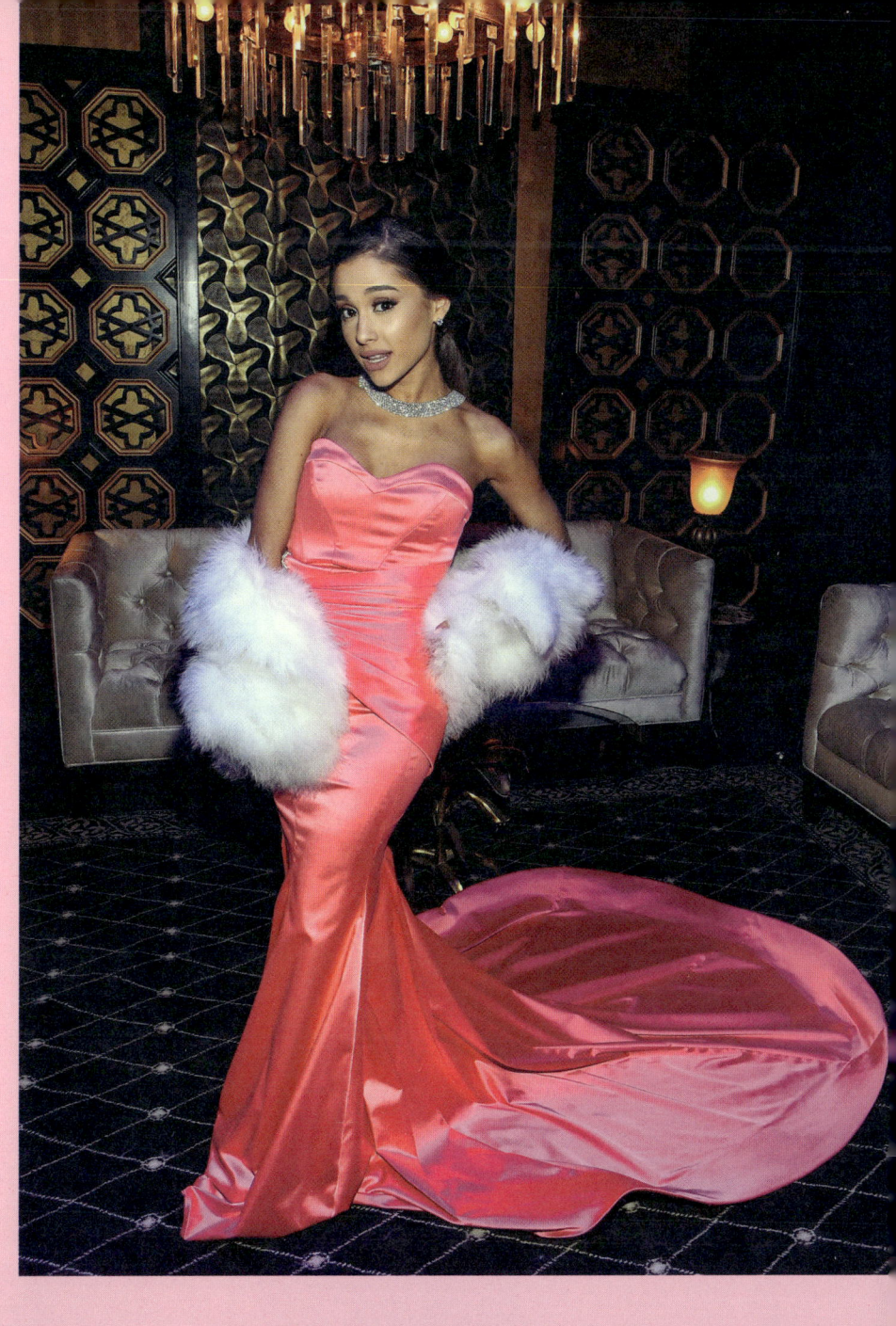

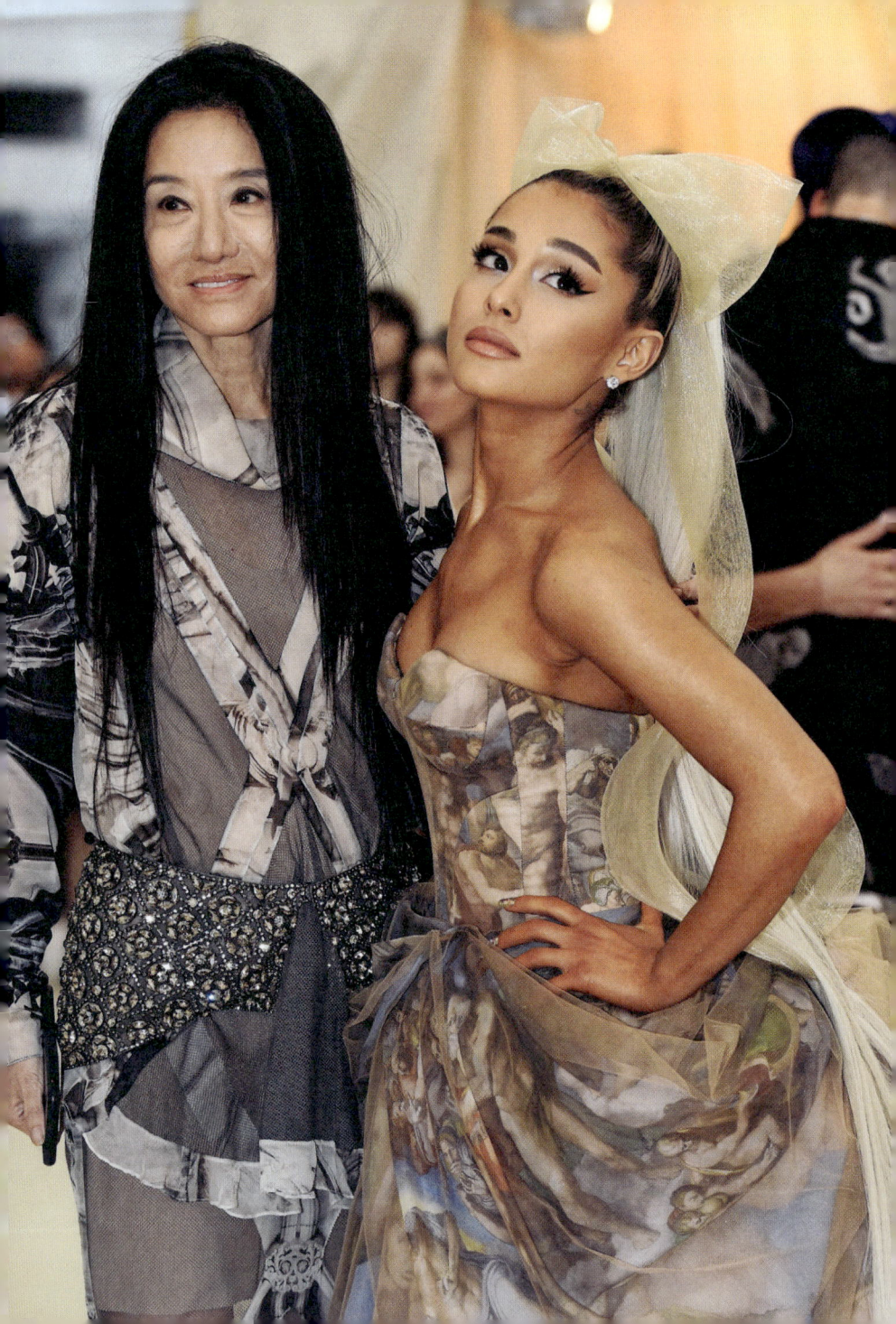

The Met Gala, May 2018

Ariana made her debut appearance at the Met Gala in 2018 and her bespoke Vera Wang gown, printed with Michelangelo's masterpieces on the Sistine Chapel, was a perfect fit for the Costume Institute's "Heavenly Bodies" theme, where she was styled like a Renaissance work of art.

She described her Met Gala Vera Wang gown as the "puff puff dream", and its replication of Michelangelo's *The Last Judgement* was "a foreshadow, a hint" of her upcoming video for 'God Is a Woman'. This was complemented by her manicure with an intricate depiction of the work on each nail, decorated with a 3D gold frame.

"It was just all about romance with her," said Law Roach to *Women's Wear Daily* in May 2018. "There is a bit of drama there, there is a silhouette that we are used to seeing her in, but of course, more elevated and more appropriate for the event. It is very recognizably Ariana Grande, for sure."

With designer Vera Wang at the Met Gala in 2018, in a Sistine Chapel dress that mirrored the aesthetics of the music video for 'God is a Woman'.

MTV Video Music Awards, August 2018

During Ariana's summer of love with Pete Davidson she honed her unique streetwear-meets-babydoll style.

It came to a pinnacle at the MTV Video Music Awards as she walked the red carpet in a metallic Venus Prototype latex chrome bustier and sparkling Le Silla "Naomi" boots while engaging in public displays of affection with an underdressed Pete, in a sweater and sneakers. The surprise choice of the night was that there was no ponytail in sight – her long dark hair was now worn down. *Vanity Fair* described her appearance as "a Madame Tussauds' version of Ariana Grande" wearing an "outfit that says Xena Princess Warrior in Space", and it would prove to be a foreshadow of the costume choices for the Sweetener world tour.

Ariana with Pete Davidson at the MTV Video Music Awards in August 2016. Her silver latex strapless dress drew comparisons to a futuristic space warrior.

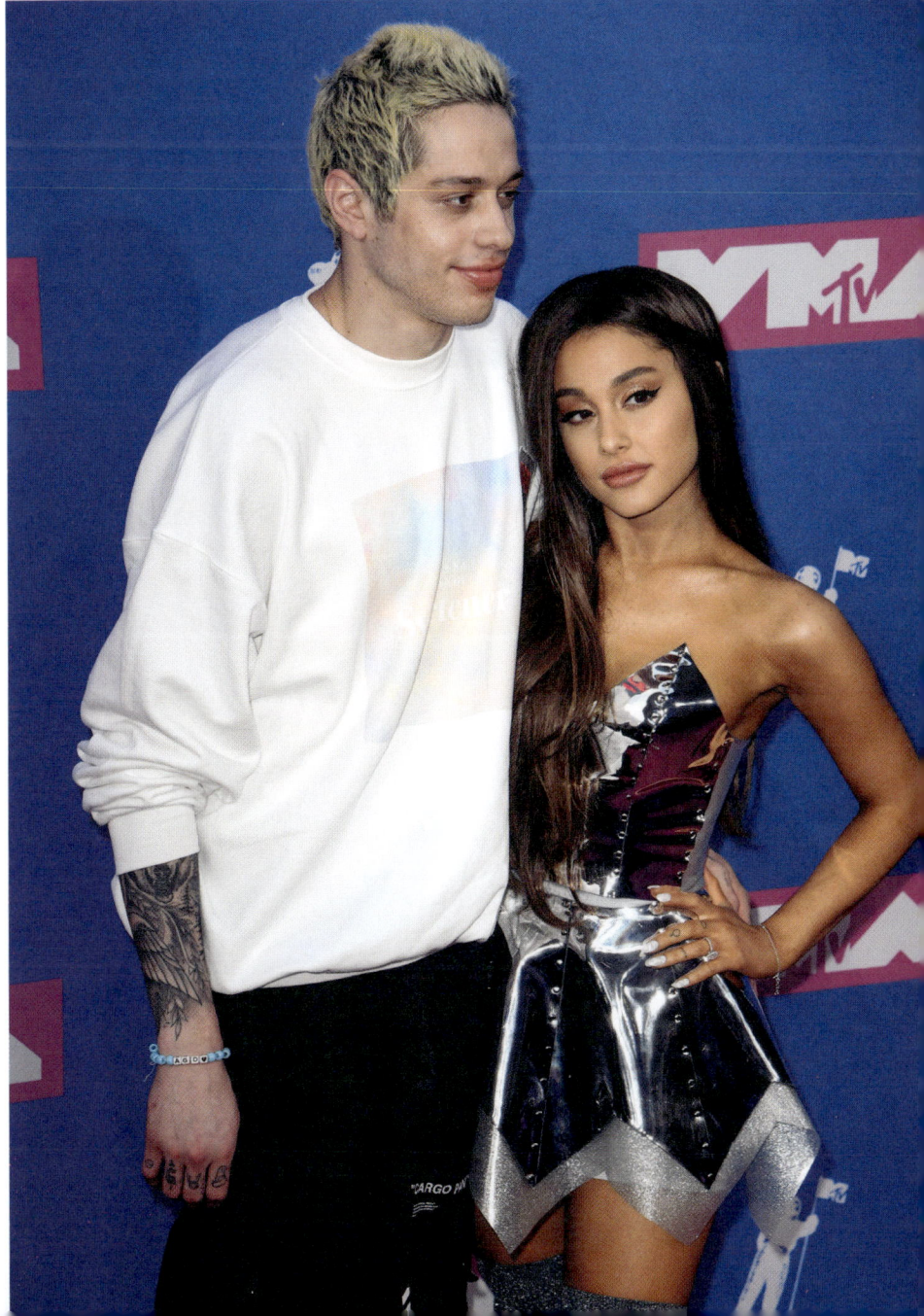

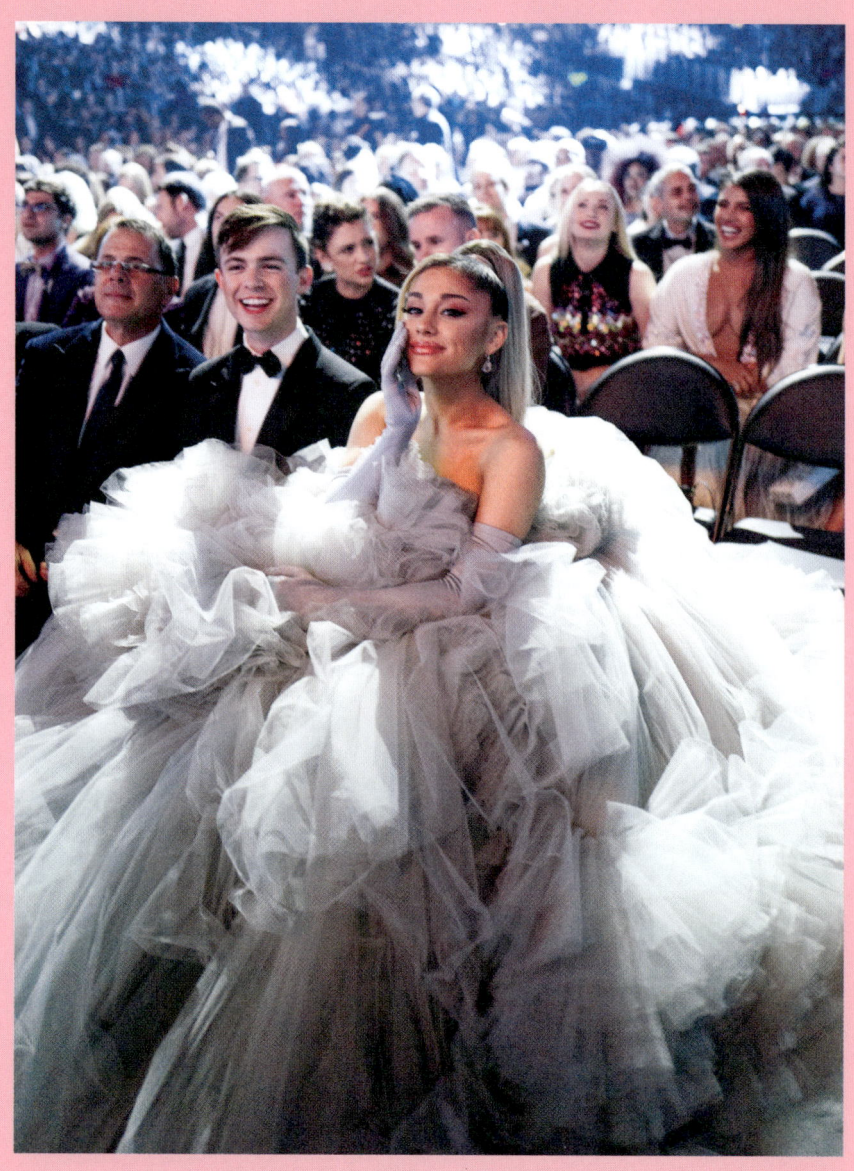

Taking up space. Ariana's 2020 Grammy Awards Giambattista Valli gown was a voluminous confection of tulle.

Billboard Women in Music, December 2018

Ariana's appearance at the *Billboard* Women in Music on 6 December 2018 was a further culmination of her style of the year as she translated her now-classic street style into event wear.

The Christian Siriano Pre-Fall 2019 puffball dress worn with Le Silla "Eva" over-the-knee stiletto boots was a perfect encapsulation of her 2018 style – the monochrome lilac, the heels, the short, voluminous dress and the waist-length dark ponytail worn as a topknot.

Grammy Awards, 26 January 2020

At the 2020 GRAMMYs, where she was nominated for five awards, Ariana arrived in a cloud of grey tulle, wearing a custom-made Giambattista Valli gown with a strapless bodice and three-tiered skirt, and with a return to the high ponytail, this time blonde.

The peak of her fairytale dressing, the gown required 400 yards of tulle and 200 hours of work to construct, and she fully demonstrated the workmanship by kneeling on the red carpet to allow the skirts to cascade around her. After posing for photos she switched into a grey Schiaparelli two-piece, with a satin top and silk folded skirt, while keeping the grey opera gloves from her first outfit: "I had two very special custom looks made and I couldn't decide," she enthused in a red-carpet interview.

And there were even more custom looks to come. For her performances she switched into a black strapless Givenchy Spring/Summer 2020 couture gown for 'Imagine' before changing into a Trashy Lingerie "Sex Kitten" short robe and Givenchy platform sandals for '7 Rings' and 'thank u, next'.

A new stylist

In 2020 Ariana hired Mimi Cuttrell, the stylist behind the sharp looks of supermodel Bella Hadid and actress and model Lily-Rose Depp, and this new pairing saw her embrace couture and archival pieces.

As a vintage fashion lover, Cuttrell raided high-end vintage boutiques and fashion house archives to find pieces guaranteed to make Ariana stand out.

OPPOSITE The second outfit worn on the GRAMMYs red carpet in 2020 – a two-piece, midriff revealing Schiaparelli gown.

OVERLEAF Performing 'Imagine' onstage at the Grammy Awards in January 2020 in Givenchy. She had multiple costume changes for the night, making up for having missed the awards in 2019.

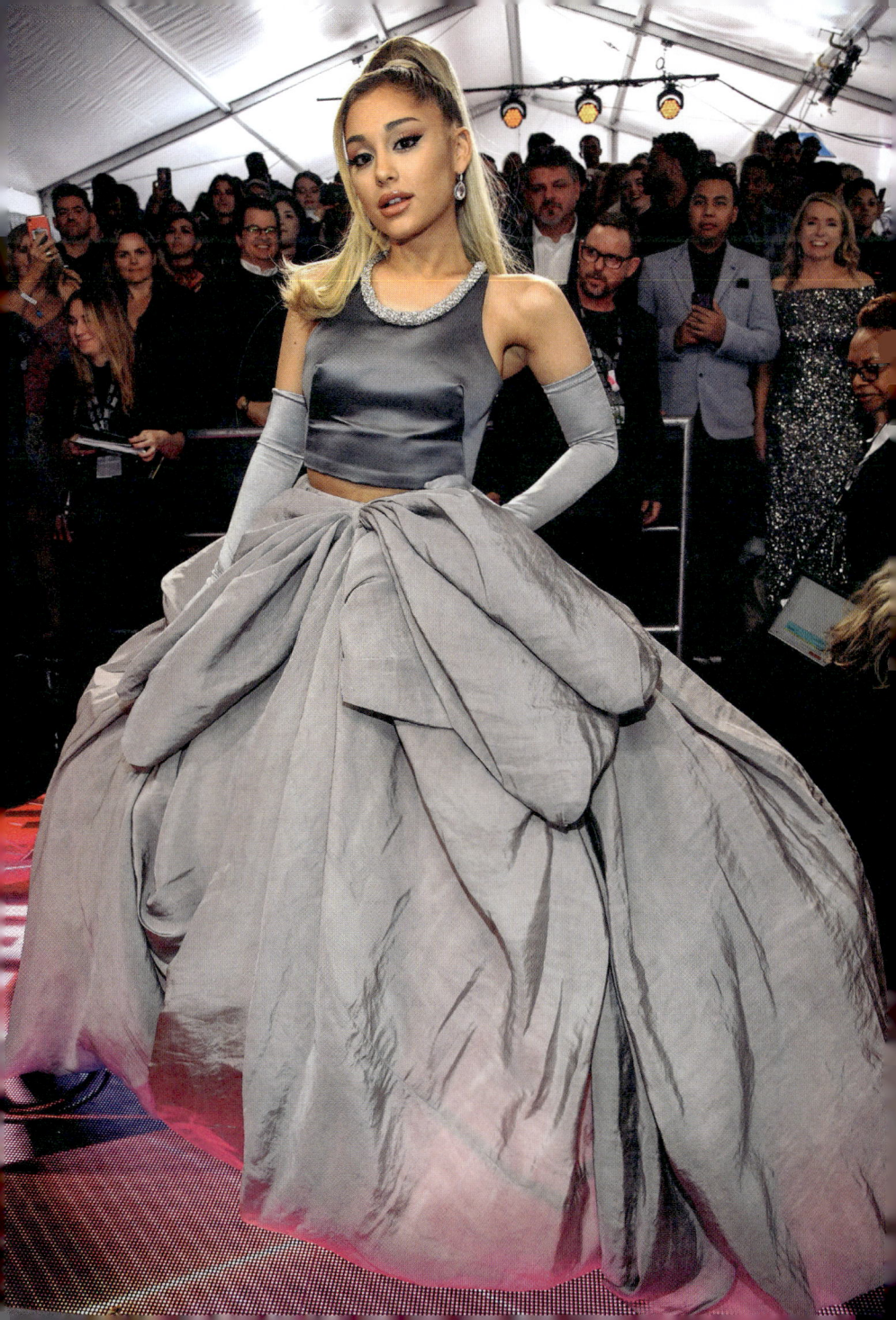

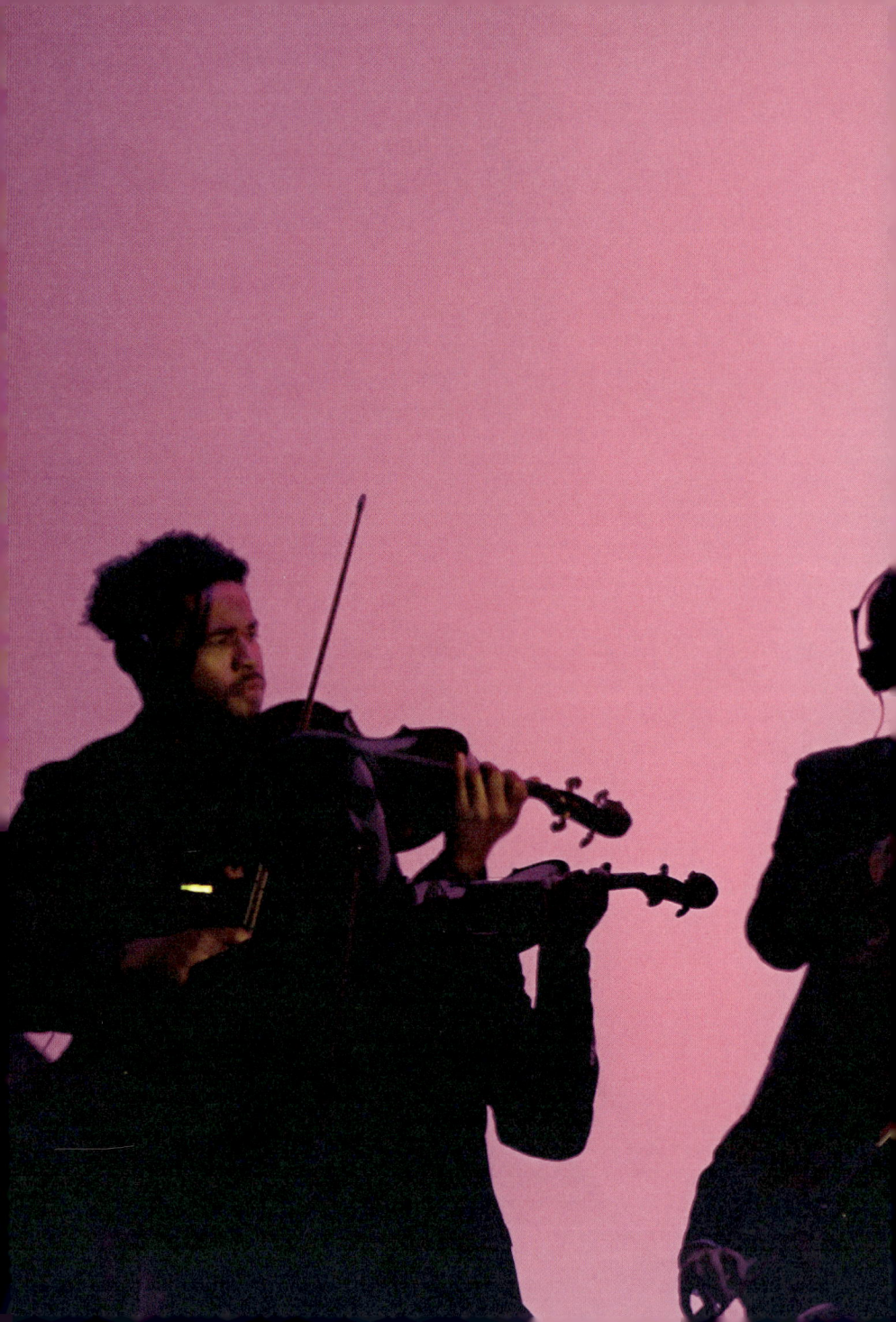

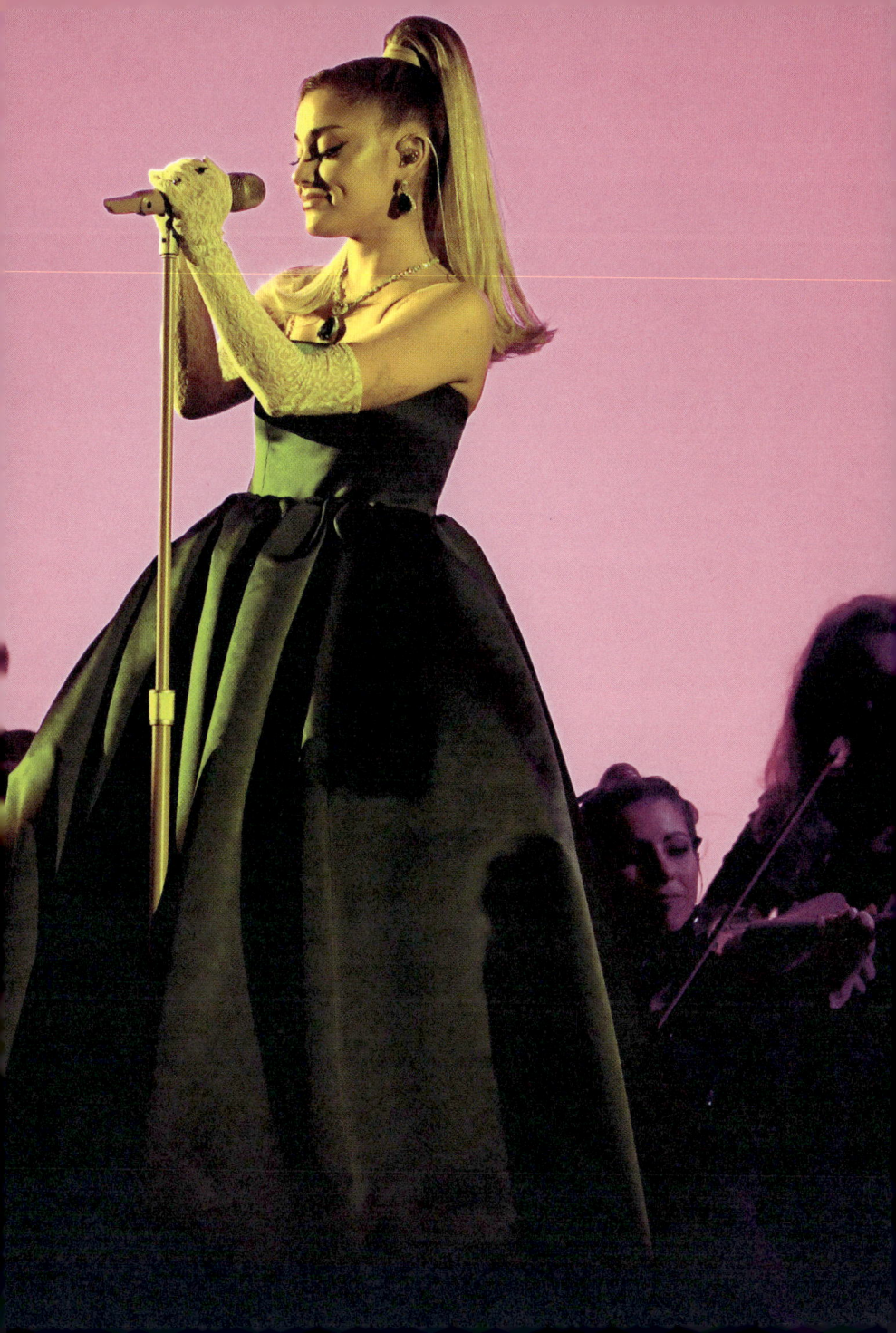

"She is evolving, and her new music has evolved and so has her look."

LAW ROACH

The Voice, 2020

For every weekly appearance on the TV talent show *The Voice*, Ariana excelled in cutting-edge fashion choices, both runway and vintage, as selected and styled by Mimi Cuttrell, who often sourced from Nina Gabbana Vintage, a favourite of singer Rihanna.

The selections followed Ariana's preferred silhouette of halternecks, minidresses and body-skimming, midriff-revealing designs from a range of designers, including a baby blue leather "Off-White" minidress by Virgil Abloh with black gloves. To perform with her fellow judges, she wore a hot pink corset, flared trousers and gloves from Prabal Gurung Autumn/Winter 2021, she chose Malaysian designer Ivan Young to custom-make a lilac satin bralet top with fringed skirt and she picked a shimmering blue-green midriff-revealing dress by Korean brand Miss Sohee.

One of the most treasured finds by Cuttrell was the exact same multicoloured Versace dress that Jennifer Garner wore in the 2004 rom-com *13 Going on 30*, from the Spring/Summer 2003 collection. In an Instagram story, the stylist revealed that the moment took six months of planning and thanked Donatella Versace for making the dress happen for Ariana's first live show for *The Voice*. Ariana closed her season by performing in the final, wearing a brilliant sunshine-yellow Valentino Spring 2010 couture gown with black gloves.

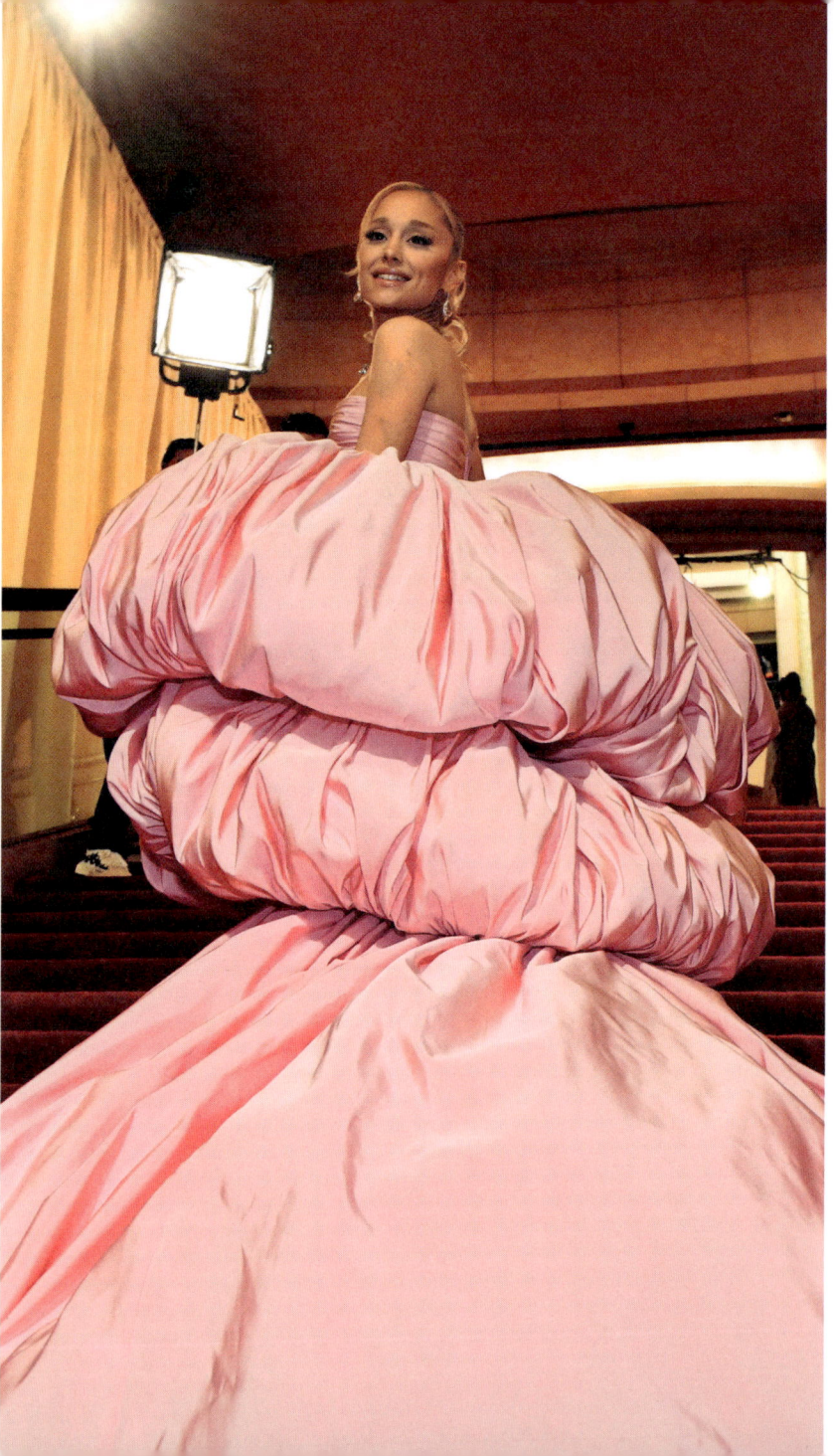

The Academy Awards, March 2024

For her first red-carpet appearance since the GRAMMYs in 2020, Ariana once again went for volume.

She arrived at the Academy Awards in a pink strapless, figure-hugging Giambattista Valli gown featuring an off-the-shoulder puff sleeve cape and long train, which she had to gather up as the fabric billowed around her. To accessorize, she wore her blonde hair scraped back and 30-carat Lorraine Schwartz diamond earrings valued at $2.5 million. The colour fitted with the Glinda-themed mood dressing for the *Wicked* press tour throughout 2024, where she promoted the film in soft shades of pink, while co-star Cynthia Erivo wore green. But at the same time, the gown drew mixed reviews. She was lambasted on social media for wearing a "cotton-candy bedspread", while *The Cut*'s Oscar gown analysis praised her simultaneously for taking a risk "for a huge gown that's *almost* too much" and for wearing what looked like "a buttercream-frosting accident happened in the piping bag".

In pink Giambattista Valli at the Academy Awards in 2024, engulfed by the billowing puffs of the train.

The Met Gala, 2024

Ariana's second appearance on fashion's most prestigious red carpet was marked by the Met Gala 2024 and this time she was also there to perform.

Mimi Cuttrell styled her to fit the "Garden of Time" theme, which connected with the Costume Institute's "Sleeping Beauties: Reawakening Fashion" exhibition. She wore a custom-made gown by Spanish brand Loewe, which once again tapped into the Renaissance with its inspiration drawn from *The Birth of Venus* and *Primavera* by Botticelli. The mother-of-pearl detail was also a tribute to Ariana's birthstone, with Lorraine Schwartz creating earrings of pear-shaped diamonds and white opals.

"I love the whimsical beauty and ethereal femininity of both paintings," Cuttrell explained to *Glamour*. "The idea that a pearl has evolved over time and is, at its essence, a 'Sleeping Beauty' really resonated with the theme of this year's Met Gala."

The whimsical Loewe gown for the Met Gala 2024 was inspired by the Renaissance art of Botticelli.

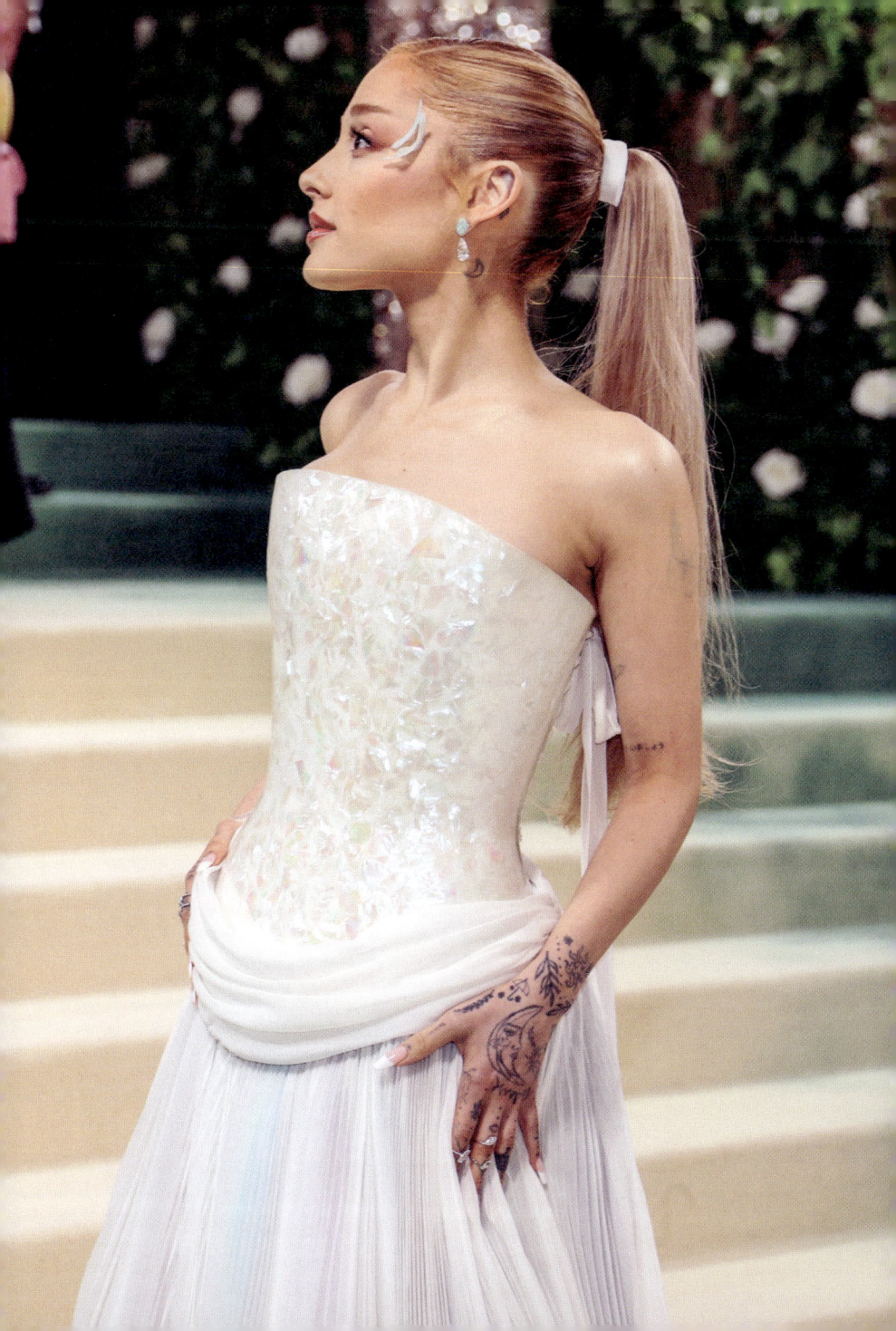

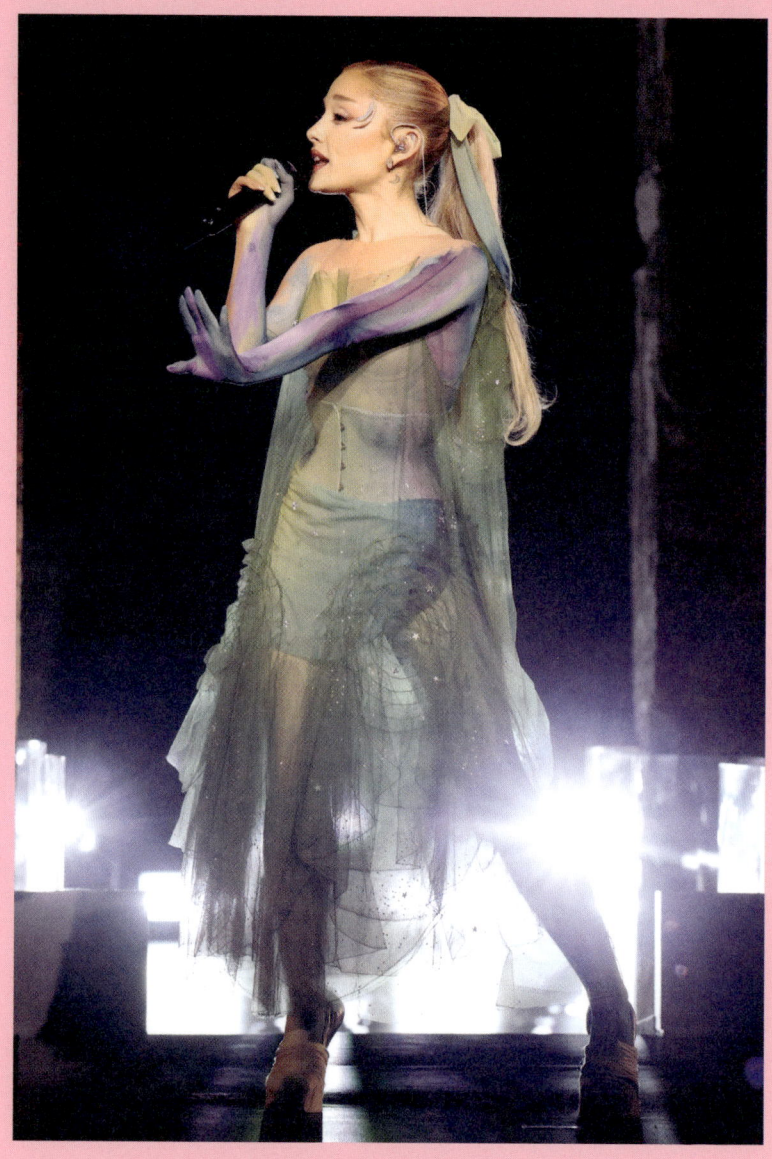

Weaving fairytales in this Maison Margiela custom-designed
forest green tulle gown to perform at the Met Gala benefit.

"I love the whimsical beauty and ethereal femininity of both paintings. The idea that a pearl has evolved over time and is, at its essence, a 'Sleeping Beauty' really resonated with the theme of this year's Met Gala."

MIMI CUTTRELL

The Paris Olympics, July 2024

At the Paris Olympics Opening Ceremony, Ariana wowed in a pale pink Audrey Hepburn-inspired satin gown with a full ballerina-length skirt. It may have been suitably Glinda-pink, but it was also in tribute to a gown worn by Hepburn in a photo taken by Norman Parkinson in Rome, 1955.

The duchess silk-satin dress was custom-made by Thom Browne and featured a drop waist with bow detail, which matched the bows in her hair. Ariana described it to British *Vogue* as "an ode to the history of French fashion and culture of the haute couture houses in Paris". She said that she and Mimi Cuttrell "drew inspiration from the beloved Audrey Hepburn and classic 1950s silhouettes to emulate an everlasting look". It was all part of her flawless mood dressing for the *Wicked* press tour and she hailed the brainstorming with Mimi to think pink so that they could "make Glinda proud".

A tribute to Audrey Hepburn and Paris while attending the opening ceremony of the Olympics in 2024.

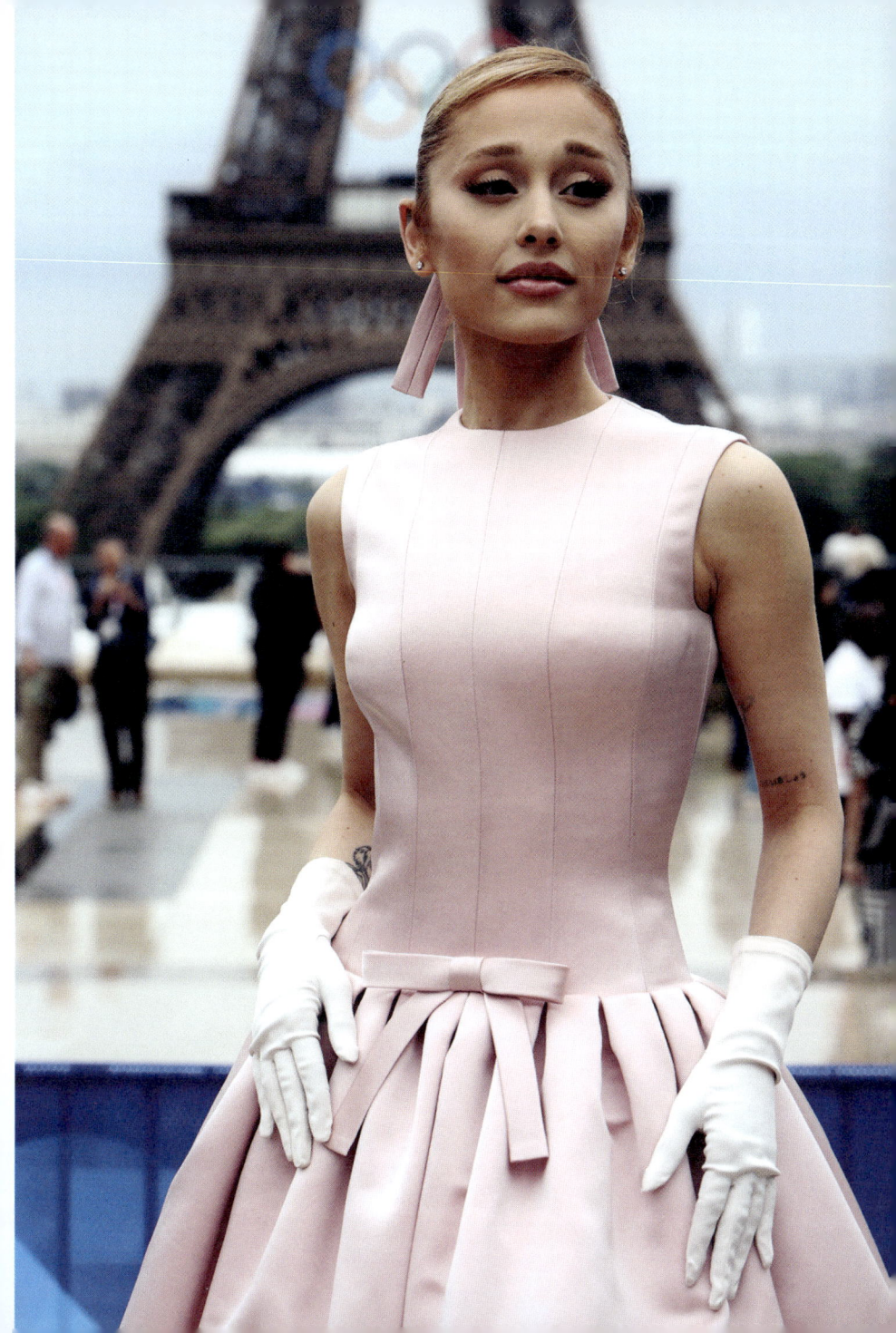

The tour looks

The Listening Sessions

Ariana's first tour, to promote her debut album *Yours Truly* (2013), was an intimate 11-date performance across North America, which she called the Listening Sessions. Her costumes were reflective of the pared-back nature of the tour and her style at the time. There were sparkling skater dresses in silver, black, red and lilac, and these were teamed with customary high heels and with her hair worn in a half ponytail, tumbling loose around her shoulders.

The Honeymoon tour

In February 2015 Ariana kicked off her first global tour, the Honeymoon tour, with concerts across North and South America, Europe and Asia. She still attracted a crowd of young fans who had first loved her as Cat Valentine and had followed her into music, and so her stage costumes didn't deviate too far from the girlish sparkles that they adored.

The *Vancouver Sun* described it as being all about "high energy and good clean fun. Grande has apparently chosen to stick with wearing the cute cat ears and straddling fan bases rather than chasing the sleaze to prove she's 'grown up'."

In a sparkling black skater dress for the *Yours Truly* Listening Sessions on 14 August 2013 in New York City.

Ariana hired Emmy Award-winning costume designer Marina Toybina to design the wardrobe. Toybina created seven sparkling showgirl outfits, including a shimmering crop top and high-waist hot pants, and a full-length sheer skirt covered with floral appliqué. As well as the feather boa and cat ears, she also brought some of the touches that would continue into later incarnations: a leotard with sweater tied around the waist, the over-the-knee boots and a black and white PVC 60s-style minidress with matching ears.

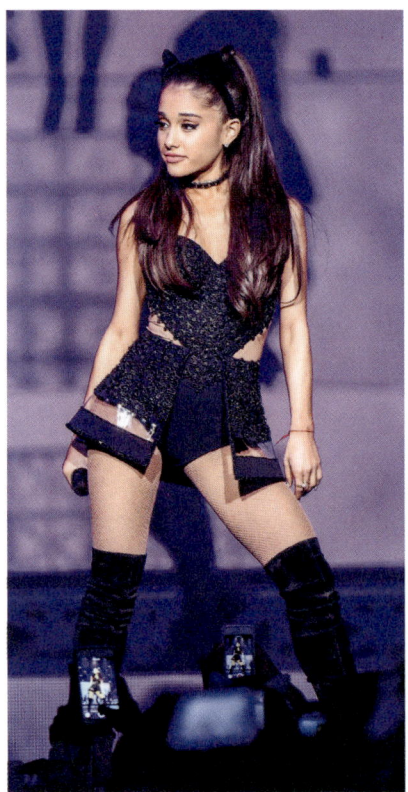

LEFT Marina Toybina designed the Honeymoon tour costumes, bringing a glamorous but cute aesthetic to the tour.

OPPOSITE On the Honeymoon tour, Ariana incorporated key touches, including the cat ears and half ponytail and a shimmering zipped sweater over her leotard.

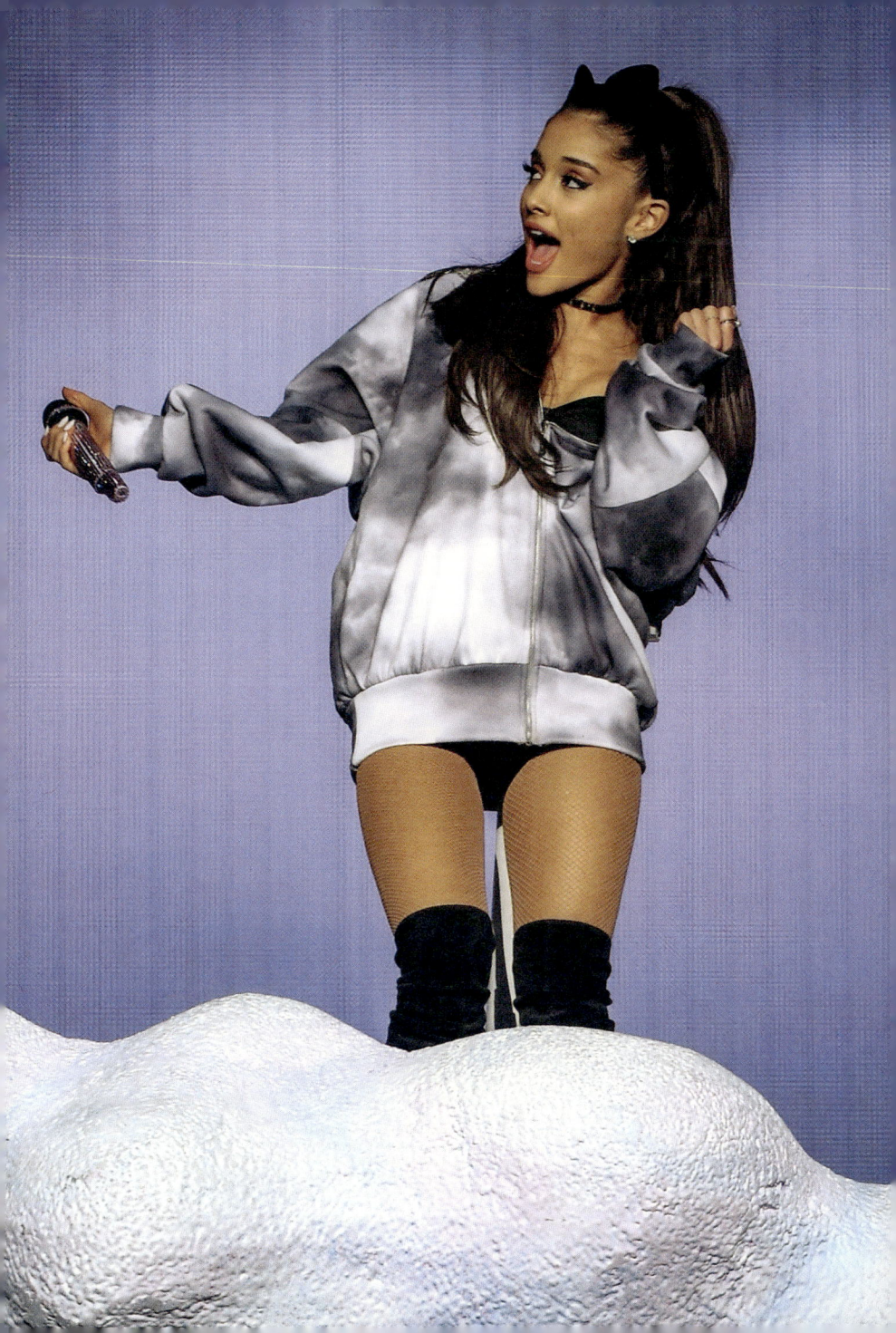

"Grande has apparently chosen to stick with wearing the cute cat ears

and straddling fan bases rather than chasing the sleaze to prove she's 'grown up'."

THE VANCOUVER SUN

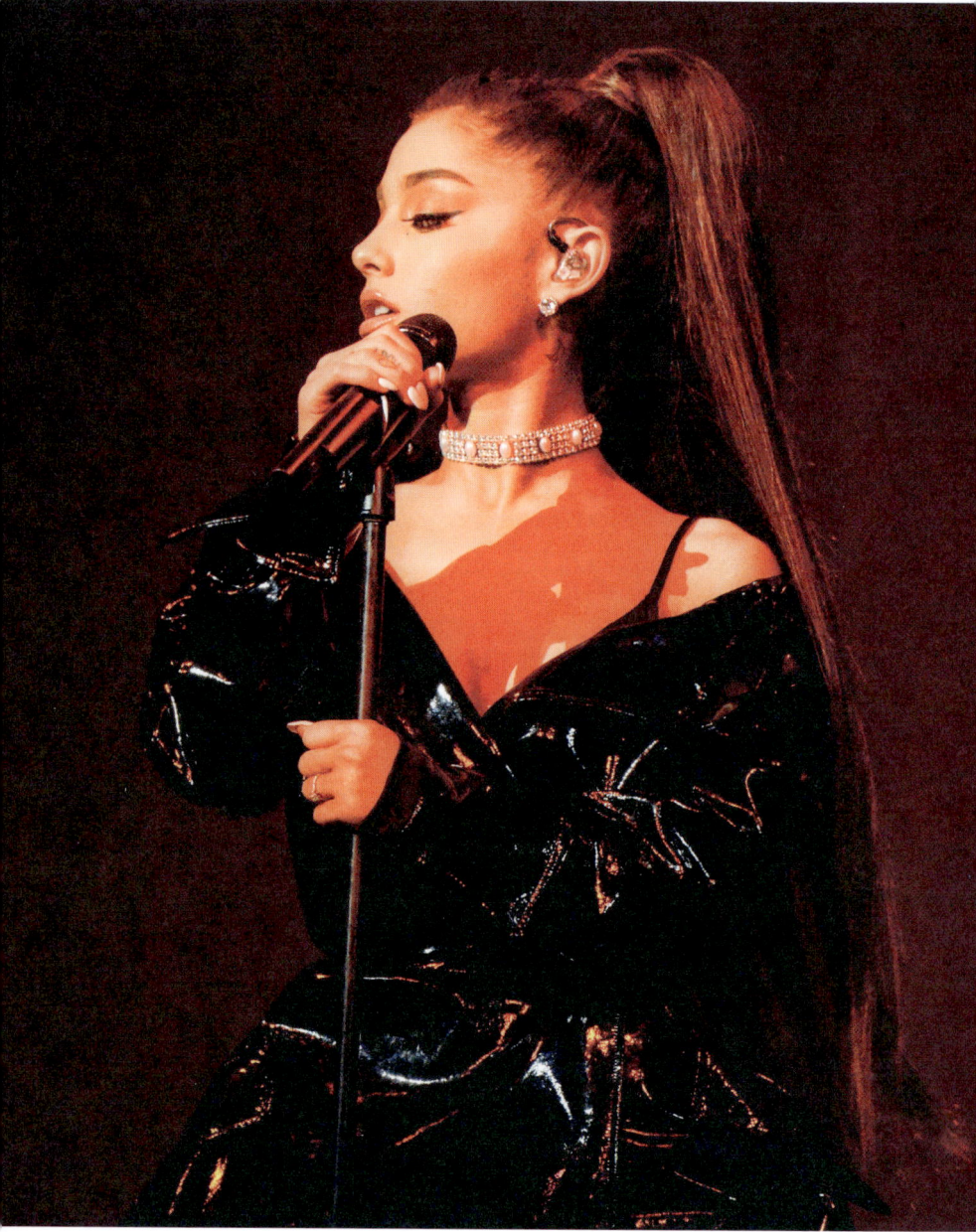

The Dangerous Woman tour

For the worldwide Dangerous Woman tour, which kicked off on 3 February 2017, in Phoenix, Arizona, Ariana recruited stylist Law Roach to create a more adult, contemporary look on stage.

Roach, who had styled the music videos 'Side to Side' and 'Dangerous Woman', followed the aesthetic set by the album for a sexy edginess that reflected street-style movements.

To keep it fresh, he worked with celebrity stylists Joey Thao and iCON Billingsley and reached out to young, diverse designers like Sergio Hudson, Michael Ngo and Bryan Hearns to continue the silhouette Ariana's fans knew and loved, but, according to Roach, "in a much more couture and elevated way." He added: "I think what Ariana is really smart about and conscious of is knowing who her fans are and letting them grow with her and not trying to outgrow them." The wardrobe treatment provided to designers set out a monochrome 90s streetwear bent, where each section of the show would tell a particular story and have its own mood.

The PVC coatdress by Sergio Hudson, worn in the finale of the Dangerous Woman tour to perform the title track, was designed to be lightweight but dramatic, and to reference the look on the album's cover.

Hearns, a 20-something graduate of the Fashion Institute of Design & Merchandising (FIDM), had previously provided pieces for Ariana for her *Billboard* magazine feature in August 2014. He met with the singer and her stylist Law Roach to go over the images, silhouettes and colours that she liked. With just a quick two-and-a-half-week timescale to get the costumes ready, he worked intensely to create the "confident, feminine and dangerous" looks. He kept her preferred shapes, of high-waisted bodysuits, shorts, skirts and crop tops, using sweatshirt fabric to keep it relaxed and leather, denim and metal buckled straps for an edginess.

As Hearns told *InStyle* magazine in February 2017: "It's about making an adult Ariana, marrying her silhouette with what's happening in fashion right now, so a big theme is sportswear – everything is oversized, there are straps everywhere, and cool hardware... It's definitely more edgy, it's more adult, but still playful and young."

One of Hearns' favourites was a white crop top and bodysuit skirt with a leather flap, worn with a bulky white puffer jacket. "It's all white and it's super crispy with thigh-high boots. It just looks really chic," he said.

LA designer Michael Ngo was tasked with translating his urban-luxe streetwear to the stage for the second act, where he created a white oversized hooded jacket and pants. The jacket and pants featured double-lacing and metal rivets which could be pulled and adjusted, and with backpack straps in the lining to allow for the off-the-shoulder look: "It was one of the first things she noticed and said she loved," said Ngo.

"*I think what Ariana is really* smart *about and conscious of is* knowing *who her* fans *are and letting them grow with her and not trying to outgrow them.*"

LAW ROACH

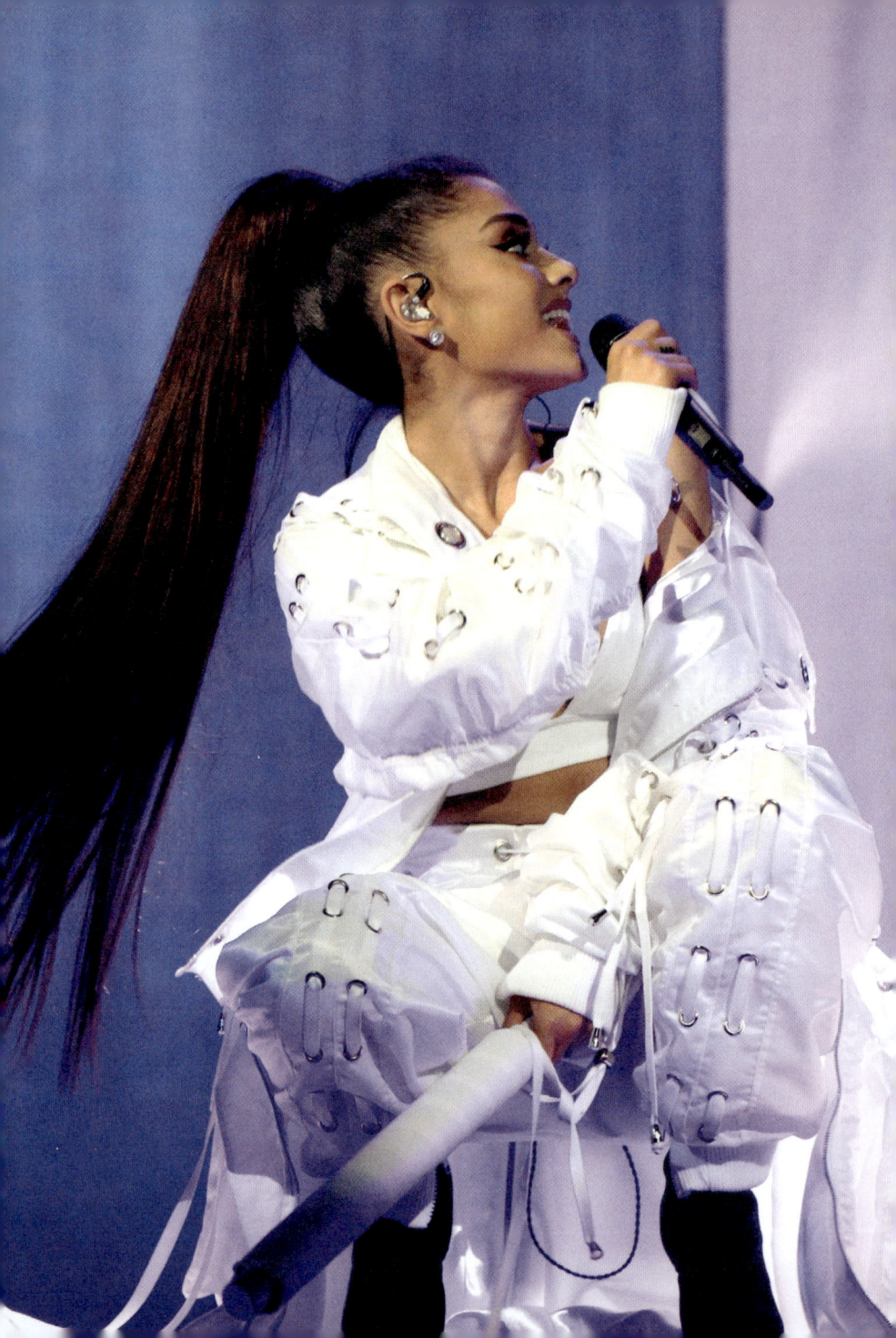

Ngo saw the Dangerous Woman tour as leaving behind the "coyness and cuteness of her past shows – there aren't any cat ears to be found on this tour. She's still very girly and playful, but her style is a lot more confident, fresh and a little bit, well, dangerous."

South Carolinian designer Sergio Hudson, winner of Rihanna's Styled to Rock fashion competition in 2013, was given the task of bringing drama to the finale with a long PVC coatdress. It served to highlight what Law Roach called her most beautiful features: "Her face, her neckline, her shoulders, her décolletage." There was also a Calvin Klein bralet, worn with a silvery grey miniskirt, and the shoes were a vital component; Ariana performed every number and dance routine in six-inch double platform heels.

In their review of the show at Madison Square Garden in February 2017, the *New York Times* hailed the singer as asserting herself "with stilettos and a soaring voice" and added that she "flaunts professionalism, not skin or profanities (though she sings a handful) and her waist-length ponytail was, as always, perfectly behaved."

The white hooded jacket and pants by Michael Ngo for the Dangerous Woman tour featured double-lacing and metal rivets that could be pulled and adjusted.

The Sweetener tour

Promoting both the *Sweetener* and *thank u, next* albums, Ariana's the Sweetener world tour took her across North America and Europe for 97 dates, opening on 18 March 2019 in Albany, New York. Given the tragedy that marked the Dangerous Woman tour, this was about recovery and resilience. The theatrical set design was built around a sphere and a large moon as a backdrop, to fit with the singer's interest in astrology and spirituality. Rather than being lit in the conventional way under a spotlight, she blended into the stage environment with colour-fusions, for a soft, cosmic aura.

Ariana's costumes, again styled by Law Roach and custom-designed by Versace and Michael Ngo, combined the ethereal with a strong, cutting-edge streetwear look. They mixed billowing with bondage, while also reflecting the lampshade skirt and boot combo that she had been championing over the last year. Roach wanted to "take her authentic blueprint and make it feel fresh and elevated." They riffed on her signatures to be "absolutely feminine and superpowerful" so that girls can see her "and realize they too can become iconic by staying authentic to who they are."

A space age tribute under a silver moon – Ariana in Michael Ngo's lavender top and chaps ensemble.

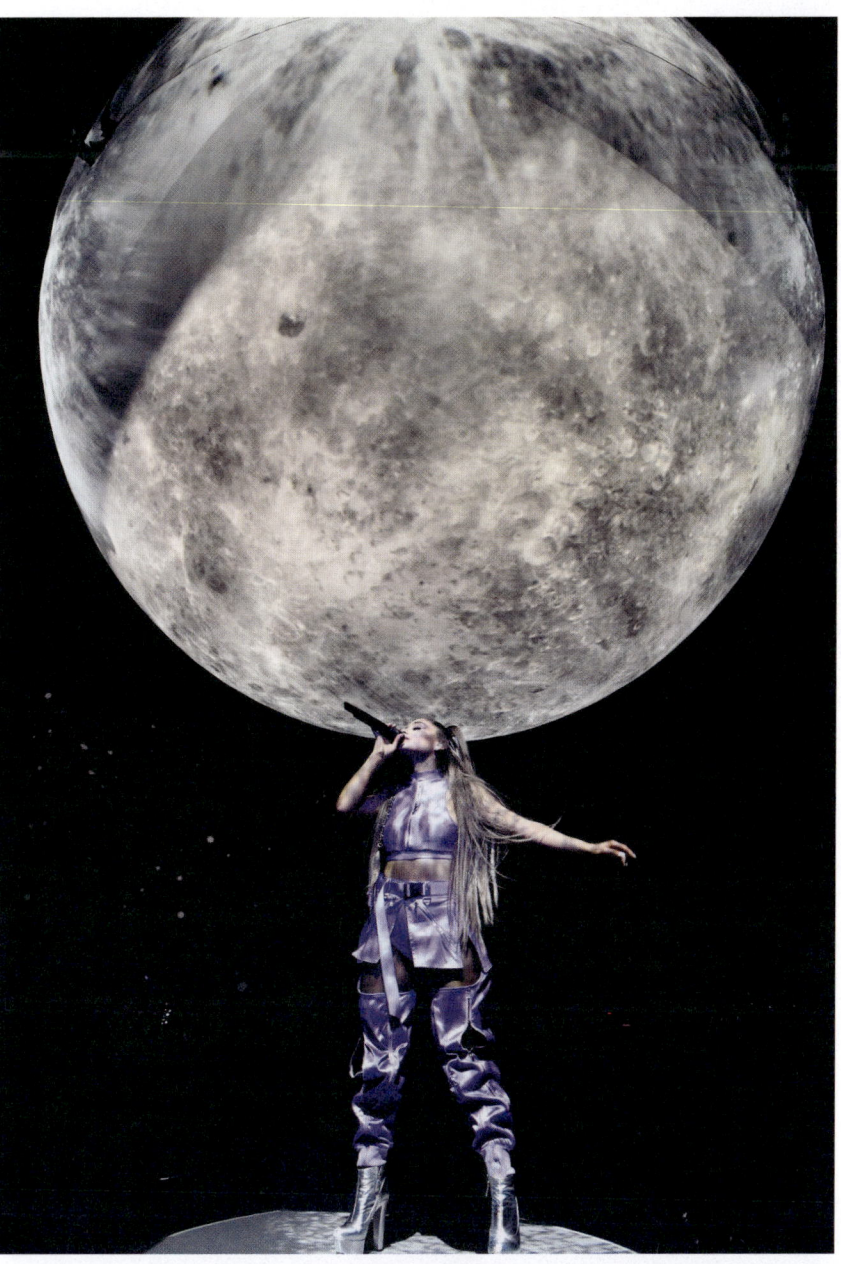

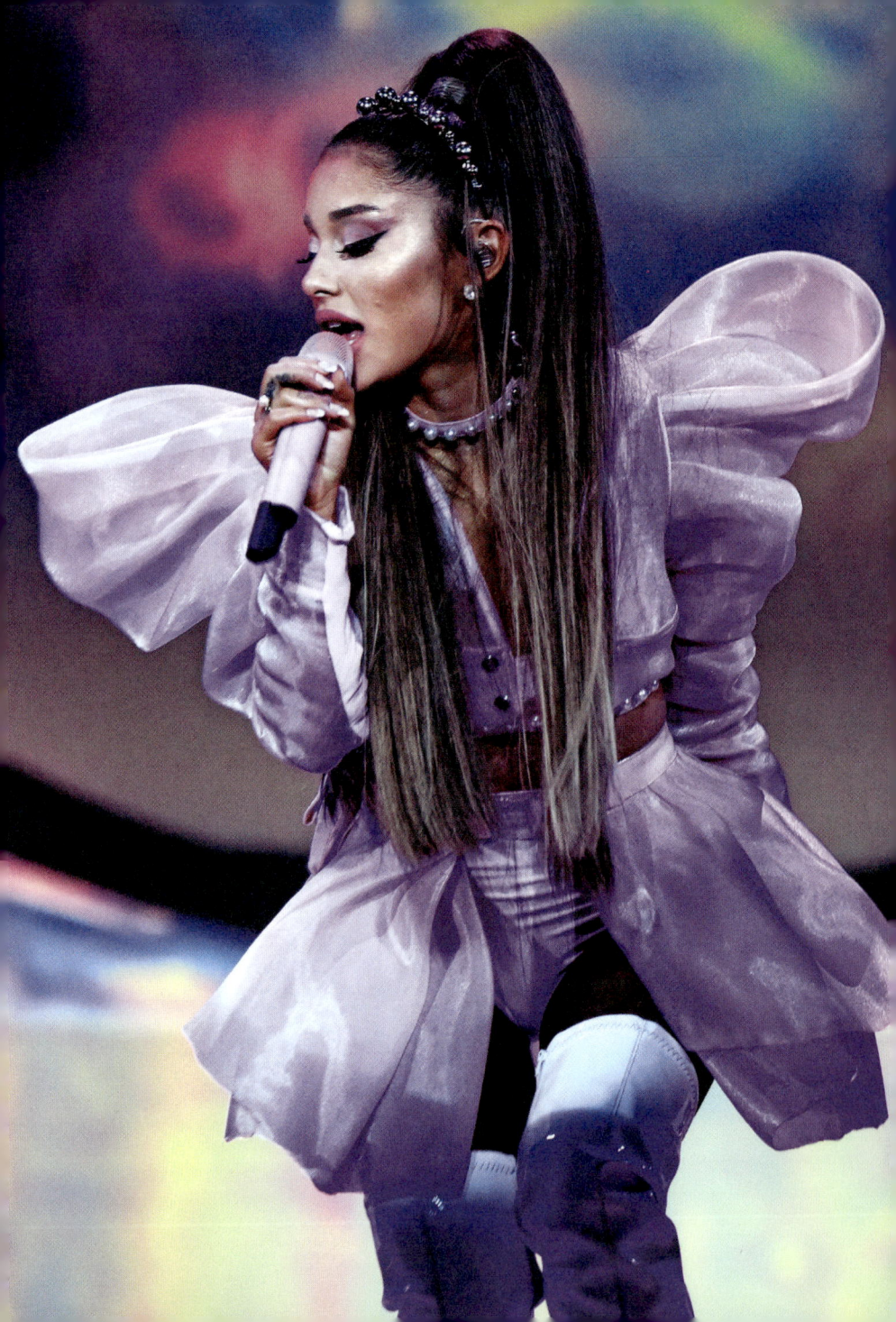

The costumes were a "warrior-princess armour", with Michael Ngo designing an orange bra top, ruched drawstring skirt and matching boots, a fantastical two-piece bubblegum pink costume – as if she was a Disney princess from another planet – and a lilac zipped crop top and miniskirt, worn with Pleaser PVC platform boots.

Opening with 'God is a Woman', she emerged in a Versace red multi-strapped top and skirt with thigh-high platform boots. Given her tribute to *Clueless* in the 'thank u, next' music video, she further referenced the style of Cher Horowitz with her own Versace-designed yellow and pink plaid skirt and bralet as she closed the show. Versace had long been a go-to of Ariana's and she thanked the brand in a social media post for "making this lil italian chic's dreams come tru".

But there was also controversy and criticism that the mood board had been lifted from Black artists, and with *RuPaul's Drag Race* star Farrah Moan and Instagram account Diet Prada leading on accusations that she had taken other designers' works without crediting them properly. Roach clapped back: "This mood board was created by me (a black man) for her. So am [I] stealing from my own culture?? She didn't style herself, people."

Ethereal in Michael Ngo's winged sleeves and skirt for the Sweetener tour, at Staples Center, Los Angeles, on 7 May 2019.

Impact

CHAPTER 4

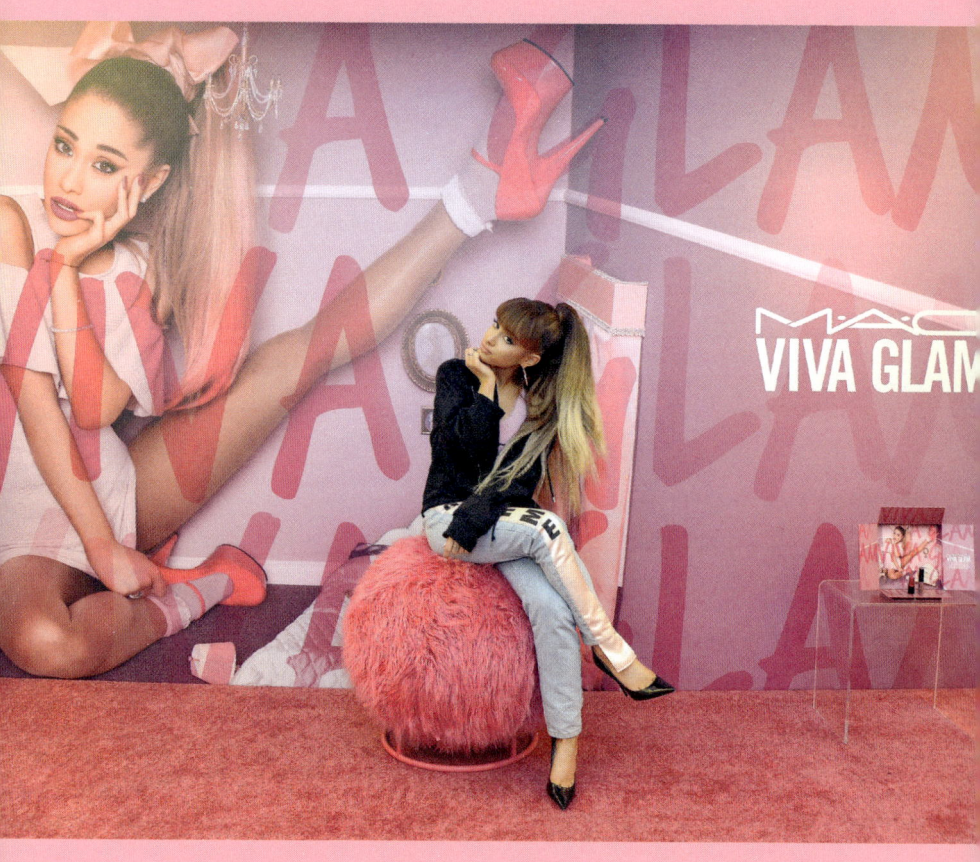

Ariana fronting the MAC Viva Glam campaign
in West Hollywood in August 2016.

Campaigns

Given her impact on fashion as she forged her own unique identity as a pop star, Ariana has been a popular choice to be the face of a range of global brands.

Their campaigns typically tapped into her unmistakable style to reach those who wished to emulate her. In October 2015 she unveiled a platinum blonde makeover to promote her new single 'Focus', which proved to be a commercial enterprise, not just for her debut perfume, Ari (a sweet, fresh scent of pink grapefruit and raspberry, with a base of musk and marshmallow) but also for the Samsung Galaxy Note 5. For the product-placement music video, where she was dressed in a La Perla moulded bodysuit, Bryan Hearns skirt and Christian Louboutin over-the-knee boots, she scribbled notes and took selfies, and even performed choreography with her back-up dancers in star-spangled "Galaxy" black leotards.

Ariana collaborated with Lipsy on a clothing line in 2016, based on her own preference for colourful skater skirts and cut-out minidresses. "We had a lot of images from Instagram and Pinterest as well as some of my favourite red-carpet looks I've worn in the past," she explained to *Miss Vogue* in February 2016. That year she also teamed up with MAC for a Viva Glam lip colour collection to raise awareness of HIV/AIDS, which was advertised with a candy-pink promotional theme to suit the femininity of her persona.

Given her love of streetwear, Law Roach helped orchestrate her collaboration with Reebok, first in 2017 while on her Dangerous Woman tour and then in 2018 for their Be More Human campaign. The campaign aimed to empower consumers to overcome barriers to become their best self, and the promotional images unveiled Ariana's newly platinum blonde hair. As well as highlighting Ariana's growth following the Manchester terrorist attack, the partnership blended seamlessly with her own casual streetwear as she posed in oversized sweaters, crop tops and leggings.

Ariana signed on as the face of Givenchy for the Autumn/Winter 2019 campaign, for which she appeared in black and white images that had an Audrey Hepburn in *Breakfast at Tiffany's* mood. The iconic French fashion house, led by British designer Clare Waight Keller, initially teased the collaboration with a silhouette of Ariana's hair and then with the hashtag #Arivenchy as she wore a series of strikingly elegant looks, including a green blazer, pleated floral gown and voluminous off-the-shoulder top.

"Givenchy is a house I have forever admired," she said in a press release. "I love this clothing and the confidence and joy it brings to the people wearing it."

Ariana also developed her own cosmetic line, r.e.m. beauty, named after both the ideal dream state and a track from *Sweetener*. First launched in 2021 and revived in 2023, it featured iridescent shimmers, bold colours and strong eyeliner for a retro, cosmic feel that replicated her own make-up looks. The advertising campaigns featured Ariana in space-age couture, such as a rare Spring/Summer 1985 Thierry Mugler silver corset, a Polo Ralph Lauren NASA white jacket from 1997 and Roberto Cavalli lurex shimmering pants, further emphasizing her partnership with stylist Mimi Cuttrell.

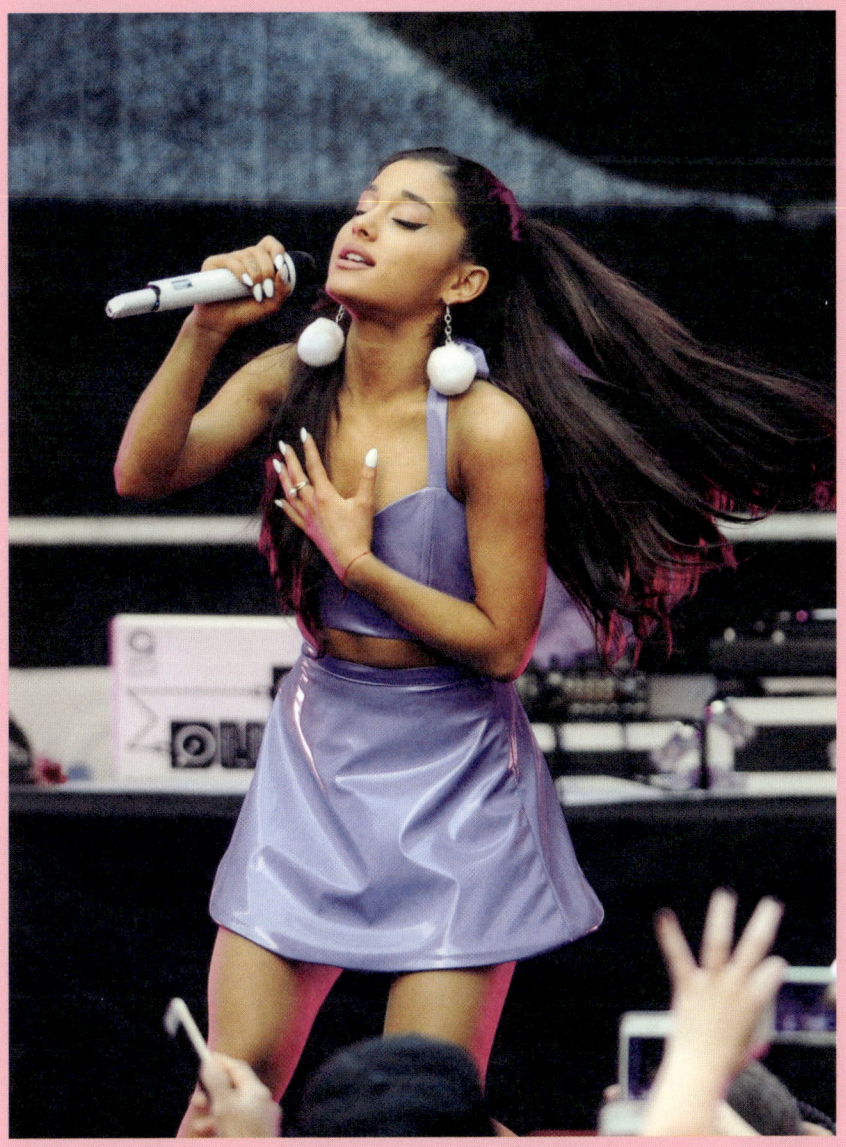

Launching the fragrance Ari by Ariana by Grande at Macy's Herald Square in New York on 16 September 2015.

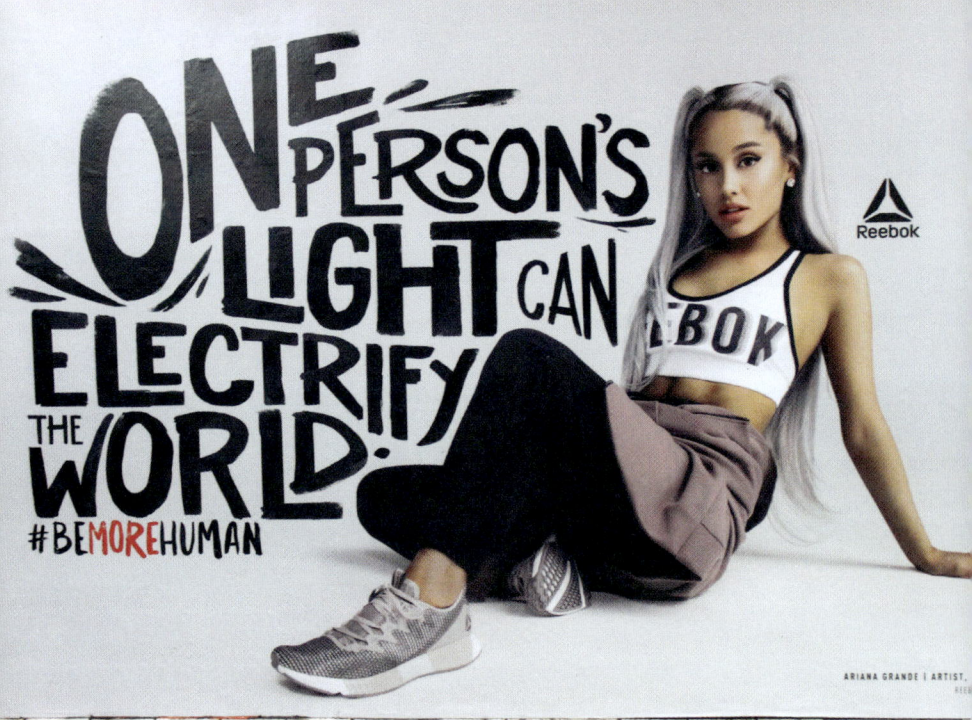

ONE PERSON'S LIGHT CAN ELECTRIFY THE WORLD!

#BEMOREHUMAN

Reebok

ARIANA GRANDE | ARTIST.

ABOVE As part of Reebok's 2018 #BeMoreHuman campaign, she was celebrated as a woman making a positive impact on the world.

OVERLEAF Bringing classic couture to the annual Academy Museum Gala in Los Angeles in October 2024, in a custom polka-dot Balmain gown based on a vintage design.

From Broadway child star to tween idol, to pop star and global icon, Ariana has grown up in the spotlight, shifting her style as she explored her own creativity and sensuality. Looking back on choices she once made, she joked to *Vanity Fair*, "I celebrate what once was," she said. "But wow."

There was sugary Audrey Hepburn, perky 1960s pop and R&B in go-go boots and shift dresses, the cat's ears and body suits, the funky street style and the cutting-edge couture. Then, entering her thirties, she transitioned from the hoodies, the over-the-knee boots and the super-high ponytail, to elegant couture. For the duration of the *Wicked* press tour in 2024, Ariana embraced method dressing by going overwhelmingly pink. "Pink was never really a part of my life until I started collecting a lot of pink pieces during the audition process," she told *Vogue* in September 2024.

As well as being the most streamed female artist of the 2010s, and having sold over 90 million records globally, Ariana has left a legacy of style that represented the mood of an era. But at the same time as achieving overwhelming success, she has also faced continued criticism of her body, her love life and even her voice.

"I was this approachable, funny redhead on Nickelodeon and everyone liked me. And then I had one too many hit records, and everyone decided that I was an evil diva. And then other terrible things happened, and all of a sudden I was this hero and this victim," she said. Throughout it all she has maintained a sweet positivity, and a desire to always be true to herself, whether that's how she navigates fame or through her wardrobe choices.

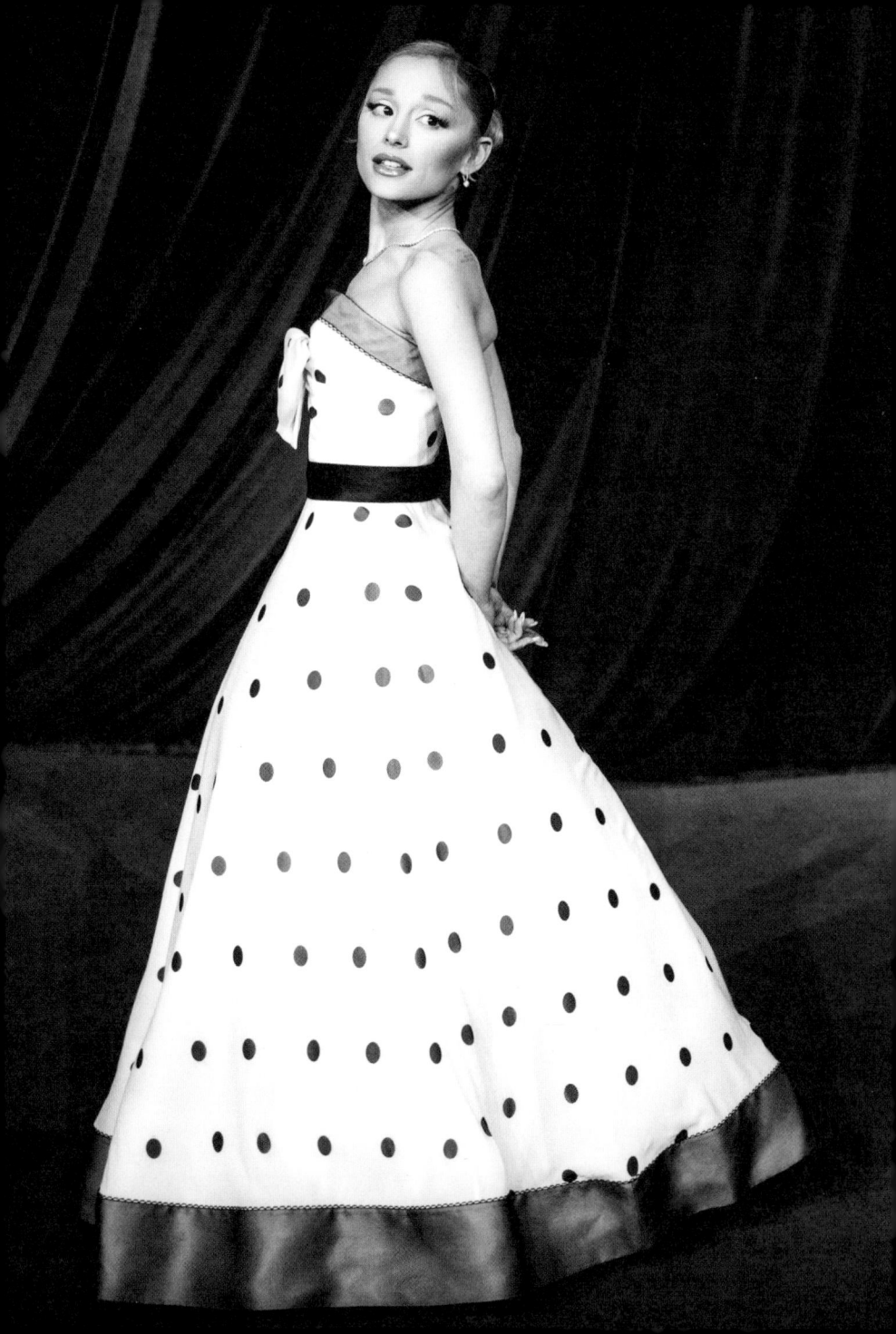

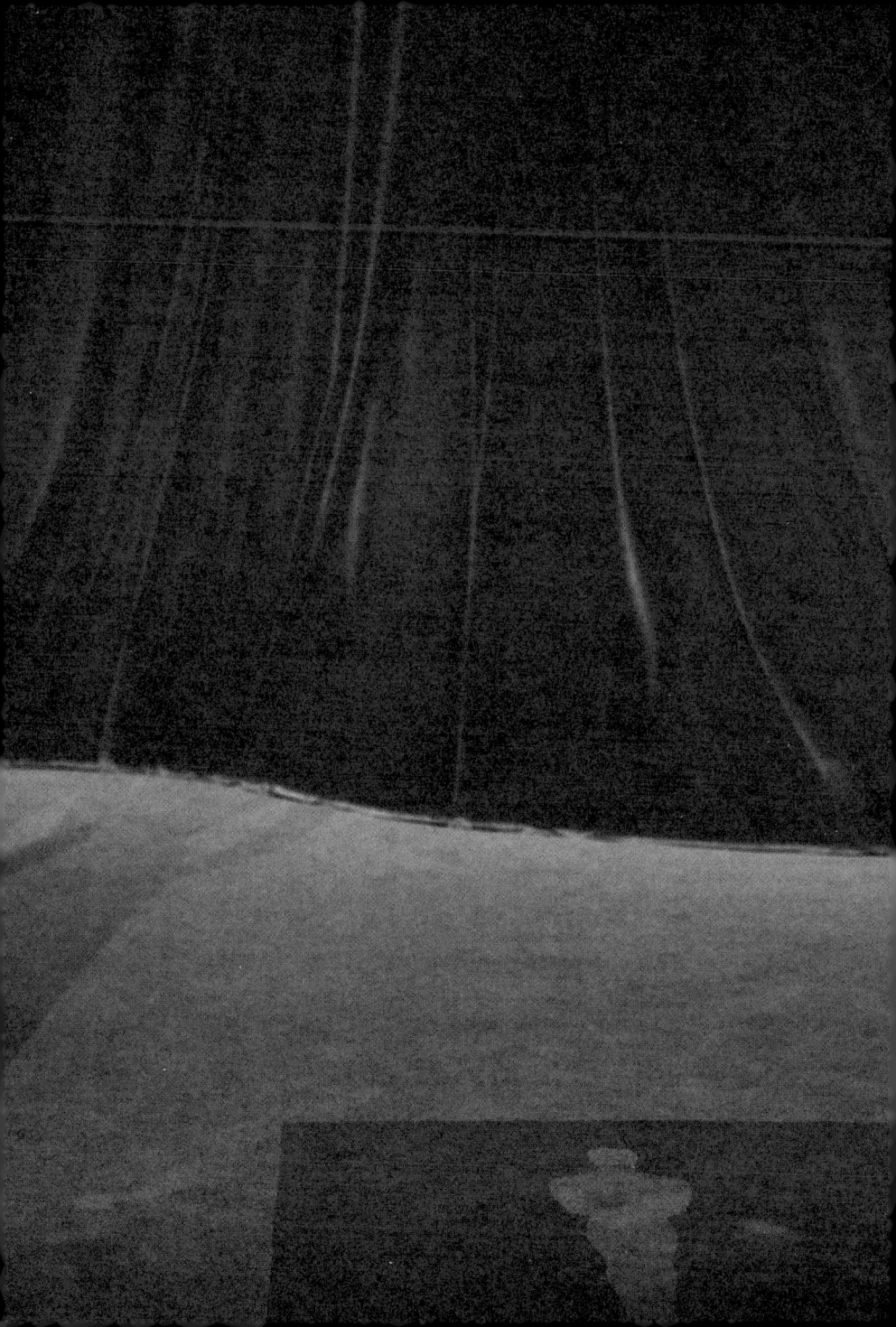

Index

Numbers in italics refer to pages with captions.

Abdul, Paula 107
Abloh, Virgil 157, 185
Academy Awards 108, 187, *187*
Academy Museum Gala *216*
Adele 27
Alaïa 107
Allure 95
Alvarez, Ricky 64
American Apparel *145*
American Music Awards 24, 60, 73, *124*, 165
Annie 23
Apple Music 1 *63–4*
Ari by Ariana by Grande 213, *215*
Ariana at the BBC 81
Arianators 118
Assago, Italy *115*
Azalea, Iggy 45, *45*, 51

B, Howie 92
babydoll 176
bags 33, 77, *145*, 154, *158*
Bailey, Jonathan 104
Balenciaga 108
ballet flats 103
balletcore 104, 108, 115, 135
Balmain 111, *216*
'Bang Bang' single *51*
basque 38
BBC 33, 81, *135*, 153
BCBG 29
Benji *145*
Bennett, LeRoy 88, 92
Berry, Maggie 172
Bieber, Justin 11, 73, 92
Big Sean 48

Billboard 60, 69
200 chart 38, 48, 56, 87, 96, 202
Hot 100 chart 84, 87
Music Awards 45, 69, *69*, 135, *141*, 162, *170*, 171
Woman of the Year 87
Women in Music *84*, *133*, 179
Billingsley, iCON 201
Birth of Venus, The 188
Bloch 107
bodysuits 63,107, 202, 213, 217
boots 8, 11, *11*, 14, 45, 55, 77, 78, 87, 104, 115, *118*, 135, *136*, *141*, 145, *145*, 148, 153, *154*, 157, 162, 176, 179, 196, 209, 213, 217
Boss RC-50 Loop Station 27
Bottega Veneta 104
Botticelli 188, *188*
'Boy is Mine, The' single 11
Brandy and Monica 111
'Break Free' single 38, 51, 52
Breakfast at Tiffany's 87, 214
Bring It On 84
Brown, Tommy 84
Browne, Thom *111*, 192
bunny ears 8, 122
Butera, Edward, father 18

campaigns *212*, 213, 214, *216*
caps 104, 107, 158
capes 96, 107
Carey, Mariah 23, 27
Carrey, Jim 108
Casadei *141*
cat ears 8, *9*, *11*, 14, 48, 52, 55, 60, 111, 118, 122, 195, 196, *196*, 198, 205, 217

Cat, Doja 96
Catwoman 111
Cavalli, Roberto 214
Chanel 33, 69, 77, 78, 153, 157, *158*
Chanel, Coco 23
Chiffons, the 38
Chu, M. 103
CinemaCon 103, *103*, 111
Coach *145*
Coachella 77, 87, 92, 135
Coldplay 11, 73
Collins, Kenley *41*
Concert for Charlottesville, A 74, 145, *147*
Converse 153, *158*
corset, lace 96, 185, 214
Cosmopolitan 55, 60
Costello, Michael 172
Covid pandemic 92, *93*, 95
Creative Arts Emmy awards 29, 162
crop tops 69, 87, 145, 171, 196, 202, 209, 214
Cut, The 187
Cuttrell, Mimi 95, 96, 108, 158, 180, 185, 187, 188, 191, 192, 214
Cyrus, Miley 11, 42, 73

Dangerous Woman album 8, 56, 73, *126*, 168, *168*
Dangerous Woman tour 8, *11*, 56, 73, 118, 201, *201*, 205, *205*, 206, 214
'Dangerous Woman' single 56, 69, 171, 172
'Dangerous Woman' video 60, 201
Davidson, Pete 11, 78, 81, *81*, 84, *136*, 157, 158, 176, *176*

de la Renta, Oscar *103*, 111
Diet Prada 209
Dion, Celine 23, 63
Dolce & Gabbana *52*, *55*, *124*
Don't Look Up 99
Doughnut-gate 64
dresses 14, *15*, 23, 27, *29*, *33*, 42, *55*, *55*, 87, 96, 111, *111*, 115, 118, 135, *141*, 142, 153, 158, 162, 179, 185, 192, 195

Easter Egg Roll 45
EDM 48, 51, 52
El Saadawi, Nawal 56
Elphaba 103
Erivo, Cynthia 103, *103*, *105*, 108, 187
Estefan, Gloria 23
Eternal Sunshine album 108
'Everyday' single 56
eyeliner 129, *132*, 214

Fader, The 74, 121
"fembot" 96
Ferg, A$AP 48
"Fireworks" necklace 69, *69*
'Focus' single 56, 213
Ford, Tom 162

Gaga, Lady 92, *93*
Gallagher, Liam 11
Gambino, Childish 48
Garfield, Andrew 104
Garland, Judy 18
Garner, Jennifer 185
GCDS 99
Gentlemen Prefer Blondes 172
Givenchy *181*, 214
Glamour 42, 188
Glinda 103, 104, 108, 111, 135, 188, 192
'God is a Woman' single 78, 209
'God Is a Woman' video *175*, *175*

Gomez, Dalton 95, 99, 104
Good Morning America Summer Concert Series *126*
Grammy Awards 29, *52*, *55*, 73, *91*, 92, 162, 168, *168*, 179–80, *179*, *180*
Grande-Butera, Frankie, brother 18, *20*, *59*, 162
Grande, Ariane
  Ariana Grande-Butera, real name 18
  Arianators 118
  diva reputation 69
  doughnut-gate 64
  Edward Butera, father 18
  first agent 27
  Joan, mother 18, *20*, *24*, 96, *129*
  Marjorie, nonna 24
  Mod aesthetic 45
  parents' divorce 18
  quotes 36–7, 43, 76, 97, 100–01, 126, 148, 161, 148, 161
  separation 104
  wedding 99
Gray, Macy 56
Gucci 96, 99

hair, colours and styles 11, 27, 74, 87, 92, *157*, 213, 214
Hanoch, Noam 64
Heap, Imogen 27
Hearns, Bryan 56, 201, 202, 213
heels 8, 11, *33*, 42, 48, 51, 64, 135, *135*, *136*, 153, 162, 168, 171, 205
Hepburn, Audrey 23, *33*, 45, *55*, 115, *132*, 192, *192*, 214, 217
highlighter 129
Honeymoon tour *115*, 135, 195–6, *196*

hoodies 145, 153, 217
Horowitz, Cher 209
Houston, Whitney 23, 27
Hudson, Sergio 201, *201*, 205, *205*

iHeartRadio Music Awards 48, *51*, 99
iHeartRadio Music Festival 9, *38*, *136*
iHeartRadio Ultimate Pool Party *119*
iHeartRadio Wango Tango by AT&T *125*, *132*
'Imagine' single 180, *180*
InStyle magazine 202
'Into You' single 56, 69, *68*, 171

J, Jessie 51
jackets 153, 157, 172, 202, 205, 214
Jay, Lilly 104
Jimmy Kimmel Live! 42
Jovani 41
'Just a Little Bit of Your Heart' single 55

Keds 153
Keveza, Romona 168, *168*
Kigu 153
KIIS FM Wango Tango 45
KISS FM 59
Kit, The 158
Klein, Calvin 56, 205
Kygo 77

Lanvin 96
Last Judgement, The 175
latex 60, 78, 118, 176, *176*
Lauren, Ralph 158
'Leave Me Lonely' single 56
Lee, Dion 96
Legally Blonde 84
leotards 115, 196, *196*, 213
'Let Me Love You' single 56

LGBTQ+ rights 14
Lipman, Monte 30
Listening Sessions tour 195, *195*
Loewe 158, *161*, 188, *188*
Lollapalooza *95*
Los Angeles Times, the 51
Louboutin, Christian 135, *145*, 213
'Love Me Harder' single 51
Lowe, Zane 63–4

MAC 213
Macy's Presents Fashion's Front Row 62
Madison Square Garden 20
Madonna 20, 23, 162
Make-A-Wish Foundation 23
make-up, cat eye 11
Manchester bombing 11, 73, 74, 145, 158, 214
March For Our Lives concert 74, *74*
Margiela Maison 103, *190*
Martin, Max 56, 77
Mase 92
McCall, Davina 81
McQueen, Alexander 60, 165, 171
Met Gala 2018 Heavenly Bodies 78, *78*
Met Gala 2024 Garden of Time *120*, 188, *188, 190*
Miami Herald 48
Michelangelo 175
midi dress 111, *161*
Miller, Mac 38, 81, *82*, 84
Minaj, Nicki 51, 52, 56, 64, 92
minidresses 8, *41, 42*, 45, 84, 92, 96, 111, *118*, 162, *165*, 185, 213
miniskirts 84, 87, 107, 115, 205
Miss Vogue 115, 213

Miu Miu 103, 135
Moan, Farrah 209
Monét, Victoria 84, 96
Monroe, Marilyn 45, 172, *172*
Montecito 99
Moschino 162
MTV Movie Awards 172, *172*
MTV Video Music Awards 41, 42, 64, 69, 70, 73, 78, 82, 92, 93, 162, *165*, 176, *176*
Mugler, Thierry 96, 111, 214
My Everything album 8, *9*, 48, 55, 95, 135
'My Everything' single *118*
'My Favorite Things' 87
'My Way' single 42

Nasty Gal 153, *153*
Nickelodeon Kid's Choice Awards 27
New York Times, the 42, 158, 205
Ngo, Michael 63, 88, 92, *95*, 116–7, *118, 136*, 201, 202, 205, 206, *206*, 209
Nguyen, Nhan-nhi "Lillian" 55
Nickelodeon 8, 27, *33*, 38, 217
Nina Gabbana Vintage 185
'No Tears Left to Cry' single 77, 121
NSYNC 92
Nylon 168

Olympic Games, Paris 192, *192*
"One Love" concert 11
One Love Manchester 73, *73*, 74
'One Last Time' single 51

Palm Springs International Film Awards 15

Parkinson, Norman 192
Perla, La 213
Phoenix 8
Pleaser *136*
Polo Ralph Lauren 214
ponytails 8, *9*, 11, 12, 14, 48, 52, 55, *55*, 77, 92, 120, 121, 122, *124*, 126, 135, *154*, 157, 158, 176, 179, 195, 205, 217
Positions album 95, 96
Positions tour 8, *11*
'Positions' video 96
Primavera 188
Primetime Creative Arts Emmy Awards 162, *162*
'Problem' *45*, 48, 51
Project Runway 41
'Put Your Hearts Up' single 30, 38

r.e.m. beauty 214
Rabanne, Paco 96
Radio Disney Music Awards 48
'Rain on Me' single 92, *93*
Rat & Boa 99, *99*
red carpet 14, 55, 56, 69, 70, 78, 162, *162*, 165, 168, 176, 180, *180*, 187, 188, 213
Reebok 214
Republic Records 30
'Right There' single 42
Roach, Law 12–13, 14, 56, 63, 69, 70, 122–23, 142–3, 166–7, 184, 203, 92, *118*, 157, 158, 165, 171, 172, 175, 201, 202, 205, 206, 209, 214
Rodarte 104, 107
Rolling Stone 30
Roxx, La 111
RUBBER COLLECTIVE 111
RuPaul's Drag Race 209

Sailor Moon 92
Saint Laurent 42, 135, *135*, 153
Sam & Cat 8, *27*, 48, 52
Saturday Night Live 52, 64, 78, 108
'Save Your Tears' single 99, *99*
Schiaparelli *180*
Schwartz, Lorraine 187, 188
Sergeenko, Ulyana 99
Seven Design Works 92
'7 rings' single 87, *180*
Shangri-Las, the 38
'Side to Side' single 56, *64*
'Side to Side' video 201
silhouettes 12, 14, 63, 96, 175, 185, 201, 202, 214
Silla, Le 77, 96, 111, 135, 141, 176, 179
Simkhai, Jonathan 171
Sinatra, Nancy 8, 45
Siriano, Christian 64, 69, *84*, *141*, 179
SiriusXM 30
Sistine Chapel 175, *175*
skirts 14, *56*, 69, 104, *135*, 179, 206, 209, *209*, 213
Slater, Ethan 104
Social Club 145
Sohee, Miss 99, 185
'Somewhere Over the Rainbow' 73
Spamalot 158, *161*
Stallion, Megan Thee 96
Stanley Cup finals 129
Stern, H. 69, *69*
street style 8, *11*, 14, 63, 69, 95, 99, 115, 118, 135, 145, 153, 157, 176, 179, 201, 202, 206, 214, 217
streetwear 8, *11*, 14, 63, 95, 99, 115, 118, 135, 145, 157, 176, 201, 202, 206, 214
'Stuck with U' single 92
sunglasses 45, 104, 158

Super Bunny 60
sweaters 8, 11, 45, 78, 81, 104, 73, 145, *145*, *147*, *148*, *153*, 158
sweatshirts 11, 55, 81, *136*
Sweetener album 77, 87, 92, 157, *157*, 206, 214
Sweetener Sessions 81, *148*
Sweetener tour 88, 92, *95*, 118, *136*, 145, 171, 176, 206, 209, *209*
Sykes, Nathan *135*, 153

Teen Vogue 171, 172
thank u, next album 84, 92, 95, 206
'thank u, next' single 84, 87, 91, *180*
'thank u, next' video 87
13 Going on 30 84, 185
Tibi 162
'34 + 35' single 96
Tiffany 87, 158
Time 52
TIME100 Gala 64, *69*
Tonight Show Starring Jimmy Fallon, The 99, 111, 141, 171
Topshop *135*, 153, *153*
Toybina, Marina *115*, 196, *196*
Trashy Lingerie *180*
tunic, lampshade 95, 140–43, 157

Valentine, Cat 26, *27*, 30, 36, 38, 121, 195
Valentino 111, 135
Valli, Giambattista 108, 165, 179, *179*, 187, *187*
Vancouver Sun, the 195, 198–9
Vanity Fair 176, 217
Venus Prototype 78, 176, *176*
Versace 52, 55, 92, 99, 111,

165, *170*, 171, 172, 206, 209
Versace, Donatella 63, 171, 185
Victorious 8, *26*, *27*, 52, 121
Viva Glam 213
Vogue 78, 84, 104, 115, 118, 121, 165, 192, 217
Voice, The 99, 185
Vuitton, Louis 15, 78, 108, 153, 157

Waight Keller, Claire 214
Wall Street Journal Magazine Innovator Awards *108*
Wang, Alexander 63, *70*
Wang, Vera 63, 78, *78*, 99, 108, 135, 175, *175*
Wanted, The 153
'Way The' single 38
Wayne, Lil 56
'We Can't Be Friends (Wait for Your Love)' single 108
Weeknd, The 48, 51, 99, *99*
Westwood, Vivienne 108
Wicked 11, 103–4, *103*, *105*, 107, 108, *111*, 135, 158, 192, 217
Williams, Pharrell 77, 115
Wimbledon 104, 107, *107*, 158
Woman at Point Zero 56
Women in Music event 132
Women's Wear Daily 99, 175

Yeezy 78, 81, *81*, 135, *136*, 145
'Yes, And?' single 107
Young, Ivan 99, 185
Yours Truly album 8, 38, 51, 95, 195, *195*

Zanotti, Giuseppe 64, 135, 168, 171
Zedd 51
Zendaya 63

Credits

The publishers would like to thank the following sources for their kind permission to reproduce the pictures in this book.

Alamy Stock Photo: MediaPunch Inc 216; /PA Images 177; /Storms Media Group 215

Getty Images: Alex Broadway 193; /Michael Buckner 50; /Larry Busacca 196, 197; /Larry Busacca/MTV1415/Getty Images for MTV; /Larry Busacca/WireImage 53; /Gilbert Carrasquillo/GC Images 120; /Charley Gallay/Getty Images for Kevin & Steffiana James 22; /Mike Coppola/Getty Images for Billboard 85; /Damebk/Bauer-Griffin/GC Images 160; /James Devaney/GC Images 109; /Dia Dipasupil 189; /Kevork Djansezian 90-91, 169, 182-183; /GC Images 156; /Charley Gallay/Getty Images for MAC Cosmetics 212; /Gary Gershoff 31; /Gotham/GC Images 80, 155; /Bruce Glikas/FilmMagic 194; /Steve Granitz/WireImage 28, 110, 170; /Jerod Harris/Getty Images for CinemaCo 102; /Dave Hogan for One Love Manchester 72; /Simon James/GC Images 32; /Robert Kamau/GC Images 135; /Jon Kopaloff/FilmMagic 33, 41; /Jeff Kravitz/FilmMagic 82-83; /Jeff Kravitz/AMA2016/FilmMagic 25, 61; /Jeff Kravitz/FilmMagic for MTV 33, 40; /Jason LaVeris 29; /Valerie Macon/AFP via Getty Images 186; /Larry Marano/Getty Images for Clear Channel 119; /Jeffrey Mayer/WireImage 163; /Kevin Mazur/Getty Images 146; /Kevin Mazur/AMA2013/WireImage 124; /Kevin Mazur/Getty Images for AG 86, 89, 94, 136, 207; /Kevin Mazur/Getty Images for American Express 149; /Kevin Mazur/Getty Images for dcp 140; /Kevin Mazur/Getty Images for iHeartMedia 98, 132; /Kevin Mazur/WireImage 9, 71; /Kevin Mazur/Getty Images for Live Nation 6-7, 11, 20-21, 57, 200, 204, 208; /Kevin Mazur/Getty Images for The Recording Academy 181; /Kevin Mazur/Getty Images for Time 65; /Kevin Mazur/MG24/Getty Images for The Met Museum/Vogue 190; /Walter McBride/Corbis via Getty Images 19; /Emilee McGovern/SOPA Images/LightRocket via Getty Images 75; /Emma McIntyre/Getty Images for Academy Museum of Motion Pictures 218-219; /Jason Merritt/Getty Images for MTV 164; /Ethan Miller 46-47; /Ethan Miller/Getty Images for iHeartMedia 39; /Neil P. Mockford/GC Images 58; /Mandel Ngan/AFP via Getty Images 147; /Marco Piraccini/Archivio Marco Piraccini/Mondadori via Getty Images 114; /Hector Retamal/AFP via Getty Images 174; /Debra L Rothenberg/FilmMagic 127; /Jun Sato/WireImage 152, 154; /SAV/FilmMagic 134; /John Sciulli/AMA2013/Getty Images for Music Choice 24; /John Shearer/Getty Images for The Recording Academy 178; /Micah Smith 34-35; /Karwai Tang/WireImage 106; /Denise Truscello/WireImage 138-139; /Jeff Vespa 54; /Slaven Vlasic/Getty Images for Macy's 62; /Theo Wargo 133; /Theo Wargo/Getty Images for Huffington Post 79; /Theo Wargo/MTV1617/Getty Images for MTV 66-67; /Matt Winkelmeyer/Getty Images for Palm Springs International Film Society 15; /Kevin Winter 68; /Kevin Winter/Getty Images for Clear Channel 49; /Kevin Winter/Getty Images for iHeartMedia 125; /Kevin Winter/Getty Images For 102.7 KIIS FM's Wango Tango 44; /Kevin Winter/MTV VMAs 2020/Getty Images for MTV

Shutterstock: Aflo 128; /Diggzy 105; /Larry Marano 130-131; /Masatoshi Okauchi 159; /Startraks 26, 144